T0305271

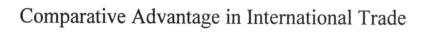

Comparative Advantage in International Trade

In memory of my parents, Lorna and Egidio Maneschi,
and of my aunt, Kathleen Fitzpatrick

Comparative Advantage in International Trade

A Historical Perspective

Andrea Maneschi

Associate Professor of Economics, Vanderbilt University, USA

Edward Elgar

Cheltenham, UK • Northampton, MA, USA

Published by
Edward Elgar Publishing Limited
Glensanda House
Montpellier Parade
Cheltenham
Glos GL50 1UA
UK

Edward Elgar Publishing, Inc.
6 Market Street
Northampton
Massachusetts 01060
USA

A catalogue record for this book
is available from the British Library

Library of Congress Cataloguing in Publication Data

Maneschi, Andrea, 1936–
    Comparative advantage in international trade: a historical
perspective / Andrea Maneschi.
    Includes bibliographical references and index.
    1. Comparative advantage (International trade)—Econometric
models. 2. International trade—Econometric models. I. Title.
HF1379.M357 1998
382'.1042—dc21   98–6258
                                                                    CIP

ISBN 978 1 85898 300 4

Printed and bound by CPI Group (UK) Ltd, Croydon, CR0 4YY

Contents

Figures

Preface and Acknowledgments

The aim of this study is to analyze the evolution of the concept of comparative advantage from the earliest times to the present day. I wish to examine how the concept itself originated, how it evolved over time, and the various interpretations of it that have been advanced in the literature. I also plan to assess its current validity in explaining an economy's pattern of specialization in light of the new trade theory that emerged in the past two decades and cast some doubt on its relevance. Although comparative advantage relates to the positive rather than the normative theory of international trade, the way in which this concept was elaborated by economists from Ricardo on was inevitably colored by their perception of the gains from trade that accrue to the trading economies or to the individual groups or classes that compose them. I have therefore made no attempt to separate positive from normative concerns, nor do I believe such a separation is desirable even if it were feasible.

A study of this kind owes a great deal to previous work in what is acknowledged to be the oldest branch of economics. In addition to the writings of the classical and neoclassical economists, I am indebted to several surveys of the history of economic thought as it relates to the theory of international trade, as well as numerous journal articles that touch on the concept of comparative advantage. I have also drawn on research of the trade-related aspects of the economic thought of David Ricardo, Enrico Barone, Vilfredo Pareto and John Rae that I have carried out in the past 15 years. In addition to integrating these papers in a unified framework, I stress important contributions made by the mercantilists, Adam Smith, 'dissenters' from the Smithian heritage such as Alexander Hamilton and Friedrich List, Mountifort Longfield, John Stuart Mill, William Whewell, Alfred Marshall, Gottfried Haberler, Eli Heckscher, Bertil Ohlin, Paul Samuelson and others. I bring the story of comparative advantage up to date by surveying recent work on the general validity of this principle, the current status of the Heckscher–Ohlin theory, neo-Ricardian trade models, and the feasibility of creating comparative advantage.

Given the length of the period that I survey and the richness of the literature on comparative advantage, I do not claim to have written a comprehensive account of the history of this important concept in the theory of international trade. My aim has been to focus on the major protagonists and the highlights of the intellectual itinerary that this concept followed from its earliest hints in Roman times down to its recent manifestations.

The idea of writing this book came to me after Pier Luigi Porta asked me to give a course with the same title at the University of Milan in May 1992. I wish to thank the persons and institutions that facilitated the task of writing it. Vanderbilt University and its Department of Economics and Business Administration allowed me a semester's sabbatical leave of absence in the Fall of 1994 to begin working in earnest on the book, and assisted me in many other ways. Ginger Leger carefully edited my manuscript so as to meet the required guidelines. Edward Elgar and his staff provided support and understanding for my delays. Peter Groenewegen sent me a helpful critique and suggestions for Chapter 3 that led me to recast parts of it, though he is not responsible for the final version. My wife and daughters provided needed emotional support throughout the preparation of the manuscript.

Parts of the following chapters previously appeared (though in altered form) in the *Cambridge Journal of Economics* (vol. 16, December 1992), the *Journal of the History of Economic Thought* (vol. 15, Fall 1993), *Oxford Economic Papers* (vol. 35, March 1983) and the *Review of International Economics* (vol. 6, February 1998) published by Blackwell Publishing Ltd. I am grateful to the editors of these journals for permission to use or quote from these papers.

1. Introduction

The principle of comparative advantage has been named the 'deepest and most beautiful result in all of economics' (Findlay, 1987a, p. 514). Paul Samuelson (1969, p. 9) believes it to be the ideal answer to a mathematician's challenge to name a proposition in the social sciences which is both true and non-trivial: 'that it is logically true need not be argued before a mathematician; that it is not trivial is attested by the thousands of important and intelligent men who have never been able to grasp the doctrine for themselves or to believe it after it was explained to them'. Despite the importance of this concept in the theory of international trade, a satisfactory definition of it is difficult to find. The term is not explicitly defined in the entry on 'comparative advantage' in the *New Palgrave Dictionary of Economics*, which simply describes it as 'the fundamental analytical explanation' of gains from trade arising from specialization and the division of labor (Findlay, ibid.). Most authors are content to describe the *effects* of specialization according to comparative advantage and to theorize about its *sources*. Comparative advantage is generally ascribed to supply-side differences between countries in their technologies (as in the Ricardian model) or in their factor endowments (as in the Heckscher–Ohlin theory). The latter explanation has come under attack because of its perceived empirical failure to account satisfactorily for the pattern of trade after World War Two, especially for the large and growing fraction of world trade that is intraindustry in nature. Partly because of this, the Heckscher–Ohlin theory has been challenged in the past two decades by a 'new trade theory' some of whose models dispense altogether with the notion of comparative advantage.

Despite this challenge, trade models based on comparative advantage continue to have pride of place in textbooks on international economics. The concept itself continues to receive plaudits, such as those quoted above, from the best minds in the profession. These plaudits, together with the doubts which the 'new trade theory' has raised regarding its current relevance to the theory of international trade, suggest the desirability of a book-length treatment of the origins and the evolution of the concept of comparative advantage down to the present day.

Chapter 2 begins by exploring various definitions of the concept of comparative advantage, pointing out its pivotal importance in the theory of international trade. A country has a comparative advantage in a given commodity when it is relatively more productive in it compared to other countries and to other commodities. Textbooks traditionally introduce this concept with examples similar to that presented by David Ricardo in his *Principles of Political Economy and Taxation*, where two commodities are produced at constant cost by one factor of production, labor. The law of comparative advantage, that a country tends to export commodities which it can produce more cheaply than other countries, is easy to demonstrate in this case since there are no 'exceptional' commodities. Complications arise when the setting becomes more general with regard to both the technology used and the numbers of factors and commodities. It is no longer true that a country necessarily exports every commodity which it can produce more cheaply before trade. Such 'antinomies' require that the law of comparative advantage be appropriately reformulated so as to guarantee its validity (Drabicki and Takayama, 1979; Deardorff, 1980; Dixit and Norman, 1980). The resulting formalization of the relationship between comparative advantage and trade flows, which is here named the Deardorff–Dixit–Norman theorem, will be used as a benchmark against which to evaluate some of the theories examined in subsequent chapters. The relationship between comparative advantage and the gains from trade is examined in both classical and neoclassical economies. The roots of comparative advantage, or reasons why a country exhibits a greater facility than others in producing certain types of goods and services, are discussed in the final section. Alternative theories of trade have been grounded in the selection of a specific feature believed to be responsible for it, such as consumer tastes, a superior technology, economies of scale or the abundance of certain factor endowments, *to the exclusion of all others*. These theories, discussed at greater length in the remaining chapters of the book, are here given a preliminary and somewhat cursory look as examples of the multifaceted manifestations of comparative advantage.

Chapter 3 begins by sketching the rudimentary rationales for international trade formulated in preclassical times. After a brief glimpse at the providentialist beginnings of trade theory, mercantilist writers are evaluated in light of some revisionist interpretations of their writings advanced in recent years. Whereas many commentators in the past accused them of being obsessed with the achievement of a positive balance of trade because they confused wealth with money, some enlightened thinkers of that period in fact developed profound insights into the workings of a competitive market economy, which were eagerly adopted by Adam Smith and the classical school. One of the achievements of the mercantilist period is the enunciation of what Jacob Viner referred to as the 'eighteenth-century rule' by which to evaluate the gains from trade. This rule is related in this chapter to the measures of the gains from trade and of comparative advantage examined in Chapter 2, and is illustrated diagrammatically.

After a brief look at the *raison d'être* of foreign trade according to the physiocrats, attention turns to the theories of trade that can be found in Adam Smith's *Wealth of Nations*. According to Smith, trade depends on a country having an *absolute* advantage in its export goods over its trading partners, in the sense that it can produce these goods at a lower real cost. This advantage is intrinsically subject to change since it derives from the division of labor and the latter's dependence on the extent of the market, whose size is increased by the addition of an export market. Smith's notion of the advantages of trade is intimately related to his views on economic development, and can thus be regarded as anticipating the new trade and growth theories examined in Chapters 9 and 10. As well as a 'productivity' theory of trade, Smith advanced a more controversial 'vent-for-surplus' theory, according to which trade is prized since it creates an outlet for goods with an insufficient domestic demand. Two other controversial issues examined in this chapter are whether Smith can be regarded as a precursor of (1) the Heckscher–Ohlin theory of trade, and (2) the concept of comparative (as opposed to absolute) advantage.

Smith's ideas on trade were rediscovered only in recent times after they were superseded by the Ricardo–Torrens theory of comparative costs, which is the subject of Chapter 4. The modern theory of international trade can be said to trace its beginnings to the enunciation of the principle of comparative advantage in the early nineteenth century. Although David Ricardo and Robert Torrens share the credit for discovering this principle, it is usually attributed to Ricardo who, in chapter 7 of his *Principles* of 1817, provided the first and justly famous numerical example of wine and cloth being traded between England and Portugal. Ricardo's 'four magic numbers' (as Paul Samuelson, an unabashed admirer of the power of this principle, called them), representing labor inputs per unit of output in each country, imply that Portugal benefits by exporting wine to England in exchange for cloth, even though she is assumed to be more productive (that is, to have a greater absolute advantage) in both sectors. The reason is that her superiority in wine exceeds that in cloth, so that it pays her to transfer resources from cloth to wine. Although Ricardo himself did not use the term 'comparative advantage' for a country's relative superiority in certain lines of activity, he attributed this superiority to 'its situation, its climate, and its other natural or artificial advantages' (Ricardo, 1951a, p. 132). Such factors are commonly subsumed under the name of 'technology', taken to be a primitive concept requiring no explanation but conditioning what Torrens aptly called the 'territorial division of labor'.

Ricardo's trade theory has an important dynamic component that has been unfortunately neglected in most accounts of it. The dynamic benefits of trade arguably eclipsed in Ricardo's mind the static benefits usually associated with his comparative cost example. The Ricardian trade-and-growth model presented in this chapter highlights these dynamic benefits, while allowing full play to each country's comparative advantage.

Despite the differences between them, classical economists and the subsequent generation of neoclassical ones concluded that free trade based on comparative advantage is the optimal commercial policy. However, there were some exceptions to the general adoption of this principle and this policy. Chapter 5 provides an interlude in the saga of the formal development of the concept of comparative advantage by examining the dissent from a free trade policy voiced by statesmen and economists who argued that the free trade doctrine does not apply to what are nowadays referred to as less developed countries. According to them, comparative advantage can be created and need not be accepted as given. Their dissent was heard soon after the publication of the *Wealth of Nations*, and gathered momentum in the first half of the nineteenth century. An early dissenter was Alexander Hamilton, Secretary of the Treasury under President Washington, who wrote the influential *Report on the Subject of Manufactures* in 1791 recommending tariff protection for the nascent American manufacturing industry. The case for protection was made even more powerfully by a Scottish economist who emigrated to Canada and then to the US, John Rae. Rae (1834) took Adam Smith to task for his cavalier dismissal of the infant industry argument for protection, and in the process of making his case against Smith he pioneered the theory of capital. Another exponent of a national system, Friedrich List (1827, 1856), articulated his views in the US and in his native Germany, and inspired nationalist policymakers in Europe and later the less developed countries.

John Stuart Mill, the last great classical economist, became convinced by Rae's rebuttal of Smith, and pleaded in his *Principles of Political Economy* of 1848 in favor of temporary protection for infant industries, giving this argument an aura of respectability among mainstream economists which it retained for a century. After Ricardo and before the neoclassical economists, Mill was the most important innovator in the theory of international trade, and his contributions are discussed in Chapter 6. In what Francis Y. Edgeworth referred to as the 'great chapter' 18 of his *Principles*, he introduced reciprocal demand as a determinant of the terms of trade. In 1852 he made certain remarkable additions to this chapter, such as his demonstration of the existence of a trade equilibrium, which most economists believe were inspired by the work of William Whewell (1850). Mill's solution for the equilibrium terms of trade depended on his assumption of unitary price elasticities of demand, and can be shown to be a special case of the general mathematical solution developed by Whewell when he translated Mill's theory into mathematics. It therefore seems appropriate to refer to a 'Mill–Whewell' law of international values. While Mill followed the Ricardian lead in attributing comparative advantage to technological differences between countries, he pointed out that each country's comparative advantage, represented by its autarky price ratio, sets limits within which the terms of trade must lie. If they coincide with a country's autarky price ratio, it neither specializes in its export commodity nor gains from trade. Echoing views expressed a century earlier by David Hume, Mill went beyond Ricardo in portraying the powerful impact of foreign trade on the work habits and skills of a country's labor force, in fact in inducing 'a sort of industrial revolution' in a previously closed economy. Chapter 6 also discusses the advances made by some of Mill's contemporaries, such as Mountifort Longfield's generalization of the Ricardian model to many commodities and the modifications of the principle of comparative advantage that began to be made towards the end of the classical era.

The marginal revolution of the 1870s brought far-reaching changes not only in the theories of value and distribution but also in international trade theory. This revolution was implemented very differently by the British and the continental European economists who analyzed its implications for trade theory. The diverse approaches taken by the first generation of neoclassical economists, represented by Alfred Marshall, Vilfredo Pareto and Enrico Barone, are described in Chapter 7. In England, Marshall (1879) rigorously formulated Mill's reciprocal demand model and illustrated it by means of offer curves. He and Edgeworth (1894) used them to analyze if a trade equilibrium is stable, and how it changes in response to technical improvements or trade taxes, but provided no additional insights into the nature of comparative advantage in the Ricardo–Mill model. Marshall later tried unsuccessfully to generalize it by lumping tradable commodities into 'representative bales' produced by a heterogeneous bundle of factors of production. By substituting this approach for the labor theory of value, he added to the longevity of the real cost approach to trade theory, which was subsequently taken up by Jacob Viner and Frank Taussig.

Marshall's method was subjected to a vigorous attack by Pareto in two remarkable papers published in Italian in the mid-1890s, and then at greater length in his *Cours d'économie politique* (1896–97). Pareto was the first to apply to two trading economies the Walrasian general equilibrium model comprising many goods and factors of production. In his *Manual of Political Economy* of 1906, he also made several contributions to the political economy of trade and protectionism, and clarified the nature of the Ricardian model. His friend Barone deserves mention as the economist who, in 1908, first drew what became the standard neoclassical diagram depicting a country's trade equilibrium and its gains from trade. He also used it to analyze the dynamic losses that can arise if the terms of trade fluctuate on either side of the autarky price ratio. This chapter closes with an appendix formalizing the generalization of the Ricardian model to many commodities effected in successive steps by H. Mangoldt, F. Edgeworth and G. Haberler. This generalization is shown to satisfy, both mathematically and diagrammatically, the Deardorff–Dixit–Norman theorem set out in Chapter 2.

Because of the differences in outlook and approach between Gottfried Haberler on the one hand, and Eli Heckscher and Bertil Ohlin on the other, it may seem surprising to juxtapose their names in Chapter 8, devoted to the second generation of pioneers of neoclassical trade theory. Aside from the coincidence that the books of Haberler (1933), in its original German, and Ohlin (1933) appeared in the same year, the rationale for this is that the theories of both economists can be regarded as applications of Walrasian general equilibrium theory to international trade. A few years earlier, Haberler (1930) had anticipated the key trade-theoretical chapter 12 of his book with a paper that generalized the constant-cost assumption of the Ricardian model to the case of increasing costs. In Austrian fashion, he envisaged comparative advantage in terms of opportunity cost, representing the quantity of goods which must be sacrificed to produce an additional unit of a particular commodity. If costs increase with the volume of production, he showed that the economy's transformation curve is bowed out rather than linear. Haberler attributed increasing costs to the existence of 'specific' factors of production, defined as those which cannot readily be shifted from one sector to another. His insights gave birth 40 years later to the specific-factors model of trade, an anticipation for which he has not been given sufficient credit in the literature. Another of Haberler's bequests was his insight that the passage of time affects an economy's trade equilibrium, as manifested by a change in the curvature of the transformation curve between the short run and the long run.

Despite the many significant contributions to the development of the concept of comparative advantage since Ricardo's *Principles*, no economist had yet formulated a full-fledged theory of trade capable of explaining why countries export certain goods and import others. This glaring lacuna in the classical and neoclassical theories of trade prompted the Swedish economists Heckscher (1949) and Ohlin (1933) to ascribe comparative advantage to a nation's resource endowments. Heckscher's paper, originally published in Swedish in 1919, is a *tour de force* setting out in crystal-clear fashion what became known as the Heckscher–Ohlin theory, which became the dominant theory of trade in the twentieth century. Assuming that technology and tastes are identical everywhere, as are the qualities of commodities and factors of production, this theory states that countries tend to export commodities whose production uses intensively their relatively abundant factors, and to import those which intensively use their scarce ones. Ohlin's aspersions on the classical model of comparative costs (he characterized the latter theory as a *deus ex machina*) were motivated by his desire to differentiate his views from those preceding them. Like Pareto whose work he admired, Ohlin expressed his trade model in an appendix in terms of a general equilibrium system with many commodities and factors of production. However, the complex set of simultaneous equations it contained, not being operational, could not be used by him to derive any of his results. The verbal theories of Heckscher and Ohlin inspired Paul Samuelson to specialize their model to two commodities, two factors and two countries (the 2 × 2 × 2 case), converting it into a small but solvable general equilibrium system. In recognition of his vital contributions to its diffusion as the mainstream theory of trade, it is now known as the Heckscher–Ohlin–Samuelson (or H–O–S) trade model. Since the latter assumes constant returns to scale, it is sometimes forgotten that Ohlin adduced in chapter 3 of his book 'another condition of interregional trade', namely economies of scale, whose importance in his mind was second only to differences in factor endowments. Ohlin also anticipated many insights of the new trade theory, such as the role of chance and history in establishing a country's trade pattern.

Chapter 9 begins by setting out the assumptions and core propositions of the H–O–S theory. This is presented for the 2 × 2 × 2 case in terms of Ronald Jones's (1965) 'magnification effect', whereby commodity price changes are magnified into the rewards of the factors intensively used to produce them, and endowment changes are magnified into the changes of the outputs of the commodities in which they are embodied. Two of the core propositions of the H–O–S theory, the Stolper–Samuelson and Rybczynski theorems, are derived in terms of these effects, and used to prove the Heckscher–Ohlin and factor price equalization theorems. The extension of the 2 × 2 × 2 Heckscher–Ohlin model to many commodities is examined to determine whether a chain of comparative advantage exists similar to that established for the classical model in Chapter 7. We also consider Jones's (1974) attempt to reconcile the Ricardian and Heckscher–Ohlin models via a multicommodity and multicountry generalization of the latter, as well as the chain of relative factor endowments proposed by Jaroslav Vanek (1968) to define a country's comparative advantage in the multifactor case in terms of its world shares of these factors. The H–O–S model is compared to the writings of Heckscher and Ohlin examined in Chapter 8, to evaluate what was gained and lost in the transition from one to the other.

Attention then shifts to a remarkable development of the past two decades, the 'new trade theory' which rose to challenge the dominant H–O–S paradigm. One reason for its emergence was the doubt cast on this paradigm by several anomalies such as Wassily Leontief's discovery after World War Two that the US exported labor-intensive rather than capital-intensive products (the so-called Leontief paradox), and the empirical finding that much of world trade is intraindustry in nature, with two-way trade taking place even within fairly narrowly defined product categories. The goods in question are mostly differentiated products produced under increasing returns to scale, and their manufacture appears to be carried out under market structures other than the perfect competition assumed by the H–O–S model, such as monopolistic competition or oligopoly (Krugman, 1990). Some authors have concluded that comparative advantage is not needed to explain trade of this type, since even economies that are identical in every respect can find it mutually beneficial to trade. The exponents of the new trade theory have in fact argued that much of world trade cannot be attributed to any of the determinants identified by the classical and neoclassical economists, such as climate, technology and the relative abundance of natural resources, labor (skilled and unskilled) or machinery. It is instead due to historical accidents such as which country first produced a commodity and exploited the related economies of scale. Since these points were made by Ohlin in 1933, the 'new' trade theory is not as new as some of its researchers have claimed.

The new trade theory was followed by a 'new growth theory' which harked back to an unfinished agenda of the growth theory of the 1950s and 1960s, and attempted to endogenize technical change rather than assume it exogenously given. Total factor productivity was empirically shown to grow at a faster rate in more open economies, and can thus be interpreted as an indicator of dynamic comparative advantage. The new trade and growth theories can claim Adam Smith as their intellectual forefather in light of Smith's insistence that an economy's productivity depends primarily on the division of labor, which itself depends on the extent of the market (including a country's export market). There is also a kinship between these theories and the thesis, advanced by the dissenters from a free trade policy considered in Chapter 5, that comparative advantage can be created (Lucas, 1993). This issue is especially important for developing countries seeking to transform their economies while reaping the benefits of the international division of labor.

Chapter 10 gathers together the threads of the determinants of comparative advantage examined in the previous chapters, and seeks to evaluate their historical and present-day importance, as well as their implications for economic policy. One of the leitmotivs of this book is the dynamic interpretation of comparative advantage that has prevailed in the past. This chapter begins by recalling that the classical economists believed comparative advantage to be inherently changeable because of technical progress, population growth on a fixed stock of land, or technological diffusion via the import of technology, skills or machinery. They also held that trade confers dynamic gains, allowing an economy to grow more quickly because of a rise in the profit rate, or to benefit from economies of scale which improve its competitiveness and the quality of its resources. The infant-industry argument for protection represents an exceptionally dynamic view of comparative advantage, giving policymakers the freedom to create it. The critiques of the concept of comparative advantage voiced in the neoclassical era are also examined. These range from Ohlin's dismissal of this theory as a *deus ex machina* to the inability of the Heckscher–Ohlin theory to produce anything similar to Ricardo's wine–cloth example, because of its assumption that technology is identical everywhere.

The validity of the Heckscher–Ohlin theory is briefly examined in light of the empirical evidence that has been collected over the past half century. This evidence casts serious doubt on two of its building blocks, the assumption of internationally identical production functions and that of identical and homothetic tastes (Trefler, 1995), and argues in favor of a synthesis of the Ricardian and Heckscher–Ohlin models. The impact of the new trade theory on the relevance of comparative advantage is assessed. Some models of the new trade theory explain intraindustry trade in terms of country size, rather than factor endowments and comparative advantage. But other models constructed by its exponents reserve an important role for comparative advantage, which is created either by a Smithian process of learning-by-doing associated with specialization and the division of labor, or by the visible hand of public policy. In such cases, one can even speak of a resurrection of Ricardian comparative advantage, endogenously determined rather than exogenously given. Since Ricardo occupies a central position in this book as the co-discoverer of comparative advantage and the economist with whom this concept has been primarily linked, a section of this final chapter examines the varieties of trade models that have been associated with his name over the past 180 years. While economists have used, and continue to use, the term comparative advantage in different and often incompatible ways, it remains an almost generally valid concept of the theory of international trade.

2. The Concept of Comparative Advantage

2.1 Searching for a definition

Since the early nineteenth century, comparative advantage has been the bedrock on which all subsequent developments in the theory of international trade have rested. Thanks to Ricardo's memorable example of cloth and wine being traded between England and Portugal, economists, the general public and even most politicians have come to accept that every nation has a comparative advantage in certain types of goods and services, though it may lack an absolute advantage in them. To arrive at a generally acceptable definition of comparative advantage is a different matter. A widespread view is that a country has a comparative advantage in commodities which it can produce more cheaply than other countries. The problem with this view is that, in the absence of trade impediments or transport costs, trade tends to equalize commodity prices in different countries. Some authors thus amend the above statement to say that the commodities in which a country exhibits comparative advantage are those which it is capable of producing more cheaply than other countries in a fictitious state of the world in which countries are isolated from each other, or self-sufficient, or in a state of *autarky*.

However, it became clear in the past two decades that even the last statement is in general erroneous, and can reflect only a *tendency*. It was shown (Drabicki and Takayama, 1979; Deardorff, 1980; Dixit and Norman, 1980) that a country does not necessarily export each commodity which it produces more cheaply in autarky than another country, or import each commodity which it produces at higher cost. Defining 'net imports' as imports minus exports (positive if a commodity is imported and negative if it is exported), all that one can claim (special cases aside) is that a country's net imports are positively *correlated* with the differences between the autarky prices in that country and in its trading partner, as expressed in the theorem stated below. Thus, a country *tends* to import commodities whose autarky prices are higher there than elsewhere, and vice versa. But in a trade equilibrium it may export (import) a commodity whose autarky price exceeds (falls short of) that abroad. Specific examples of this have been offered by Drabicki and Takayama, and (in algebraic terms) by Dixit and Norman. A general explanation of this phenomenon is that exports and imports are the solution of a general equilibrium system which can reflect complex relations of complementarity and substitutability between commodities, either on the production or the consumption side.

Most textbooks of international trade illustrate comparative advantage by means of Ricardo's own example quoted below in Chapter 4, or of a similar example based on four numbers representing the productivity of labor (or its inverse, the labor needed per unit of output) in two sectors in each of two countries. Comparative advantage is then evinced by the commodity which each country produces relatively cheaply. If the two countries' autarky price ratios differ, there is no ambiguity regarding the commodity in which each exhibits a comparative advantage. But the addition of even one extra commodity means that autarky price ratios can no longer be used as guides to comparative advantage. Bilateral comparisons of relative prices for pairs of commodities are misleading. This was shown by Ethier (1984, p. 137) as follows. Let us adopt the convention (here and elsewhere in this book) that variables in lower case letters relate to the home country, and those in upper case letters to the foreign country. Assume that the autarky price ratios for three goods (1, 2 and 3) in the home and foreign countries are such that

$$p_1/P_1 < p_2/P_2 < p_3/P_3. \tag{2.1}$$

A pairwise comparison of goods 1 and 2 leads to the prediction that the home country exports good 1 and imports good 2. A pairwise comparison of goods 2 and 3 similarly suggests that it exports good 2 and imports good 3. Since a country cannot simultaneously export and import the same good, this procedure is clearly faulty.

Ethier (ibid.) showed that even the weaker statement that autarky prices form a 'chain of comparative advantage' is in general invalid. Thus, suppose that the autarky prices of n commodities are such that

$$p_1/P_1 < p_2/P_2 < ... < p_n/P_n. \tag{2.2}$$

In general there is no borderline commodity j such that the home country exports all goods from 1 to j, and imports all goods from $j+1$ to n, although this may happen in special cases such as the multicommodity Ricardian model discussed in Chapter 7.

Deardorff (1980) and Dixit and Norman (1980, chapter 4) showed that comparative advantage is still a meaningful concept if it is interpreted in the weaker sense that nonnegative *correlations* exist between a country's net imports of commodities and (i) their autarky prices, (ii) the differences between their autarky prices and their free trade prices, and (iii) the differences between their autarky prices and those of its trading partner. As we shall see, these correlations follow from the demonstration that the value of each country's net imports at autarky prices is non-negative. This, in turn, is based on the inference that the community's utility level is at least as high after trade as before it.

Let m_i denote the net import of commodity i, which is an import if $m_i > 0$ and an export if $m_i < 0$. The corresponding net import vector of the home country is m, and its output, demand (= consumption) and price vectors are y, d and p. Subscripts $i = 1, \ldots , n$ refer to the n commodities which enter the above vectors. Superscripts a and t refer to a country's autarky and trade equilibria. The *inner product* of two n–dimensional vectors a and b, written ab, is equal to the sum of the products of their corresponding elements a_i and b_i, or $ab = \sum_{i=1}^{n} a_i b_i$. The authors mentioned above proved what will be referred to as the Deardorff–Dixit–Norman (DDN) theorem:

Deardorff–Dixit–Norman theorem: The inner products $p^a m$, $(p^a - p^t)m$ and $(p^a - P^a)m$ are non-negative.[1]

This theorem is proved as follows. Given that the home country consumes the bundle d^t in the trade equilibrium even though its autarky bundle was available to it, d^t must be at least as expensive as d^a at autarky prices, or

$$p^a d^t \geq p^a d^a. \qquad (2.3)$$

The output bundle y^a, chosen at the autarky prices p^a, maximizes the home country's GNP at those prices, so that

$$p^a y^a \geq p^a y^t. \qquad (2.4)$$

The consumption of each commodity in autarky must equal its output, or $y^a = d^a$, so that (2.3) and (2.4) can be combined to yield

$$p^a d^t \geq p^a d^a = p^a y^a \geq p^a y^t. \qquad (2.5)$$

From the double inequality (2.5) and the definition of net imports, $m = d^t - y^t$, we obtain

$$p^a m \geq 0. \tag{2.6}$$

The second part of the theorem is obtained by subtracting from (2.6) the balance of trade constraint

$$p^t m = 0, \tag{2.7}$$

which results in

$$(p^a - p^t) m \geq 0. \tag{2.8}$$

The third part is obtained by applying (2.6) to the foreign country (whose net import vector is $M = -m$) as well as to the home country, and adding these two inequalities to yield

$$(p^a - P^a) m \geq 0. \tag{2.9}$$

(Q.E.D.)

The DDN theorem establishes a positive correlation between the components of the vector m and those of each of the vectors p^a, $(p^a - p^t)$ and $(p^a - P^a)$. A country therefore imports commodities which tend to have the following attributes: (1) higher than average autarky prices, (2) autarky prices which exceed their free trade prices, and (3) autarky prices exceeding those in the foreign country.

The first part of the theorem is illustrated for the two-commodity case in Figure 2.1, whose horizontal axis measures home country imports (exports) of good 1 to the right (left) of the origin, while the vertical axis measures its imports (exports) of good 2 above (below) the origin. The ray SOS' defines the home country's autarky price ratio, its slope with the vertical axis measuring the relative price of good 2 in terms of good 1. It is tangent at point O to the home country's offer curve AOD.[2] If the international terms of trade are defined by the ray OT, indicating a lower price of good 2 compared to autarky, point A represents the home country's equilibrium trade vector, consisting of exports BO $(= -m_1)$ of good 1 and imports AB $(= m_2)$ of good 2. Taking good 1 to be the numeraire (unit of account), the value of net imports at autarky prices is $m_1 + (p_2/p_1)^a m_2 = -BO + BC = OC$, confirming the nonnegative sign of what will be referred to as the 'DDN index'. If the terms of trade were given by OD instead of OT, the corresponding trade bundle would be point D, with the home country exporting good 2 in exchange for good 1. The value at autarky prices of its net imports in terms of good 1 would again be positive and equal to OC.

Figure 2.1   The DDN index in the two-commodity case

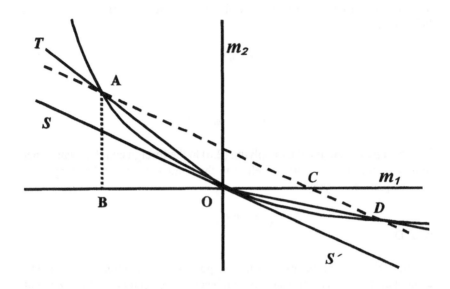

In order to illustrate the DDN theorem diagrammatically in the multicommodity case, the correlations which it implies are first rewritten as follows. Let $\rho = (\rho_i)$ be the vector of ratios of the home country's autarky prices to the corresponding world prices, so that

$$\rho_i = p_i^a/p_i^t. \qquad\qquad (i = 1, \dots , n) \quad (2.10)$$

Let $V_m = (V_{mi})$ be the vector of net imports valued at world prices, so that

$$V_{mi} = p_i^t\, m_i. \qquad\qquad (i = 1, \dots , n) \quad (2.11)$$

Then inequality (2.6) can be rewritten as[3]

$$\rho V_m \geq 0. \qquad\qquad (2.12)$$

Renumber commodities so that the first k are imported while the remaining $n - k$ are exported. If $m_i > 0$, let $\underline{m}_i = m_i$ ($i = 1, \dots , k$) denote home country imports of commodity i; if $m_i < 0$, let $x_i = -m_i$ ($i = k + 1, \dots , n$) denote the exports of i. Then (2.12) can be rewritten as

$$\sum_{i=1}^{k} \rho_i(p_i^t \underline{m}_i) \geq \sum_{i=k+1}^{n} \rho_i(p_i^t x_i). \tag{2.13}$$

By (2.7), $\sum_{i=1}^{n} V_{mi} = 0$, or

$$\sum_{i=1}^{k} p_i^t \underline{m}_i = \sum_{i=k+1}^{n} p_i^t x_i. \tag{2.14}$$

Hence the import-value weighted average of the ρ_i ratios of the commodities imported by the home country is greater than or equal to the export-value weighted average of the ρ_i ratios of its exported commodities.

The correlation between the components of ρ and V_m, which is equivalent to that between p ª and m, is depicted in Figure 2.2, where the vertical axis plots ρ_i and the horizontal axis represents V_{mi}. The values at world prices of home country imports (exports) of commodity i are plotted to the right (left) of the origin. Points in the right-hand (left-hand) quadrant represent commodities imported (exported) by the home country. Inequality (2.13) implies that the sum of the rectangles (not drawn) subtended by the points in the right-hand quadrant exceeds the sum of those subtended by points in the left-hand quadrant. Because of (2.14), the sum of the bases of the rectangles in the right-hand quadrant, total imports at world prices, equals the sum of the bases of those in the left-hand quadrant, total exports at world prices. (2.13) and (2.14) imply that the import-value weighted average of the heights ρ_i of the rectangles in the right-hand quadrant exceeds the export-value weighted average of the heights of the rectangles in the left-hand quadrant. In other words, the average ratio of the autarky prices of imported commodities to their free trade prices exceeds the corresponding ratio for exported commodities.

Let P be the vector of ratios of the foreign country's autarky prices to the corresponding world prices, so that

$$P_i = P_i^a/p_i^t. \qquad (i = 1, \dots, n) \tag{2.15}$$

Inequality (2.9) can then be rewritten as

$$(\rho - P) V_m \geq 0, \tag{2.16}$$

or as

$$\sum_{i=1}^{k} (\rho_i - P_i)(p_i^t \underline{m}_i) \geq \sum_{i=k+1}^{n} (\rho_i - P_i)(p_i^t x_i). \tag{2.17}$$

Hence the import-value weighted difference between the ratios ρ_i and P_i of the commodities imported by the home country is greater than or equal to the export-value weighted difference between them of its exported commodities.

Figure 2.2   Correlation between autarky prices, free trade prices and net imports

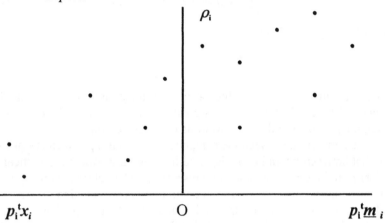

Figure 2.3   Correlation between autarky price differences and net imports

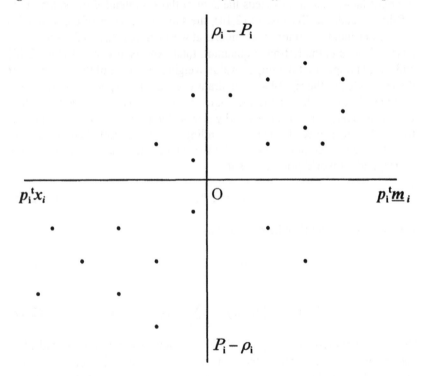

The correlation between the components of $(\rho - P)$ and V_m, which is equivalent to that between $(p^a - P^a)$ and m, is depicted in Figure 2.3, where the vertical axis plots $(\rho_i - P_i)$ and the horizontal axis is the same as in Figure 2.2. Inequality (2.17) implies that the sum of the areas of the rectangles (not drawn) subtended by points in the NE and SW quadrants exceeds the sum of the areas of those subtended by points in the NW and SE quadrants. Commodities represented by points in the NE and SW quadrants are exported by the country where they are cheaper in autarky; those in the NW and SE quadrants are exported by the country where they are dearer in autarky. The existence of commodities falling in the latter category weakens, but does not invalidate, the non-negative correlation between $(p^a - P^a)$ and m postulated by the DDN theorem.

Note finally that inequality (2.8) can be rewritten as

$$(\rho - 1)V_m \geq 0, \tag{2.18}$$

where 1 is an n–component vector of 1's. A diagram reflecting the correlation between $(\rho_i - 1)$ and V_{mi} would be spread over four quadrants, like Figure 2.3.

Another issue of interest is the relationship between the free trade price vector p^t and the autarky price vectors p^a and P^a. The inequality corresponding to (2.6) for the foreign country is $P^a M \geq 0$. Substituting $M = -m$ into this and combining it with (2.6) and (2.7), we obtain

$$p^a m \geq 0 = p^t m \geq P^a m. \tag{2.19}$$

Hence p^a and P^a lie on opposite sides of the hyperplane defined by $p^t m = 0$.[4] However, inequality (2.19) does not in general imply that

$$p^a \geq p^t \geq P^a, \tag{2.20}$$

that is, that the free trade price vector lies 'between' the two autarky price vectors. While this holds in the case of a two-commodity model, when commodities number three or more it is possible that the free trade prices of some commodities violate (2.20) by falling short of, or exceeding, the corresponding autarky prices in *both* countries. This is another of the antinomies pointed out by Drabicki and Takayama (1979). We can thus conclude that a country may not only export a commodity whose autarky price exceeds the other country's, but that the world price of a traded good may exceed (or fall short of) the pre-trade prices in both countries. Inequality (2.19) does, however, imply that the free trade price vector is wedged loosely (but not strictly) between the two autarky price vectors. The same message is conveyed by (2.8) and by the corresponding inequality for the foreign country.

2.2 Comparative advantage and the gains from trade

Since its inception, the notion of comparative advantage has been associated with the gains resulting from international trade. Starting with Adam Smith, the classical economists frequently merged the positive and normative aspects of trade. Ricardo expressed this with his well-known dictum that

> it is quite as important to the happiness of mankind, that our enjoyments should be increased by the better distribution of labour, by each country producing those commodities for which by its situation, its climate, and its other natural or artificial advantages, it is adapted, and by their exchanging them for the commodities of other countries, as that they should be augmented by a rise in the rate of profits. (Ricardo, 1951a, p. 132)

Conceptually, however, the normative and positive aspects of trade theory can and should be kept distinct, since a nation can engage in trade without gaining from it. A given degree of comparative advantage, as measured by the DDN index p^*m, can be associated with varying degrees of gains from trade.[5]

Two indices are commonly used to provide a monetary measure of the 'gains from trade', or change in economic welfare resulting from the opening of trade in a previously closed economy: the equivalent variation (EV) and the compensating variation (CV). The CV is the amount of income that must be taken away at the set of free trade prices to restore welfare to its autarky level, whereas the EV is the income which must be given at the original set of autarky prices to attain the level of welfare associated with free trade. The CV is often preferred to the EV to depict the gains from trade since it allows their decomposition into production gains and consumption gains.[6] It is convenient to define the CV and the EV in terms of a community's expenditure function $e(p, u)$, which denotes the minimum amount of expenditure needed to attain the level of utility u at the set of prices p. The CV associated with the passage from autarky to free trade is given by

$$CV = e(p^t, u^t) - e(p^t, u^a).$$ (2.21)

The EV, the alternative measure of welfare change, takes p^a rather than p^t as the reference price vector, and is defined as

$$EV = e(p^a, u^t) - e(p^a, u^a).$$ (2.22)

Figure 2.4   DDN index and equivalent variation in a neoclassical economy

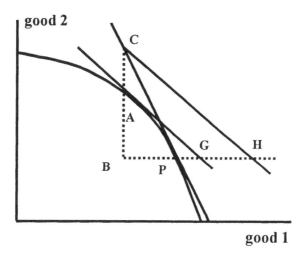

The above formulas for the CV and EV assume that the compensation (or equivalence) is of the Hicksian type, such that the community is just able to achieve the pre- or post-trade levels of welfare respectively. If the 'equivalence' underlying the EV is instead of the Slutsky type, EV_S, the community is able to buy the free trade consumption bundle at the autarky prices.[7] Substituting in (2.22) $p^a d^t$ for $e(p^a, u^t)$, and $p^a d^a$ for $e(p^a, u^a)$, we obtain

$$EV_S = p^a (d^t - d^a). \tag{2.22a}$$

To establish the relationship between EV_S and the DDN index $p^a m$, we note that

$$\begin{aligned} p^a m &= p^a(d^t - y^t) = p^a(d^t - d^a) + p^a(y^a - y^t) \\ &= EV_S + p^a(y^a - y^t) \ge EV_S, \end{aligned} \tag{2.23}$$

since, from (2.4), $p^a(y^a - y^t) \ge 0$. Hence, the DDN index overestimates or, in the limit, equals the Slutsky EV. To obtain a graphical illustration of their relative magnitudes, Figure 2.4 depicts a neoclassical economy with a strictly concave production possibility frontier (PPF). Its autarky equilibrium is at point A, where the price ratio is given by the slope of the line AG. The terms of trade are equal to the slope of the line PC, and the production and

Figure 2.5   DDN index and equivalent variation in a classical economy

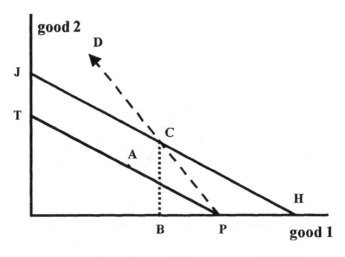

consumption points in the trade equilibrium are P and C. If the exportable good 1 is the numeraire, the Slutsky EV (2.22a) is measured by the difference GH between the values of the consumption bundles C and A at autarky prices. The trade vector consists of exports BP (= $-m_1$) of good 1 and imports CB (= m_2) of good 2. The DDN index, representing the value of net imports at autarky prices in terms of good 1, is $m_1 + (p_2/p_1)^a m_2 = -\text{BP} + \text{BH} = \text{PH}$. Since this exceeds EV_S by the distance PG, we confirm that in a neoclassical economy the DDN index overestimates the Slutsky EV of the gains from trade.

Figure 2.5 depicts a 'classical' economy with a linear PPF, TP, and autarky equilibrium at A. The autarky price ratio is given by the slope of TP. If the terms of trade are given by the slope of the ray PD, the economy specializes in good 1 at point P. Assume that consumption occurs at point C located on the consumption possibilities frontier PD, so that CBP is the trade triangle. If the line JCH is drawn parallel to TP, the value of the DDN index $p^a m$ in terms of good 1 is again BH − BP = PH. But in this case the Slutsky EV is also equal to PH, so that in a classical economy the DDN index also serves as a measure of the gains from trade.[8]

The reason why the DDN index can measure the gains from trade in a classical economy, but overestimates them in a neoclassical one, is not far to seek. If, in Figures 2.4 and 2.5, the autarky price ratios were by chance equal and the trade triangles were congruent, the respective DDN indices would take the same value. In Figure 2.4, EV_S would fall short of its value in Figure 2.5, since an economy with a concave PPF which is induced to specialize is less efficient in transforming the importable good into the exportable one than one with a linear PPF. The reason is that this transformation is subject to increasing costs, which are analogous to the 'difficulty of production' to which Ricardo alluded in chapter 2 of his *Principles of Political Economy and Taxation*. In Ricardo's case, the pressure of population on the land causes the margin of cultivation to be pushed out. As agricultural output expands, its price rises in terms of manufactures. It is somewhat paradoxical that, in international trade textbooks, it is Figure 2.5 that is commonly associated with Ricardo's name rather than Figure 2.4. This paradox is examined in Chapter 4, which discusses the Ricardian system, as well as Chapter 8, which considers the concave PPF which Gottfried Haberler introduced in 1930 in order to generalize the classical model.

For the model illustrated in Figure 2.5, a new interpretation of the EV and hence of the DDN index is provided in Chapter 3. When that index is expressed in terms of labor rather than a commodity numeraire, it coincides with what Viner (1937) labeled the eighteenth-century rule for assessing the gains from trade.

2.3 The causes of comparative advantage

The DDN theorem establishes correlations between a country's net import vector and the vector of home country autarky prices, or of the difference between the latter and foreign country autarky prices or free trade prices. Much of the theory of international trade seeks to explain such correlations by identifying the *proximate* sources of comparative advantage, that is, the economic reasons why some countries tend to have lower autarky prices for certain commodities than for others, and hence to export them. A common feature of the models based on comparative advantage is that the latter is derived from *differences* between countries, whether in tastes, technology, factor endowments or other characteristics. This has been intuited and stated in a variety of ways since the earliest times, as in the providentialist or universalist view of trade examined in Chapter 3. David Hume (1955, p 79) anticipated Adam Smith and David Ricardo when he argued that 'nature, by giving a diversity of geniuses, climates, and soils, to different nations, has secured their mutual intercourse and commerce, as long as they all remain industrious and civilized'.

If two economies are identical in every respect, or if one of them is a blown-up replica of the other and their tastes are identical and homothetic, their autarky prices are equal and there is no incentive for them to trade. In order for comparative advantage to exist, in the immortal French words, *c'est la différence qui compte.* It subsequently dawned on economists that comparative advantage is a sufficient but not a necessary condition for trade. As discussed in Chapters 9 and 10, the 'new trade theory' which revolutionized international economics in the past two decades stresses the notion that trade need not be based on differences between two trading partners, but can in fact be more intense the greater the similarity between them. Over a century before this theory emerged, some economists, pamphleteers and policymakers had argued that comparative advantage can be created, and need not be accepted as originating from a country's current characteristics. The views on the promotion of industries entertained by the mercantilists and by three major advocates of a national system will be examined in Chapters 3 and 5 respectively. When modeling any of the main sources of comparative advantage, it is assumed that the others are inoperative, so that in all other respects countries are identical. This *ceteris paribus* condition is a familiar one to students of economics. In its absence, a given source of trade can be counteracted by one of the other sources.

The first major source of trade, international differences in tastes, is self-explanatory. If two countries are identical except that one has a more pronounced taste for certain commodities, that country has a higher pre-trade price for them and hence tends to import them in exchange for commodities that are more in demand in its trading partners. The considerable differences which have been observed in countries' expenditure patterns suggest that this can be an important cause of international trade, even if convergence in per capita incomes combined with an international demonstration effect can dampen these differences over time.

The remaining reasons for trade relate to supply-side rather than demand-side differences between countries. A second reason for differences in autarky prices, emphasized by the classical economists, is that techniques of production vary among countries because of inherent characteristics such as 'climate', location, skills, factor endowments, and (as Ricardo put it) 'other natural or artificial advantages'. Differences in country-specific suitabilities for the production of commodities were taken to be a primitive datum, seldom explained in terms of more fundamental causes. Ricardo did not elucidate the rationale for technological differences among countries, which he represented by labor productivities. But he realized that these are not given once and for all, and allowed for what are now referred to as 'reversals of comparative advantage', which lead a country to export a commodity it used to import and vice versa. One reason for such reversals may be technological discoveries, as if England were 'to discover a process for making wine, so that it should become her interest rather to grow it than import it' (1951a, p. 137). An equally important source of modifications in the technology used, mentioned in the previous section, is the increased 'difficulty of production' of commodities such as 'corn' which occurs when a country's population grows and the extensive (or intensive) margin of cultivation is pushed out. As will be stressed in Chapter 4, the associated variations in a country's land-labor endowment ratio were never far from the classical economists' minds as a significant determinant of comparative advantage.

This brings us to a third major explanation of comparative advantage that was advanced by the Swedish economists Eli Heckscher (1949) and Bertil Ohlin (1933). Countries differ not because of technology, which is assumed to be everywhere the same, but because factor endowments are distributed unevenly among them. A country tends to export commodities whose production utilizes intensively those factors with which it is relatively well endowed, and to import those which intensively utilize factors that are relatively scarce in it. Some classical economists (including Adam Smith) anticipated Heckscher and Ohlin to a certain extent by relating factors' abundance to their cheapness, and hence to the export of commodities embodying their services. The Heckscher–Ohlin theory of trade has been the 'mainstream' explanation of trade in the post-war period and is examined in Chapters 8 and 9. In the multicommodity case, this theory asserts that the factor intensity of a country's net exports is *correlated* with its relative factor abundance. It is an eminently plausible explanation of many types of trade such as that in primary goods which, being inherently land-intensive, can only be exported by countries where land is abundant. The 'availability' theory of trade of Kravis (1956) is a first cousin of the Heckscher–Ohlin (or possibly of the Ricardian) theory. It stipulates that a country exports a resource or commodity which happens to be available there and not elsewhere. Such availability can be interpreted as an extreme example of absolute (or comparative) advantage, which is infinitely great for the commodity in question.

The Heckscher–Ohlin theory is nowadays customarily presented in the rigorous though simplified form which Stolper and Samuelson ([1941] 1949) and Samuelson (1948, 1949) imparted to it for the 2 × 2 × 2 case. The Heckscher–Ohlin–Samuelson (H–O–S) model is highly effective for pedagogical purposes, but had the stultifying effect of focusing attention on the two-factor version of the theory. The 'Leontief paradox' that emerged from Wassily Leontief's empirical test of the theory for the US economy (examined in Chapter 9), based on capital and labor as the only two primary factors, led to many subsequent attempts to evade the straitjacket of the two-factor case.

Additional major explanations of trade include the cheapening of commodities resulting from economies of scale, external economies and dynamic increasing returns ('learning by doing'). Some of these can be traced back to Adam Smith, who insisted that the division of labor and its productivity-enhancing benefits are limited by the extent of the market. Such explanations were not neglected by subsequent classical economists, or neoclassical ones such as Marshall, but were ruled out of court by the H–O–S theory of trade, which postulated constant returns to scale and an unchanging technology. It is ironic that Ohlin himself – in contrast to the reductionist versions of his theory – was fully aware of the importance for trade of economies of scale, and his 1933 book elaborated in some detail on their supplementary role in stimulating trade flows. This rationale for trade is inconsistent with comparative advantage, since a country's production costs can be lower simply because it was the first to start producing a commodity. Its acquired expertise allows it to become the low-cost world producer even though other countries, with an earlier start, could have had lower production costs. Learning by doing may allow such countries to realize their potential comparative advantage in a line of production for which they are suited. The important distinction between actual and potential comparative advantage is explored in Chapters 5 and 9.

The explanations of trade discussed so far often operate jointly rather than in isolation from each other. Moreover, any one of them can undergo modification as the economy evolves. Not only is this true of Ricardian comparative advantage, as pointed out above, but of other theories such as that based on factor endowments, which can change because of endogenous growth or migration. These explanations by no means exhaust all possible rationales for trade. Chapter 3 begins by considering several theories advanced in pre-classical times, and ends with the rich menu of choices offered by the putative founder of the classical school, Adam Smith.

Notes

1. This theorem suggests a non-negative 'correlation' between the vectors which constitute each of these inner products, using that term in the sense of a relationship rather than a correlation coefficient. However, Deardorff (1980) has shown that a suitable choice of numeraire yields nonnegative correlation *coefficients* only between m and either $(p^a - p^t)$ or $(p^a - P^a)$. The weak inequalities used below to prove this theorem allow for the possibility that a country's demand vectors coincide in trade and autarky, so that it neither gains nor loses from trade. If its demand vector changes as it passes from autarky to trade, the theorem can be strengthened to postulate that the above inner products are strictly positive, as in Deardorff (1994a).
2. As Deardorff (1980, p. 948) pointed out, 'autarky prices provide a supporting hyperplane for the set of all possible trades'.
3. This reformulation of (2.6) corresponds to Corollary 1 of Deardorff (1980).
4. Woodland (1982, p. 208) makes the equivalent point that one of the autarky price vectors forms an acute angle with that hyperplane and the other an obtuse angle.
5. See Maneschi (1998a).
6. See Dixit and Norman (1980, pp. 71–2) and Cornes (1992, chapter 9).

7. On the difference between Hicks and Slutsky compensations, see Varian (1992, pp. 135–7).
8. Note, however, that even in the classical case the DDN index continues to overestimate the EV if the latter is defined in the Hicksian way.

3. Theories of International Trade up to Adam Smith

3.1 The providentialist beginnings of trade theory

The analogy between an individual's need to trade with other individuals and a nation's need to trade with other nations, in both cases due to their lack of self-sufficiency, was stressed by the ancient Greeks, starting at least with Plato. The city-state of Plato's time, even more than present-day nation-states, did not have a diversified economy and needed to trade with other states in order to acquire the resources or commodities it lacked. This need to interact with other states, in order to compensate for a state's own deficiencies, had the positive result of stimulating the division of labor. The attendant increases in productivity, which became the centerpiece of Adam Smith's *An Inquiry into the Nature and Causes of the Wealth of Nations* (1976), were a benefit of trade of which the Greeks were fully aware.

The Greeks and Romans were aware of the advantages of certain types of soil for the cultivation of particular crops, leading to agricultural specialization. Parts of the ancient world were well known for certain prized products which could not be obtained elsewhere. Before itemizing them, Virgil listed the properties of the land with which his 'never-satisfied farmer' must become familiar in order to be successful:

> The land's peculiar cultivation and character,
> The different crops that different parts of it yield or yield not.
> A corn-crop here, grapes there will come to the happier issue:
> On another soil it is fruit trees, and grass of its own sweet will
> Grows green. Look you, how Tmolus gives us the saffron perfume,
> India its ivory, the unmanly Sabaeans their incense,
> The naked Chalybes iron, Pontus the rank castor,
> And Elis prize-winning mares.
> Nature imposed these laws, a covenant everlasting,
> On different parts of the earth right from the earliest days when
> Deucalion cast over the tenantless world the stones

From which arose mankind, that dour race.

(Virgil, *The Georgics*, Book I, 1990, p. 28)[1]

The notion that 'nature imposed these laws, a covenant everlasting, on different parts of the earth right from the earliest days' implies that specialization, and hence comparative advantage, are frozen for ever. It is consistent with the static view of its determinants which later became associated with Eli Heckscher and Bertil Ohlin. The suitability of the land to 'the different crops that different parts of it yield or yield not', and the availability of certain commodities in some parts of the world but not others, suggest both the restrictiveness of mother nature and the advantages she has granted to some locations over others.

The economic mutualism associated with trade was given a religious dimension in the Christian era. The perceived need for a state to rely on other states for some of the commodities it requires was interpreted as part of a plan of divine providence to foster a spirit of cooperation and amity between different peoples. Following Viner (1972), we can speak of a 'providentialist' theory of trade, or alternatively of a 'doctrine of "Universal economy", a phase of the more general doctrine of the "universalism" of mankind' (Viner, 1991, p. 41). This consists of two interrelated parts: that providence encourages different peoples to trade as a means of promoting solidarity between them, and creates the incentive for this by scattering resources unevenly throughout the globe. Viner has traced the first full statement of this thesis to a teacher in Antioch in the fourth century AD, Libanius, who was pagan but paradoxically taught two of the earliest Church Fathers, St. Basil and St. John Chrysostom. Through them and later theologians it entered the Christian tradition. Viner cites the following statement of Libanius, translated from the Greek original:

> God did not bestow all products upon all parts of the earth, but distributed His gifts over different regions, to the end that men might cultivate a social relationship because one would have need of the help of another. And so he called commerce into being, that all might be able to have common enjoyment of the fruits of earth, no matter where produced. (Viner, 1972, pp. 36–7)

This notion was adopted by some theologians, but not by others who associated all kinds of trade with greed, exploitation and luxury. Even after Libanius' formulation had become a mainstream Christian view in the high Middle Ages, it was rejected by some scholastics for religious or moral reasons, some of which had been voiced much earlier. According to them, self-sufficiency was viewed as preferable to economic dependence on foreigners. Contact with the latter was likely to introduce objectionable customs, including the worship of foreign gods and a taste for luxuries, to engender envy and even to breed wars. The greatest of the scholastics, St. Thomas Aquinas, on the one hand espoused Libanius' providentialist view, but on the other hand was suspicious of contact with foreigners on non-economic grounds. On economic grounds, he praised the ideal of self-sufficiency, but also conceded that even a perfect city may require the services of merchants to import needed goods or to dispose of surpluses.

The providentialist view of trade has resurfaced through the centuries down to recent times, and was sometimes rediscovered by proponents who were not aware of its ancient lineage. According to Viner, economists who advocated it include Robert Torrens, Nassau Senior, Johann H. von Thünen and John Rae, author of *New Principles on the Subject of Political Economy* (1834). This list omits Ricardo, who in his *Essay on Profits* (1951b, p. 31) observed that 'if the weather is injurious to one soil, or to one situation, it is beneficial to a different soil and different situation; and, by this compensating power, Providence has bountifully secured us from the frequent recurrence of dearths'. While this rationale for trade stresses the need for international economic mutualism and suggests the gains to be derived from it, it does not of itself give any indication of comparative advantage. Libanius and his followers spoke of the differential geographic availability of products. From the seventeenth century on, this was extended to differences in the endowments of factors of production, climate, skills and tastes. In the twentieth century, its progeny was the Heckscher–Ohlin theory of trade, which will be evaluated in Chapters 8 and 9.

In the absence of any analytic underpinnings for comparative advantage, some writers in the sixteenth and seventeenth centuries sought to interpret the dictates of providence in decidedly nationalistic terms. Their suggestions, of which Viner cites some revealing examples, smack much more of mercantilism than of providentialism.[2] French polemicists argued that since providence had made France the only economy able to produce a full range of necessities, France's imposition of severe import restraints did not violate its dictates. English polemicists argued for self-sufficiency in sectoral rather than economy-wide terms. Given that providence had blessed England with a plentiful supply of raw wool, they contended that it must have intended the wool to be processed into woolens. It would be a sign of ingratitude to God to suppose that he had withheld from the English the 'aptness of wit' needed to manufacture cloth. These and similar examples led Viner to ask:

> How do such writers discover in advance, when the interests of rival nations conflict, which nation providence will choose to prefer, and how is it that they almost invariably find that

it is their own nation? I suppose the answer is that pious patriotism is a natural product of the psychological propensity to find affinity between cherished ideas. (Viner, 1972, p. 44)

While providentialist thought can point to economic and non-economic gains from trade, it turns into special pleading when the issue of comparative advantage is raised. This underlines the need for an analytic theory of trade.

The providentialist theme reappeared in altered form during the French Enlightenment under the name *doux commerce*. The origins and vicissitudes of this term have been ably investigated by Hirschman (1977). He cites a reference to the providentialist theory in *Le parfait négociant* (1675) by Savary, who went on to say that 'this continuous exchange of all the comforts of life constitutes commerce and this commerce makes for all the gentleness (*douceur*) of life'. Subsequently Montesquieu opined that 'it is almost a general rule that wherever the ways of man are gentle (*moeurs douces*) there is commerce; and wherever there is commerce, there the ways of men are gentle' (cited in Hirschman, 1977, p. 60). Hume followed him in this view, while ascribing to trade other advantages examined below.[3] Trade came to be regarded as a peaceful, inoffensive occupation associated with the 'polished nations' of Western Europe, and the idea that wealth is compatible with virtue is fundamental to Adam Smith's *Wealth of Nations*.[4] However, Hirschman (1977, p. 62) has wryly noted that 'the persistent use of the term *le doux commerce* strikes us as a strange aberration for an age when the slave trade was at its peak and when trade in general was still a hazardous, adventurous, and often violent business'. This leads us to examine the mercantilist attitude towards trade theory and trade policy.

3.2 Mercantilism and the theory of trade

Given the length of time over which it lasted (from the sixteenth to the second half of the eighteenth century), the way it was interpreted in different countries and the fact that even in the same country it never became a school of thought in the conventional sense of the term, it is difficult to associate a specific theory of trade with the writings of what Adam Smith called 'the commercial, or mercantile system'. Heckscher (1930, p. 337) stressed the policy side in his definition of mercantilism, which 'in the sense of a policy and doctrine of protection represents the most original contribution of the period in question to economic policy and the one which has retained more sway over men's minds than any other'. Viner (1968, p. 439) similarly described mercantilism as 'a doctrine of extensive state regulation of economic activity in the interest of the national economy'. In his monumental earlier study (1937), he provided an in-depth analysis of the mercantilist writings on foreign trade issues.[5] One of the main contributions stressed by Viner was the eighteenth-century rule for the gains from trade, which paved the way for subsequent developments in the theory of comparative advantage and is discussed in the next section. Even critics of the mercantilists such as Schumpeter (1954) have pointed out that they developed several useful concepts which entered the international economics literature, such as the balance of payments and the balance of trade. The correction of disequilibria in the balance of trade, the difference between exports and imports, has remained to this day a fundamental concern of policymakers.

Much ink has been spilled on the reasons why so many mercantilists appeared obsessed with achieving a favorable balance of trade. Most commentators in the past adopted a negative attitude towards this policy goal as well as the analytical contributions of this period. Some maintained that mercantilists wished to promote exports and discourage imports in order to accumulate the difference in the form of bullion (precious metals). This policy aim was allegedly epitomized in the title of Thomas Mun's ([1664] 1954) classic contribution to the mercantilist literature, *England's Treasure by Forraign Trade, or the Ballance of our Forraign Trade Is the Rule of our Treasure*, first published in 1664 but written some 40 years earlier. Ever since Adam Smith criticized them virulently in Book IV of his *Wealth of Nations*, and perhaps in good part because of this criticism, mercantilists have been accused of confusing wealth with money, despite the fact that some explicitly referred to the Midas fallacy. The accumulation of precious metals over an indefinite period of time seems indeed a peculiar national policy target, and whether such a goal is feasible was questioned in mercantilist times even before David Hume formulated the price specie flow mechanism. One of the earliest defenses of the mercantilists came from J. M. Keynes (1936, p. 336) who, in his desire to find anticipations of his own views, related a positive balance of trade to an economy's need for liquidity, and its implications for the interest rate and for investment. A later interpretation was that an important goal of the 'reform mercantilists' was the generation of a high rate of employment, and that a 'balance of labor', or 'foreign paid incomes', or the 'export of work' was the chief force underlying their concern with the balance of trade.[6]

Some revisionist writers, stressing the continuity between scholastic and mercantilist thought, as well as between mercantilist and classical thought, have recently concluded that the mercantilists should be viewed in a far more positive light.[7] They claim that 'it is impossible to portray [mercantilism] as a simple defense of protectionism and authoritarian economic policies sponsored by the state' (Magnusson, 1993, p. 9), and argue 'against the notion that the favourable balance of trade should be looked upon as a mere consequence of an asserted confusion between money and wealth. Such a folly is hardly observable in the mercantilist literature' (Magnusson, 1994, p. 159). Their research claims that the mercantilists advocated a favorable trade balance for a multiplicity of reasons, the accumulation of precious metals being of decidedly secondary importance. Foremost in their minds was to bring about an allocation of resources in line with what they perceived to be the primary goals of a developing economy, one of which was the export of manufactures with high value added. What seems certain is that the mercantilists already thought of the economy as a system, or as a complicated machine, in which variables such as the balance of trade must be related to other economic variables of far greater interest to them.

These revisionist writers reject the interpretation of mercantilism as a mere advocacy of protectionism. Despite some inconsistencies to which the mercantilists were subject, many of them were critical of contemporary state policies, and some eloquently supported a policy of free trade, as well as the dissolution of state-sponsored monopolies. Conversely, Adam Smith and several subsequent members of the classical school endorsed certain policies that can only be labeled as mercantilist. Magnusson (1993) has argued that what was occurring during this period was nothing less than a 'mercantilist revolution', satisfying the four criteria for a revolution in economic thought set out by Hutchison (1978). Hutchison (1978, 1988) has even questioned if a 'Smithian revolution' occurred at all! Smith and his *Wealth of Nations* were heavily indebted to innovations made over the previous century by writers such as Galiani, Cantillon, Tucker, Mandeville, Gervaise, Hume and other figures of the Scottish Enlightenment. Owing to Smith's animosity towards mercantilism, some of the very writers from whom he drew inspiration have sometimes (paradoxically) been tarred with the same brush as less enlightened thinkers.

While granting that the mercantilist writers 'began to lay the foundations of the general theory of international trade that was to take shape in the last decades of the eighteenth and the first decades of the nineteenth centuries', Schumpeter (1954, pp. 348, 367, 369) charged that 'the bulk of the literature is still essentially preanalytic, and not only that, it is crude'. Moreover, 'nobody seems ... to have had any inkling of the principle of comparative costs'. This last dictum is overly harsh. An economist of the mercantilist era who had more than an inkling of the sources of comparative advantage, its shifts over time, and the close relationship between trade and economic development, is Josiah Tucker, who engaged David Hume in what is known as the 'rich country–poor country' debate.[8] Tucker was anxious to correct Hume's contention that rich countries would suffer from the competition of poor ones because of the latter's low wage and price levels. Following their correspondence through an intermediary mutual friend, Lord Kames, Tucker ([1774] 1973, p. 177) claimed that 'though I cannot boast that I had the Honour of making the Gentleman [Hume] a *declared* Convert, yet I can say ... he has wrote, and reasoned, as if he was a Convert'.[9] Tucker argued (pp. 184–7) that rich countries compensated for their higher wages and prices by the superiority acquired through 'general Application, and long Habits of Industry', as evidenced *inter alia* by established trade and credit; a great variety of tools and machinery; good roads and other types of infrastructure; experienced, skilled and knowledgeable factors; a more advanced division of labor; a greater capacity for making technical improvements and undertaking long-term and large-scale investments; a more competitive market structure; a more prosperous home market; and a lower rate of interest. These characteristics are much more backward or simply do not exist in poor countries. Tucker was led to enunciate

> as a general Proposition, which very seldom fails, That *operose* or *complicated Manufactures* are cheapest in rich Countries;–and *raw Materials* in poor ones: And therefore in Proportion as any Commodity approaches to one, or other of these *Extremes*, in that Proportion it will be found to be cheaper, or dearer in a rich, or a poor Country ... [Moreover] there are certain *local* Advantages resulting either from the Climate, the Soil, the Productions, the Situation, or even the natural Turn and peculiar Genius of one People preferably to those of another, which no Nation can deprive another of. (Tucker [1774] 1973, pp. 188, 193)

Tucker's notion of comparative advantage in developed (rich) and developing (poor) countries coincided with that espoused by many mercantilists, who spoke of a country's 'riches' as either 'natural' or 'artificial', the former coming from the earth and the latter from 'manufactories' (Magnusson, 1994, p. 154). The territorial division of labor which Tucker envisaged was destined to be one that most economists thereafter would accept as natural. As described in Chapter 5, even a 'nationalist' economist like Friedrich List maintained that tropical countries have no 'vocation' for manufacturing. But unlike List, Tucker was referring to rich and poor countries with comparable climates, and reached the more positive conclusion that 'the very same Country may be relatively both richer and poorer than another at the very same Time, if considered in different Points of View' ([1774] 1973, p. 194). Thus a poor country may produce certain manufactures more cheaply than a rich one, as illustrated by the fact that Scotland and Ireland were more productive than England in linen manufacture thanks to a head start of more than half a century. These and other thought-provoking observations, as well as his support of free trade, guarantee for Tucker a position of honor among pre-Smithian economists.

The Hume–Tucker debate shows that economists, already in the eighteenth century, perceived the fluid nature of comparative advantage, noting that its evolution over time determines the relative economic status of nations. In his essay 'Of Commerce', Hume (1955, p. 14) observed that 'commerce with strangers ... rouses men from their indolence' and that 'imitation soon diffuses all those arts; while domestic manufactures emulate the foreign in their improvements, and work up every home commodity to the utmost perfection of which it is susceptible'. As noted in Chapter 6, a century later J. S. Mill held a similar view of the advantages of trade. In 'Of the Jealousy of Trade', Hume argued (1955, pp. 78–9) that 'the encrease [sic] of riches and commerce in any one nation, instead of hurting, commonly promotes the riches and commerce of all its neighbours.... Every improvement, which we have since [two centuries ago] made, has arisen from our imitation of foreigners.... Notwithstanding the advanced state of our manufactures, we daily adopt, in every art, the inventions and improvements of our neighbours'. His contention that 'imitation soon diffuses all those arts' showed great insight, and is still reflected two centuries later in the expression 'international diffusion of technology'. Hume also maintained that no country should worry that other countries can improve their techniques to such an extent that they no longer demand any of its products, seeing that 'nature, by giving a diversity of geniuses, climates, and soils, to different nations, has secured their mutual intercourse and commerce, as long as they all remain industrious and civilized' (1955, p. 79). The diversity among nations thus implies that each can expect to retain a comparative advantage *vis-à-vis* its trading partners. Hume's attribution of comparative advantage to different 'geniuses, climates, and soils' was later echoed by Smith, Ricardo and other classical economists.

Returning to Schumpeter's contention that the mercantilists had no interest in the notion of comparative advantage, any failing in this regard should be attributed to the *Zeitgeist* rather than to any theoretical inaptitude. Mercantilism was defined by Viner (1968, p. 439) as 'a doctrine of state intervention in economic life, but of state interventionism of a special pattern and with some special objectives'. It sometimes involved a detailed regulation of foreign trade, with policy tools differentiated by type of import and export. Exports of manufactures – particularly those with a high labor content – were encouraged, those of agricultural goods and raw materials were discouraged, while the export of machinery was condemned since it allowed foreigners to become productive in lines of activity regarded as a domestic preserve. Imports were tolerated if they involved goods domestically not available or raw materials that could be worked up into wrought goods, or if they represented a *quid pro quo* from a country willing to allow entry to domestic exports. Imports of luxuries or of finished manufactures were discouraged. Export bounties and import restrictions were graduated according to these criteria. Trade incentives included allowing private companies to monopolize certain foreign (as well as domestic) markets, or even to administer colonies. Some of these protectionist policies resemble those adopted after World War Two by developing countries pursuing industrialization via import substitution.[10]

Mercantilist thinkers tended to think of trade in a diametrically opposite way to modern trade theorists. The latter argue about the sources of comparative advantage, and go on to examine how a country which specializes according to it is likely to gain from trade. Mercantilists thought first in terms of policy goals, such as output, employment or national power, and went on to devise appropriate sectoral priorities to achieve them. Comparative advantage thus took on a normative hue, being a question of prescription rather than description. This perspective is understandable given the mercantilists' goals and the constraints facing them. Of course, Adam Smith had strong objections to the 'folly and presumption' of statesmen when they favor one sector over another, instead of leaving such choices to individuals motivated by their private interests under the guidance of the invisible hand.

3.3 Gains from trade and the eighteenth-century rule

One of the remarkable contributions of the mercantilist period was the articulation of what Viner has called the 'eighteenth-century rule' for the gains from trade, according to which 'it pays to import commodities from abroad whenever they can be obtained in exchange for exports at a smaller real cost than their production at home would entail' (Viner, 1937, p. 440). While it is true that this 'rule' gives no indication of the sources of comparative advantage, it offers a powerful rationale for specialization in accordance with its dictates. The gains from trade it implies are presented below in simple mathematical terms and illustrated graphically. Viner provided several instances where this rule was used by British writers. Although he dated the rule from 1701, an even earlier instance of it occurred in 1673, when Samuel Fortrey argued against restrictions on the export of corn. He claimed that the export of cattle was more remunerative since it could purchase a greater amount of corn: 'for the profit on one acre of pasture, in the flesh, hide, and tallow of an Ox ... is so much greater value abroad, than the like yield of the earth would be in corn' (Fortrey, 1673, p. 17; cited by Magnusson, 1994, p. 101).

Viner quoted the following numerical example of the rule by the unknown (to him) author of *Considerations on the East-India Trade* of 1701, who has been since identified by Macleod (1983) as Henry Martyn:[11]

If nine cannot produce above three Bushels of Wheat in *England*, if by equal Labour they might procure nine Bushels from another Country, to imploy these in agriculture at home, is to imploy nine to do no more work than might be done as well by three; ... is the loss of six Bushels of Wheat; is therefore the loss of so much value. (Martyn, [1701] 1954, p. 583)

Martyn provided a more poetic illustration of the gains from trade when he described the advantages of importing foreign commodities in terms of the discomfort which the inhabitants of the importing country can avoid:

> Our Wants at home might be supply'd by our Navigation into other Countries, the least and easiest Labour. By this we taste the Spices of *Arabia*, yet never feel the scorching Sun which brings them forth; we shine in Silks which our Hands have never wrought; we drink of Vineyards which we never planted; the Treasures of those Mines are ours, in which we have never digg'd; we only plough the Deep, and reap the Harvest of every Country in the World. (Martyn, [1701] 1954, p. 585)

Another instance of Viner's rule occurred much later in Turgot's 'Letter on the "Marque des fers"' of 1773:

> To persist in opposing ... [the advantages of free trade] from a narrowminded political viewpoint which thinks it is possible to grow everything at home, would be to act just like the proprietors of Brie who thought themselves thrifty by drinking bad wine from their own vineyards, which really cost them more in the sacrifice of land suitable for good wheat than they would have paid for the best Burgundy, which they could have bought from the proceeds of their wheat. (Quoted in Groenewegen, 1983a, p. 591)

The eighteenth-century rule was subsequently used by Adam Smith to illustrate the gains from trade.[12] In his famous comparative cost example, Ricardo (1951a, chapter 7) also appealed to it to illuminate the gains from trade, when he argued that Portugal could obtain more cloth by exchanging some of her wine for English cloth than by manufacturing the cloth herself, even though her labor was more productive in cloth than English labor. Viner did not believe that Ricardo's principle of comparative costs went much further than that:

> Such gain from trade is always possible when, and is only possible if, there are comparative differences in costs between the countries concerned. The doctrine of comparative costs is, indeed, but a statement of some of the implications of this rule, and adds nothing to it as a guide for policy ... This explicit statement that imports could be profitable even though the commodity imported could be produced at less cost at home than abroad was, it seems to me, the sole addition of consequence which the doctrine of comparative costs made to the eighteenth-century rule. (Viner, 1937, pp. 440–41)

The eighteenth-century rule reflects the benefits of trade viewed as an indirect method of production. Consider this in the context of a two-commodity economy where good 1 is exported, good 2 is imported and labor is the only factor of production. Let the superscripts a and t represent the autarky and trade equilibria. If a_i is the amount of labor needed to produce one unit of good i, one unit of labor can produce either $1/a_2$ units of good 2 or $1/a_1$ units of good 1, which can be exchanged for $(1/a_1)(p_1/p_2)^t$ units of good 2 at the terms of trade $(p_1/p_2)^t$. This trade is beneficial as long as

$$(1/a_1)(p_1/p_2)^t > 1/a_2, \tag{3.1}$$

or

$$(p_1/p_2)^t > a_1/a_2 = (p_1/p_2)^a, \tag{3.1a}$$

which implies that the terms of trade exceed the price ratio under autarky, a_1/a_2. In Martyn's numerical example of 1701 quoted by Viner and reproduced above, the LHS of inequality (3.1) amounts to 1 bushel of wheat per unit of labor, while its RHS is only ⅓ bushel, so that trade results in a gain of ⅔ bushel of wheat per unit of labor employed.

The gains from trade implied by inequality (3.1) are expressed per unit of labor shifted from the importable to the exportable sector. Under 'classical' technological assumptions, the corresponding total gains from trade to the nation can be shown to be proportional to the Deardorff–Dixit–Norman (DDN) index defined in Chapter 2 and to the equivalent variation (EV) of the gains from trade. In light of Adam Smith's dictum that 'what every thing is really worth to the man who has acquired it ... is the toil and trouble which it can save to himself, and which it can impose upon other people' (Smith, 1976, p. 47), it seems consonant with the eighteenth-century rule to express the gains from trade in terms of the total labor saved when m_2 units of good 2, rather than produced directly, are imported in exchange for exports x_1 of good 1. The economy allocates a_1x_1 units of labor in order to pay for imports which would have cost it a_2m_2 units of labor to produce directly. Since the balance of trade constraint implies that $x_1 = (p_2/p_1)^t m_2$, the saving in terms of 'real cost' (here represented by labor) effected by trade is

$$a_2m_2 - a_1x_1 = a_1m_2[a_2/a_1 - (p_2/p_1)^t]. \tag{3.2}$$

Since autarky prices are proportional to labor coefficients, the value of the trade vector at autarky prices in terms of good 1 is

$$p^a m = (a_2/a_1)m_2 - x_1 = m_2[a_2/a_1 - (p_2/p_1)^t]. \tag{3.3}$$

Figure 3.1   Gains from trade according to the eighteenth-century rule

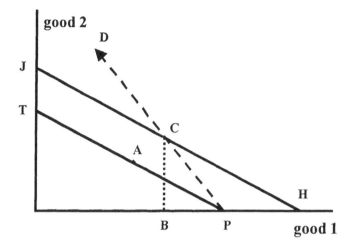

Equation (3.2) is equal to (3.3) multiplied by a_1. The difference is merely due to the different units of account, which are labor in (3.2) and good 1 in (3.3). As was shown in Chapter 2, (3.3) is also equal to the Slutsky EV in terms of good 1. If the gains from trade according to the eighteenth-century rule are measured in terms of the amount of labor saved by engaging in trade, they are therefore proportional to the DDN index as well as to the EV.

These expressions are illustrated in Figure 3.1, which reproduces for convenience Figure 2.5. The slope of the linear transformation curve TP defines the economy's autarky price ratio, and its consumption possibilities frontier is DP, whose slope is the terms of trade. It was shown in Chapter 2 that if P and C are the free trade production and consumption points, the value of the trade bundle at autarky prices in terms of good 1, $p^a m$, is equal to PH as well as to the EV of the gains from trade. Since CB is the imports of good 2 and BP the exports of good 1, the gains from trade can also be measured, according to the eighteenth-century rule, by the difference between the amount of labor which would have been needed to produce the consumption bundle C and the amount used for production at point P. If d_i and y_i are the demand for and output of good i, these gains from trade are given by $a_1 d_1^t + a_2 d_2^t - a y_1^t$ $= a_2 m_2 - a_1 x_1$, which is identical to (3.2). Geometrically, the amount of labor required to produce bundle C would have been that associated with the hypothetical transformation curve JH, so that the 'distance' (in terms of labor employed) between it and the economy's actual transformation curve TP (to which JH is parallel) measures the gains from trade.

The substantial identity between the DDN index of comparative advantage $p^a m$, the EV of the gains from trade and the eighteenth-century rule can be generalized to a multicommodity classical model. However, the eighteenth-century rule fails in the case of a neoclassical multifactor technology, since there is no longer a measure of real cost which aggregates the heterogeneous factors of production into a single number. Indeed, this is the fundamental rationale for Gottfried Haberler's (1936) advocacy of opportunity cost in terms of foregone output instead of 'real cost' as a measure of the value of marginal changes in commodity output, discussed in Chapter 8. But if we assume a single factor, labor, subject to constant returns, the eighteenth-century rule remains a valid and intuitively plausible measure of the gains from trade, three centuries after its initial formulation.

3.4 Physiocracy and the theory of trade

Physiocracy, whose etymological meaning is 'rule of nature', was a manifestation of the French Enlightenment and constituted the first full-fledged school of political economy. The insights of its adherents into the nature of economic activity and the ideal role of the state owed much to capable anticipators such as Richard Cantillon and Pierre de Boisguilbert. The physiocrats regarded their contemporary A. R. J. Turgot, if not as a full-fledged member, at least as a strong sympathizer. Under the leadership of François Quesnay, who contributed several articles to the *Encyclopédie*, they launched a frontal attack against mercantilist doctrine and articulated a program of reform for the French economy, which included freedom of both domestic and foreign trade. In the short span of two decades (beginning in 1756) over which they were active, the physiocrats influenced the British classical school and Adam Smith in particular, who spent three years in France from 1763 to 1766 and met several of them. The enduring legacies of physiocracy include the characterization of a competitive economy as one in which individuals pursuing their self-interest allow society's welfare to be maximized, and a depiction of the circular flow of commodities between the principal classes of society.[13] This circular flow was depicted and quantified in the *tour de force* of Quesnay known as the *tableau économique*, which gave rise to such heterogeneous descendants as Marx's schema of simple reproduction, neoclassical general equilibrium analysis and Leontief's input–output table. Capital expenditures in the form of advances to farmer-entrepreneurs constituted an integral part of the process of production, and laid the foundations for the classical theory of capital. More controversial contributions of the physiocrats were their distinction between productive and unproductive labor, which Adam Smith and the classical school adopted after redefining these categories; their belief (taken over from Cantillon) that agriculture is the sole productive sector of the economy in the sense of yielding a surplus over cost; and, as a consequence of this, their advocacy of a single tax on land to replace the multiplicity of contemporary taxes.

Given the physiocrats' importance in the filiation of economic ideas, it is surprising and somewhat disappointing that they failed to take an interest in and contribute to the theory of international trade.[14] While the mercantilists had given an overwhelming importance to a country's foreign trade because (*inter alia*) of its favorable effects on the pattern of economic activity, the physiocrats focused attention on agriculture. The circular flow of commodities when agriculture is the linchpin of the economic system can be depicted more easily in a closed-economy setting, as illustrated by the *tableau économique*. The physiocrats regarded foreign trade, on a par with domestic trade and manufacturing, as a 'sterile' activity. They even argued that a large volume of foreign trade is harmful, although this was tempered with the belief that this volume was in any case likely to shrink as the economy developed. They did recognize the benefits of specialization, granting that 'each country was considered as endowed with "produits privilégiés" which, because of natural conditions or national aptitudes, it could produce more "cheaply" than other countries' (Bloomfield, [1938] 1994, p. 222). Moreover, they acknowledged the providentialist function of foreign trade in promoting international economic solidarity. Foreign trade also served to dispose of unwanted surpluses as exports, or to offset shortfalls in production via imports. But these views, as we have seen, were hardly novel or specific to them.

In spite of their failure to advance the theory of international trade, the physiocrats were staunch advocates of freedom in both internal and external trade. While other individuals had previously advocated this policy, it was the first time it was endorsed by a cohesive school of economists. The physiocrats regarded freedom in foreign trade as part of the natural order, going hand in hand with their doctrine of *laissez-faire* and their efforts to reduce all impediments to internal trade. They were especially strong advocates of the freedom to export grain. Stringent regulations had prevented grain exports until 1764 and had become the subject of heated debate. This export ban was one of the many mercantilist measures which the physiocrats wanted to abolish as detrimental to the interests of the agricultural classes with which their primary sympathies lay. The free export of grain would allow its price to maintain a satisfactory level (*bon prix*) even at times of abundant harvests whereas an export ban would cause its price to fall, damaging both the profitability of agriculture and the prosperity of the nation. As Vaggi (1987a, p. 874) argues, '[the physiocrats] looked to a positive balance of trade for French agriculture, since France should have become the granary of Europe

... [and] ... regarded foreign trade as necessary only because the French domestic market was too small and too poor to guarantee the profitable sale of French corn'. Given the importance of agriculture in their system, one is tempted to conclude that the physiocrats' enthusiastic advocacy of free grain exports prevented them from forging any analytical progress with a theory of international trade that extends to economic sectors they regarded as 'sterile'.[15]

3.5 Adam Smith's theory of foreign trade

Adam Smith's masterpiece, *An Inquiry into the Nature and Causes of the Wealth of Nations*, is the founding document of the classical school of economic thought. One of Smith's critics has argued that 'no matter what he actually learned or failed to learn from predecessors, the fact is that the *Wealth of Nations* does not contain a single *analytic* idea, principle, or method that was entirely new in 1776'. But he also described Smith as 'the most famous of all economists', and his book as 'the most successful not only of all books on economics but, with the possible exception of Darwin's *Origin of Species*, of all scientific books that have appeared to this day' (Schumpeter, 1954, pp. 181, 184). Despite Smith's virulent attack on mercantilism, especially in Book IV of the *Wealth of Nations*, Schumpeter and other commentators are correct in maintaining that many of the components of his system of thought were derived from numerous writers of the mercantilist period which preceded him, as was discussed in section 3.2. His system of thought was also a product of the Enlightenment, and as such shared many elements in common with the equally remarkable systems elaborated by Cesare Beccaria and A. R. J. Turgot at about the same time. Schumpeter (1954) spoke of the 'triumvirate' of Beccaria, Smith and Turgot, all of whom set down their views of political economy in the form of treatises. Groenewegen (1983b) listed the numerous sources and authorities that these authors shared, and concluded that the intellectual foundations of classical political economy were truly international in nature. Due to the much longer span of time which he was able to devote to its elaboration, Smith's treatise is without doubt 'the most polished, most elaborate and most coherent' of the three (Groenewegen, 1983b, p. 53). Smith displayed a unique genius in his ability to synthesize the novel and profound insights contained in the economic literature of the previous century. His book contains an unrivaled depiction of the *modus operandi* of a functioning market economy, accompanied by richly supportive historical illustrations of the economic principles he enunciated.

Smith's attitude toward foreign trade and his reasons for why nations specialize in certain commodities must be examined in the context of his view that the exchange of commodities is a root cause of specialization and of the division of labor in a market economy. It is useful to contrast the *Wealth of Nations* with subsequent economic treatises beginning with David Ricardo's *Principles of Political Economy and Taxation*, which contain one or more chapters devoted to the theory of foreign trade. Despite the frequent references to foreign trade in the *Wealth of Nations*, it does not contain any chapters with that title, perhaps because Smith viewed foreign trade as a member of the genus of trade broadly defined, whether between countries, individuals, regions of a country, or town and country. Whereas Ricardo differentiated the theory of domestic values from that of international values, on the assumption that factor mobility is much greater in the domestic than in the international context, Smith made no such assumption. Also, as Myint (1977, p. 233–4) has noted, 'Smith's theory of foreign trade is closely interwoven with his theory of economic development which permeates the *Wealth of Nations* ... [it] is not confined to the chapters on the mercantile system and the colonies in Book IV; it is widely scattered all through the book'.

Smith's most significant statements on foreign trade occur in the early chapters of Book IV where he launched his broadsides against mercantilism. The gains from foreign trade are highlighted in chapter 2, entitled 'Of Restraints upon the Importation from foreign Countries of such Goods as can be produced at Home'. Positive and normative elements of trade theory (with the emphasis on normative ones) are treated simultaneously by Smith. This contrasts with the present-day practice of setting out the 'positive' theory of international trade, outlining the reasons for specialization, as a prelude to the 'normative' theory dealing with the benefits of free trade and the welfare implications of trade impediments.

Absolute advantage

The basis of a country's ability to export certain goods resides in what Smith calls its 'advantage' in them, a word which (together with the adjective 'advantageous') occurs repeatedly in chapter 2 of Book IV. After discussing the specialization which characterizes the work of tailors, shoemakers and farmers, Smith argued in favor of buying in the cheapest market, whether its advantage over other markets is natural or acquired:

> All of them find it for their interest to employ their whole industry in a way in which they have some advantage over their neighbours, and to purchase with a part of its produce ... whatever else they have occasion for. What is prudence in the conduct of every private family, can scarce be folly in that of a great kingdom. If a foreign country can supply us with a commodity cheaper than we ourselves can make it, better buy it of them with some part of the produce of our own industry, employed in a way in which we have some advantage. (Smith, 1976, p. 457)

The natural advantages which one country has over another in producing particular commodities are sometimes so great, that it is acknowledged by all the world to be in vain to struggle with them. By means of glasses, hotbeds, and hotwalls, very good grapes can be raised in Scotland, and very good wine too can be made of them at about thirty times the expence for which at least equally good can be brought from foreign countries ... Whether the advantages which one country has over another, be natural or acquired, is in this respect of no consequence. As long as the one country has those advantages, and the other wants them, it will always be more advantageous for the latter, rather to buy of the former than to make. (Smith, 1976, p. 458)

Other than by means of examples (or ironic counterexamples designed to expose the fallacies of mercantilism, as in the case of raising grapes in Scotland), Smith did not elaborate much on the sources of a country's 'advantages'. He provided some early hints in the *Wealth of Nations* when he discussed the growth of corn and the production of manufactures in Poland, France and England. He singled out a country's 'soil, climate, and situation' (1976, p. 17) as crucial determinants of its competitiveness in manufactures, which include silk manufactures and coarse woolens. The language David Ricardo used some 40 years later is almost identical to Smith's, and of the same degree of vagueness, since he attributed a country's specialization to 'its situation, its climate, and its other natural or artificial advantages' (Ricardo, 1951a, p. 132).

Smith based foreign trade on what is now called *absolute advantage*, according to which a country exports commodities that it can produce at a lower real cost than its trading partners. This is implicit in the examples which he gave, such as the one of grapes which, if produced in Scotland, would cost 30 times their cost elsewhere. Unlike Ricardo, he offered no numerical examples of the costs of two commodities in two countries, which might have suggested to him (as they did to Ricardo) the notion of *comparative* advantage. If each country has an absolute advantage in its export good, this is hardly necessary. Whether Smith can be said to have intuited the concept of comparative, as opposed to absolute, advantage is examined briefly below.

Qualitative and quantitative advantages

Smith's examples of international trade make the obvious point that countries export commodities in which they have or acquire an absolute advantage. According to Hollander (1973, p. 274), 'advantages are sometimes defined in *qualitative* terms as for example the climate of France which is more suitable for vines than is that of Scotland ... and for silks than is that of England ... However, there is also a recognition of *quantitative* differences in factor endowments'. In spite of this important distinction, Hollander overlooked it when he later maintained (pp. 283–4) that 'in effect, [Smith's] analysis defined each country's "advantage" in terms of its relative factor endowments'. Bloomfield ([1975] 1994, p. 113) also quoted some passages from the *Wealth of Nations* which support the interpretation that '[Smith] lays down with remarkable clarity the elements of the proposition later to be made famous by Heckscher and Ohlin'.[16] Such passages, drawn from what Schumpeter (1954, p. 187) has called 'the great and justly famous chapter "Of Colonies"', include the following:

> Land is still so cheap, and, consequently, labour so dear among them [the American colonies] that they can import from the mother country, almost all the more refined or more advanced manufactures cheaper than they could make them for themselves. (Smith, 1976, p. 582)

> Agriculture is the proper business of all new colonies; a business which the cheapness of land renders more advantageous than any other. They abound, therefore, in the rude produce of land, and instead of importing it from other countries, they have generally a large surplus to export. (Smith, 1976, p. 609)

Smith also noted that high wages need not be prejudicial to a country's ability to export because of offsetting trends in other factor prices:

> In countries which are fast advancing to riches, the low rate of profit may, in the price of many commodities, compensate the high wages of labour, and enable those countries to sell as cheap as their less thriving neighbours, among whom the wages of labour may be lower. (Smith, 1976, p. 114)

But the natural prices of factors of production, on which commodity prices depend, are not governed solely by relative factor endowments. According to Smith, 'the natural price [of commodities] itself varies with the natural rate of each of its component parts, of wages, profit, and rent; and in every society this rate varies according to their circumstances, according to their riches or poverty, their advancing, stationary, or declining condition' (1976, p. 80). Book III of the *Wealth of Nations* elaborates on the 'natural progress of opulence', noting that 'the cultivation and improvement of the country, ... which affords subsistence, must, necessarily, be prior to the increase of the town, which furnishes only the means of conveniency and luxury' (1976, p. 377). The specialization of the colonies in agricultural goods can thus be set down to an early stage of economic evolution rather than to a particular constellation of factor endowments. Dynamic considerations of this type stand in marked contrast to the underlying basis of the Heckscher–Ohlin theory.[17]

Another point of contrast is found in Ohlin's assumption that production functions are internationally identical, whereas Smith makes no such assumption. Hollander's *qualitative* advantages which one nation has over another (and depend on its 'soil, climate, and situation') are incompatible with it, so that a country's advantage cannot be defined solely in terms of factor proportions. In this respect, Smith's position is similar to Ricardo's, who attributed comparative advantage to unexplained differences in technology or factor endowments among countries. While factor endowments clearly play an important role in Smith's trade theory (as in his example of trade between North America and England), they may be overridden or reinforced by qualitative factors. To view Adam Smith as a forerunner of Heckscher and Ohlin seems therefore a rather strained interpretation of his position. As argued in section 8.2, a similar remark applies to other forerunners of their theory, including the few identified by Ohlin himself.

Did Adam Smith anticipate comparative advantage?

Bloomfield ([1975] 1994, p. 111) pointed out that 'almost at the beginning of his book [Smith] does make a statement that could have been developed into a theory of comparative costs, but fails to follow through'. In support he quoted part of the following passage, where Smith first argued that technical progress tends to occur at a faster rate in manufacturing than in agriculture:

> This impossibility of making so complete and entire a separation of all the different branches of labour employed in agriculture, is perhaps the reason why the improvement of the productive powers of labour in this art, does not always keep pace with their improvement in manufactures. *The most opulent nations, indeed, generally excel all their neighbours in agriculture as well as in manufactures; but they are commonly more distinguished by their superiority in the latter than in the former.* Their lands are in general better cultivated, and having more labour and expence bestowed upon them, produce more, in proportion to the extent and natural fertility of the ground. But this superiority of produce is seldom much more than in proportion to the superiority of labour and expence. *In agriculture, the labour of the rich country is not always much more productive than that of the poor; or, at least, it is never so much more productive, as it commonly is in manufactures.* The corn of the rich country, therefore, will not always, in the same degree of goodness, come cheaper to market than that of the poor. (Smith, 1976, p. 16; emphasis added)

The italicized sentences claim that richer nations are more productive than poorer ones in both manufactures and agriculture, but their superiority in the former exceeds that in the latter. In modern language, they have an absolute advantage in both industries, but a comparative advantage in manufacturing. What is still missing in Smith's formulation is a statement that, in terms of relative prices, the poor country's corn will be cheaper than the rich country's, in place of his much weaker contention that 'the corn of the rich country ... will not always ... come cheaper to market than that of the poor'. Also missing is any discussion of how the terms of trade are determined. Smith's formulation is thus comparable to that of Torrens quoted in Chapter 4, but markedly inferior to Ricardo's as a statement of comparative costs.[18]

It is for this reason that Smith's theory of foreign trade has often been regarded as inferior to Ricardo's (Bloomfield [1975] 1994). On the other hand, Myint (1977, p. 234) has posed the question: 'Granted that Smith's principal concern is with long-run economic development rather than with the static allocative efficiency of resources, is his failure to discover comparative costs really a serious handicap to his work as a trade theorist?' Myint proceeded to list five 'theoretical costs that Ricardo and J. S. Mill paid for the privilege of discovering and formalizing the comparative costs theory' and concluded that 'Smith escaped all these disadvantages'! (ibid.). As pointed out in Chapter 4, Myint's statement gives an exaggerated notion of the role which the theory of comparative costs in fact played in Ricardo's theorizing on foreign trade, and is more applicable to some of Ricardo's followers.

The 'productivity' theory of trade

Myint (1958, p. 318) identified two distinct theories of trade in Adam Smith. The first of these, the 'productivity' theory discussed in this subsection, can be related to absolute advantage, as long as this is interpreted in dynamic terms. Its connection in Smith's mind to the 'vent-for-surplus' theory, to be discussed in the next subsection, can be inferred from the fact that both theories are mentioned in the following well-known passage where Smith describes the gains from trade:

> Between whatever places foreign trade is carried on, they all of them derive two distinct benefits from it. It carries out that surplus part of the produce of their land and labour for which there is no demand among them, and brings back in return for it something else for which there is a demand. It gives a value to their superfluities, by exchanging them for something else, which may satisfy a part of their wants, and increase their enjoyments. By means of it, the narrowness of the home market does not hinder the division of labour in any particular branch of art or manufacture from being carried to the highest perfection. By opening a more extensive market for whatever part of the produce of their labour may exceed the home consumption, it encourages them to improve its productive powers, and to augment its annual produce to the utmost, and thereby to increase the real revenue and wealth of the society. (Smith, 1976, pp. 446–7)

The 'productivity' theory of trade, a term suggested to Myint by the second half of this passage, is consonant with the *leitmotiv* of the *Wealth of Nations*, the division of labor and its crucial role in fostering a country's 'wealth'. The division of labor depends on the extent of the market, which is enhanced (subject to transport costs, for which Smith explicitly allows) when an export market is added to the domestic one.[19] By stimulating the division of labor, trade enhances the level of productivity. Hence a country's absolute advantage in any sector, instead of exogenously given, is endogenously determined by its development path, which is in turn affected by its trade pattern. Smith illustrated the productivity theory by referring to the advantage that Europe derived from the discovery of America:

> By opening a new and inexhaustible market to all the commodities of Europe, it gave occasion to new divisions of labour and improvements of art, which, in the narrow circle of the ancient commerce, could never have taken place for want of a market to take off the greater part of their produce. The productive powers of labour were improved, and its produce increased in all the different countries of Europe, and together with it the real revenue and wealth of the inhabitants. (Smith, 1976, p. 448)

In other words, free trade is a *sine qua non* for a wider extension of the market and the enhanced division of labor this implies. Productivity differentials introduced by a country's trade-and-development path clearly belong to the category of 'qualitative' advantages, and reinforce the above conclusion that the quantitative advantages associated with its factor endowments play a supporting, but not a determining, role in establishing its trade pattern. The productivity theory of trade can also be contrasted with neoclassical trade theory, according to which a given technology and given stocks of factors of production yield a production possibility frontier, and trade simply results in the economy moving along this frontier in accordance with comparative advantage. Myint (1958, p. 319) pointed out that 'the Adam Smithian process of specialisation ... involves adapting and reshaping the productive structure of a country to meet the export demand, and is therefore not easily reversible', in contrast to the usual assumption that the movement of resources associated with trade is completely reversible. The productivity theory of trade thus suggests a pattern of cumulative causation whereby a nation's advantages, which initially give rise to trade, are themselves modified by trade via an irreversible feedback process.[20]

The vent-for-surplus theory of trade

The vent-for-surplus theory, which is twinned with the productivity theory in the passage quoted above, has had a much more controversial history. The term was coined by J. S. Mill (1920, p. 579) in his critique of Smith's use of it as a possible justification for trade. As noted in section 6.4, Mill called it 'a surviving relic of the Mercantile Theory', since it tends to attribute benefit to exports rather than to imports, 'as if not what a country obtains, but what it parts with, by its foreign trade, was supposed to constitute the gain to it' (ibid.). Ricardo had previously also criticized Smith's underlying assumption that a sector's capacity remains unutilized unless it is channeled into exports, since this was inconsistent with Smith's (and Ricardo's) adherence to Say's Law. Even some self-proclaimed admirers of Smith have rejected this theory or downplayed its significance.[21]

Defenders of it have included Williams ([1929] 1949), Myint (1958, 1977) and Kurz (1992). In his sweeping critique of the classical doctrine of international trade, Williams cited England as an example of a country whose 'international trade is her *raison d'être*' ([1929] 1949, p. 264) and argued that, by specializing in manufacturing for the export market, her production structure and her very factor endowments were conditioned by the pattern of trade. If she were cut off from foreign markets, it is difficult to see how these factors could effortlessly shift *à la* Ricardo–Mill into import substitute industries, since 'specialization is the antithesis of mobility, in this case of domestic movement of productive factors ... What Mill overlooked was the entire absence, under assumptions of predominant foreign trade, of comparable alternatives in purely domestic production; for by the very fact of specialization for foreign trade such alternatives could not logically exist' (pp. 263–5).

Myint (1958) related the vent-for-surplus theory to the conditions prevailing in less developed economies in the nineteenth century, and argued that their development can be accounted for by increasing export demand leading to the utilization of previously idle capacity. But since this output expansion occurred with fixed technical coefficients rather than a changing technology, this theory should be kept distinct from the productivity theory of trade. The rationale Myint offered for it is that 'the concept of a surplus productive capacity above the requirements of domestic consumption implies an inelastic domestic demand for the exportable commodity and/or a considerable degree of internal immobility and specificness of resources' (1958, p. 322). In a later paper, Myint (1977) drew attention to Smith's contention that the vent-for-surplus theory applied even to the 'landed nations' of Western Europe such as France and England. Since Smith stated that agriculture as well as manufacturing was characterized by excess capacity, Myint was correct in arguing that a nation's need for a vent for surplus can arise for reasons other than increases in productivity.

An imaginative interpretation of the vent-for-surplus theory has recently been advanced by Kurz (1992), who attributed it to the phenomenon of joint production. The lack of sufficient domestic demand for one of the joint products requires it to be disposed of via exports. Kurz cited a passage from chapter 11 of Book I, 'Of the Rent of Land', where Smith, referring to animals which provide both meat and clothing, noted that 'if there was no foreign commerce, the greater part of [the clothing materials] would be thrown away as things of no value' (1976, p. 178). Smith mentioned some other examples of joint production, mostly from agriculture, but all those cited by Kurz occur in the same chapter 11 of Book I, and there is no mention of joint production in the many passages discussing vent for surplus elsewhere in the *Wealth of Nations*. Although Kurz's rationale for a vent for surplus is ingenious and may apply to particular types of trade, there is insufficient textual evidence for it to be a general explanation of this phenomenon.[22]

Too much energy may have been devoted in the literature to teasing out the meaning of Smith's vent-for-surplus theory of trade. Its being conjoined with the productivity theory in the passage quoted above gives the edge to those who see these theories as two sides of a coin. It seems reasonable to infer that the learning by doing and economies of scale associated with specialization in a manufacturing economy could yield a productive structure whose full utilization is predicated upon exports.

An embarrassment of riches?

As was subsequently true of the British classical school, Smith was concerned more with the normative than the positive side of trade. Several influential commentators have concluded that Adam Smith's contribution to the theory of international trade was slight at best and erroneous at worst.[23] Bloomfield, Myint and others have provided a more balanced perspective by showing that Smith's trade theory, while not rigorous, is very broad in scope and intimately connected with his theory of economic development. Its cornerstone, absolute advantage, is not impervious to the passage of time, but is path dependent on the economy's evolution. Smith's productivity theory is particularly compelling and establishes him as the intellectual forefather of the new theories of international trade discussed in Chapters 9 and 10. Since absolute advantage is closely connected with a country's qualitative as well as its quantitative characteristics, it is somewhat dubious to view Smith as a precursor of the Heckscher–Ohlin theory of trade. Of course, Smith was correct to point out that relative factor abundance and the associated factor prices have an effect, sometimes a decisive one, on trade flows, but the latter are mostly dominated by productivity advantages related to the division of labor. Given his implicit assumption of less than full capacity utilization, Smith's vent-for-surplus theory is not logically incorrect, as was maintained by Ricardo and Mill, and many authors have attempted to provide a justification for it. When it is related to the productivity theory, vent for surplus carries with it the plausible implication that economies of scale can be fully exploited only if the export market is added to the domestic one. The various strands of Smith's trade theory make it much richer than the neoclassical theory which followed it a century later. For this reason it has enjoyed a renaissance since Myint resurrected it from oblivion, and has been heralded as a precursor of recent innovations in the literature of trade and economic development.

Notes

1. The action of Deucalion, son of Prometheus, is one of the Greek creation myths, whereby he repeopled the earth after a great flood by casting stones behind him. These turned into the Stone People who 'rescue[d] the earth from the desolation left by the flood' (Edith Hamilton, *Mythology*, p. 74). The second part of this passage from Virgil's *Georgics*, in its translation by John Dryden, was quoted by John Rae as the 'embryo' form of a view which he accused Adam Smith of propagating. This is that 'in the same manner as by the poet, the products of different regions are spoken of by political economists, as bestowed on them by nature, are termed natural productions, and the attempt to transfer them to other sites, is held to be a procedure in opposition to the designs of providence, whose intentions, it is asserted, in giving them these productions, were, that the inhabitants of different countries should exchange the products of their several territories with one another' (Rae, 1834, p. 257). Rae's objections to this view are set out in Chapter 5.
2. Viner (1937, pp. 100–103; 1972, pp. 42–5).
3. In his essay 'Of Commerce', Hume (1955, p. 13) argued that 'if we consult history, we shall find, that, in most nations, foreign trade has preceded any refinement in home manufactures, and given birth to domestic luxury'.
4. See Dickey (1993) and Gomes (1987, pp. 121–3).
5. See also Allen (1968), Blaug (1985, chapter 1), Schumpeter (1954, Part II, chapter 7), Spengler (1960) and Wu (1939, chapter 2). Also of interest is Allen (1970) and the subsequent critique of Coats (1973), with Allen's (1973) rejoinder.
6. For this interpretation of mercantilist policy, see Johnson (1937) and Grampp (1952).
7. See Hutchison (1988) and Magnusson (1993, 1994). Magnusson (1993) is a collection of articles by economists and historians presenting a variety of interpretations of mercantilism.
8. See Tucker ([1774] 1973), Semmel (1970, pp. 14–19) and Elmslie (1995).
9. In this and subsequent quotations in this book, any italicized words or phrases were italicized in the original text, unless I point out that the emphasis is mine.
10. For a comparison between mercantilist policies and the import substituting policies followed by some less developed countries in the postwar period, see Spengler (1960, pp. 50–52).
11. See Irwin (1996, p. 56).
12. As Bloomfield ([1975] 1994, p. 458) pointed out, Viner (1937, pp. 440–41 and 104–6) was incorrect when he implied that Smith was unaware of this rule. See Smith (1976, III.i.1 and IV.ii.12), where the former paragraph from the *Wealth of Nations* refers to the gains from trade between 'town' and 'country', and the latter to those from foreign trade.
13. See *inter alia* Schumpeter (1954, Part II, chapter 4) and Vaggi (1987a, 1987b).
14. The reasons for this have been ably analyzed by Bloomfield ([1938] 1994) and Gomes (1987, pp. 116–21), to whom this section is indebted.
15. According to Peter Groenewegen, ' extended free trade for the Physiocrats was largely confined to rural exports to create the market which made productivity gains profitable' (private communication).
16. Viner (1937, pp. 500–507) criticized Ohlin for his statement that the English classical school had failed to attribute specialization to relative factor abundance. He cited Smith as one of the classical writers whom Ohlin (1933) failed to add to his list of precursors of his own theory,

which consisted only of Sismondi and Longfield.

17. Similarly, in the chapter 'Of the Wages of Labour', Smith stated that 'it is not the actual greatness of national wealth, but its continual increase, which occasions a rise in the wages of labour. It is not, accordingly, in the richest countries, but in the most thriving, or in those which are growing rich the fastest, that the wages of labour are highest' (1976, p. 87).

18. Two recent papers by Elmslie and James (1993) and Elmslie (1994) take a new look at Smith's trade theory and examine *inter alia* the issue of whether Smith had a theory of comparative costs.

19. The division of labor and its dependence on the extent of the market are discussed at the very beginning of the *Wealth of Nations* in Book I, chapters 1–3.

20. The importance of feedback processes and cumulative causation in Smith's theory of trade is also highlighted by Elmslie and James (1993) and Elmslie (1994)

21. According to Hollander (1973, p. 276), 'mere lip-service was paid by Smith to the vent-for-surplus doctrine'. Bloomfield ([1975] 1994, p. 472) concluded that 'there still remains something of a mystery as to the exact meaning of Smith's "surplus-produce" argument, at least when applied to Britain and other more "developed" countries of Europe. It is probable that more may have been read into this argument than Smith in fact intended'.

22. For a similar view of the limits of Kurz's rationale for Smith's vent for surplus, see Elmslie (1996).

23. Bloomfield cites such opinions expressed by Bastable, Robbins, Viner, Angell, Heckscher and others, and notes that other economists have simply ignored Smith's contributions to trade theory. Bloomfield's own conclusion is that 'admittedly, Smith was not a great trade theorist, but he comes up, on the whole, with a performance that deserves respectful consideration' ([1975] 1994, p. 111).

4. David Ricardo, Robert Torrens and the Discovery of Comparative Advantage

The discovery of the concept of comparative advantage by Robert Torrens and David Ricardo, and its association with Ricardo even though Torrens had enunciated it two years earlier, are the subject of this chapter. Their respective formulations and the question of priority in this discovery are discussed in section 4.1, as is the suggestion that neither of them, but James Mill, was in fact the first to unearth this new rationale for the existence of and gains from trade. Section 4.2 argues that Ricardo's famous example of comparative advantage arising from the trade of cloth and wine between England and Portugal should be integrated with his insights into the dynamic benefits which accrue to a country that imports wage goods, and is thereby able to lower the money wage and raise the rate of profits. Section 4.3 documents this further by citing some of the numerous passages in Ricardo's *Principles* that discuss international trade and nearly always do so in connection with trade in corn. This is consistent with the policy implication with which Ricardo's name is primarily associated, the abolition of Britain's Corn Laws. Section 4.4 sets out a model of Ricardian trade which combines the dynamic thrust of the gains from trade that are implied by Ricardo's theory of rent with his formulation of comparative advantage. Section 4.5 highlights the fact that Ricardian comparative advantage determines both the direction of trade when two countries exchange corn against manufactures, and their ability to reap dynamic benefits from it. Their trade pattern as they approach the stationary state causes their factor endowments to be endogenously determined.

4.1 The Ricardo–Torrens theory of comparative advantage

1815 was a banner year in the history of economic thought. Edward West, Thomas Robert Malthus and David Ricardo formulated what subsequently became known as Ricardian rent theory. While Ricardo, in the Preface to his *Principles of Political Economy and Taxation* (Ricardo, 1951a), generously acknowledged the precedence of the first two economists in the formulation of this theory, and each economist stressed somewhat different aspects, it is now associated with his name. This discovery was destined to influence profoundly the direction which classical political economy was to take. The same year, 1815, saw the first enunciation by Robert Torrens of the equally important principle of comparative advantage, according to which a country can benefit by importing a commodity even if it is able to produce it at a lower real cost than its trading partner. The reason is that it has an even greater (that is, a *comparative*) advantage in the export commodity used to pay for this import. While there has been much debate as to whether the principle of question should be attributed to Ricardo or Torrens (or even to James Mill), 'as so often happens in the history of thought, the greater name drives out the lesser one' (Samuelson, 1969, p. 4). Just as in the case of *Ricardian* rent theory, we speak of *Ricardian* comparative advantage. But there is no denying that Torrens was the first to formulate this principle in print in his *Essay on the External Corn Trade*, where he argued that even if England can produce corn more efficiently, it may be to her advantage to import it from Poland:

> If England should have acquired such a degree of skill in manufactures, that, with any given portion of her capital, she could prepare a quantity of cloth, for which the Polish cultivator would give a greater quantity of corn, than she could, with the same portion of capital, raise from her own soil, then, tracts of her territory, though they should be equal, nay, *even though they should be superior*, to the lands of Poland, will be neglected; and a part of her supply of corn will be imported from that country. For, *though the capital employed in cultivating at home, might bring an excess of profit, over the capital employed in cultivating abroad*, yet, under the supposition, the capital which should be employed in manufacturing, would obtain a still greater excess of profit; and *this greater excess of profit would determine the direction of our industry*. (Torrens, 1815, pp. 264–5; emphasis added)[1]

Ricardo's own statement of the principle of comparative advantage was published two years later in chapter 7 of his *Principles*. In spite of Torrens's precedence in print, this has become the *locus classicus* of the law of comparative advantage known to all students of international economics. Ricardo's example involving the trade of wine and cloth between England and Portugal had the advantage over Torrens's formulation of being expressed in terms of what Samuelson (ibid.) has called the 'four magic numbers' representing the amounts of labor needed to produce wine and cloth in each country:

England may be so circumstanced, that to produce the cloth may require the labour of 100 men for one year; and if she attempted to make the wine, it might require the labour of 120 men for the same time. England would therefore find it her interest to import wine, and purchase it by the exportation of cloth.

To produce the wine in Portugal, might require only the labour of 80 men for one year, and to produce the cloth in the same country, might require the labour of 90 men for the same time. It would therefore be advantageous for her to export wine in exchange for cloth. This exchange might even take place, notwithstanding that the commodity imported by Portugal could be produced there with less labour than in England. Though she could make the cloth with the labour of 90 men, she would import it from a country where it required the labour of 100 men to produce it, because it would be advantageous to her rather to employ her capital in the production of wine, for which she would obtain more cloth from England, than she could produce by diverting a portion of her capital from the cultivation of vines to the manufacture of cloth.

Thus England would give the produce of the labour of 100 men, for the produce of the labour of 80. (Ricardo, 1951a, p. 135)

John S. Chipman has pointed out that Ricardo's wording is far from felicitous. The first paragraph 'is a *non sequitur*, since nothing so far has been said about Portugal; indeed, the argument could be turned around merely by redefining the units of measurement'. The first two sentences of the second paragraph are 'equally unsatisfactory, except when read in conjunction with the first' (Chipman, 1965a, pp. 479–80). The words 'therefore' appearing in the second and fourth sentences of the above passage are misleading. The same is true of the 'thus' with which the third paragraph begins, since Ricardo provided no justification for setting the terms of trade between England and Portugal at one unit of wine for one of cloth. Although these terms of trade happen to be roughly halfway between their autarky price ratios, which are 90:80 in Portugal and 100:120 in England (expressed in quantity of wine per unit of cloth), this is an arbitrary assumption.[2] Only with J. S. Mill's law of reciprocal demand, to be discussed in Chapter 6, was this vacuum in Ricardo's formulation of a trade equilibrium satisfactorily filled.

If we now compare Ricardo's formulation with that of Torrens, we see that both authors justify trade using arguments consistent with the eighteenth-century rule defined by Viner and discussed in Chapter 3. According to Torrens, England could obtain a greater quantity of corn in exchange for her cloth than she could raise with the same resources directly from her own soil. And according to Ricardo, Portugal could obtain more cloth by producing wine and exchanging it for English cloth, than 'by diverting a portion of her capital from the cultivation of vines to the manufacture of cloth'. Each country gains from trade irrespective of whether it has an absolute advantage or disadvantage in its export commodity over its trading partner.[3] As Viner pointed out,

[the] explicit statement that imports could be profitable even though the commodity imported could be produced at less cost at home than abroad was, it seems to me, the sole addition of consequence which the doctrine of comparative costs made to the eighteenth-century rule. Its chief service was to correct the previously prevalent error that under free trade all commodities would necessarily tend to be produced in the locations where their real costs of production were lowest. (Viner, 1937, p. 441)

Being clothed in numbers, Ricardo's example allowed subsequent economists to calculate the two countries' autarky price ratios and speculate where between them the terms of trade would be located. This gave it a decisive advantage over Torrens's non-numerical example.

According to some commentators, Ricardo's imperfect formulation of the law of comparative advantage, and the fact that he never referred to it again in his writings, tend 'to cast some doubt as to whether he truly understood it; at best, his version is carelessly worded' (Chipman, 1965a, p. 480). Others (J. Hollander, 1910, 1911; Viner, 1937, pp. 443, 487–8) have instead wondered if Torrens truly grasped its implications, although Robbins (1958, pp. 33–4) seems to have effectively disposed of such qualms. On the question of priority, the contention of Robbins (1958, p. 32) that 'Torrens was first in the field' is incontrovertible. It is harder to give credence to a claim Torrens made in the Preface to the third edition of his *Essay on the External Corn Trade*, concerning some propositions he had put forward ('the Author believes for the first time') in its first edition: 'these principles [which include comparative advantage] Mr. Ricardo adopted into his very valuable work upon Political Economy and Taxation; and they form, in some measure, the ground-work of his chapters upon foreign trade, and of his doctrines on the influence of taxation upon the export and import of commodities' (Torrens, 1827, pp. vii–viii). It is true that Ricardo's *Essay on the Influence of a Low Price of Corn on the Profits of Stock* (Ricardo, 1951b), which was published on the same day (24 February 1815) as the first edition of Torrens's *Essay on the External Corn Trade*, contained no reference to comparative advantage. Moreover, we know that Ricardo was impressed with Torrens's pamphlet.[4] But according to Robbins,

that is not to say that we need to accept the suggestion, also put forward in [the preface of the third edition of Torrens's *External Corn Trade*], that Ricardo was in any way indebted to Torrens in this connection. We have seen already how surprised Ricardo was at Torrens' complaint of insufficient acknowledgement; and all that we know of Ricardo, his generosity and his honesty, his transparent candour, compels the conclusion that if he had been conscious of any debt in this connection he would certainly have acknowledged it. (Robbins, 1958, p. 32)

The superiority of Ricardo's formulation of the law of comparative advantage over Torrens's is universally acknowledged. According to Viner (1937, p. 442) 'Ricardo is entitled to the credit for first giving due emphasis to the doctrine, for first placing it in an appropriate setting, and for obtaining general acceptance of it by economists'. Chipman (1965a, p. 482) noted that 'Ricardo succeeded to a greater extent than Torrens in relating the principle to a larger theoretical system'. Robbins has argued that

> in admitting [Torrens's] claim to priority of publication, we are not in any way assessing the relative merits of the two treatments or the degree of influence which they respectively exercised. Needless to say, on both these counts the verdict must go to Ricardo. Both in respect of full elaboration and in respect of subsequent influence there can be no comparison between Torrens' paragraph and Ricardo's chapter. (Robbins, 1958, pp. 32–3)

Regarding Torrens's formulation, Robbins (1958, p. 23) added that 'as pure analysis it still lacks the final emphasis upon the comparison of ratios which is the ultimate essence of this principle'. It is also curious that Torrens's paragraph occurred, almost casually or as an afterthought, on pp. 263–4 of a rather long pamphlet (Torrens, 1815), and that he did not see fit to stress its novelty or importance. This suggests that he had no inkling of the revolutionary implications this principle was destined to have.

Who first used the terms 'comparative advantage' and 'comparative cost'? According to Viner (1937, p. 443), 'Torrens ... incidentally first used the term "comparative cost" in connection with the doctrine' in the fourth edition of the *Essay on the External Corn Trade*. Viner also notes (ibid.) that J. Hollander (1911) claimed that 'James Mill first used the word "comparative" in connection with the theory of international trade', and that Ricardo in his *Principles* used the phrases 'comparative disadvantage as far as regarded competition in foreign markets' and 'comparative facility of its production', the latter in connection with the production of raw produce in America and Poland (1951a, pp. 172, 374). Viner overlooked another statement of Ricardo (1951a, p. 263), that 'a new tax too may destroy the comparative advantage which a country before possessed in the manufacture of a particular commodity'. I have found no reference to comparative advantage or cost in the first edition of Torrens's *Essay* (1815), although the phrase 'comparative advantages' appeared several times in its fourth edition (Torrens, 1827, pp. 396, 423, 427). The phrase 'comparative cost' also entered this edition (p. 401), as Viner noted. But by then this concept was hardly novel, since years earlier, in his article 'Colony' in the *Encyclopaedia Britannica* and in his *Elements of Political Economy* (Mill, 1818, 1821), 'James Mill ... had published complete statements embellished with the comparison of cost ratios'

(Thweatt, 1976, p. 215). It is not rewarding to pursue further this question of priority since, as Viner (1937, p. 443) persuasively argued, 'terminological usage by the classical economists must have been so influenced by their oral discussion as to make the record of priority in print have little bearing on the question of priority in use'.

Thweatt's observation recalls his tantalizing suggestion that James Mill was in fact responsible for formulating the principle of comparative advantage.[5] After pointing out that Ricardo's formulation of this principle was defective while Torrens's was incomplete, Thweatt (1976, p. 229) contends that 'if it was not Ricardo who was responsible for incorporating the law of comparative advantage into mainstream political economy, it must have been one of his disciples – and so it turns out'. He notes that economists such as George Stigler and Carl Shoup expressed surprise at the fact that Ricardo made no subsequent use of this principle,[6] and argues that among Ricardo's disciples, James Mill stood out for his advocacy of the Ricardian principle of comparative advantage, which he illustrated with a wealth of numerical examples. He observes (pp. 226–8) that Ricardo's trade model is really a trade-and-growth model whose validity depends on absolute advantage and can thus dispense with comparative advantage. He also points to the peculiar choices Ricardo made for the labor productivities of the two commodities traded by England and Portugal, where England is less efficient than Portugal in producing both cloth and wine, and ends up importing wine.[7] Three pages earlier Ricardo had listed wine (as well as velvets and silks) among 'the commodities consumed by the rich' whose importation has no effect on the profit rate. And yet for Ricardo the *raison d'être* of liberalizing England's foreign trade, as elaborated below, was to raise her rates of profit and capital accumulation, which could be achieved only by importing a wage good such as corn.

Thweatt (1976, pp. 229, 231) cited O'Brien's (1970, p. 191) finding that 'McCulloch never accepted the theory of comparative costs as expounded by Torrens and Ricardo', and pointed out that Torrens in later years 'often merely repeated what Ricardo and Mill had already published'. After coyly asking the question, 'Is it so unlikely that Mill could have been responsible for the inclusion of the page-long account of the principle of comparative costs in Ricardo's chapter on foreign trade?', he went on to argue that 'if then we do not owe the early development of the doctrine of comparative advantage to Ricardo, Torrens, or McCulloch, then almost by elimination it must be due to the efforts of James Mill' (1976, pp. 221–2, 232). While this suggestion is not devoid of plausibility, it has been rejected by Hollander (1979, p. 462), who cited a letter by Mill explicitly attributing the principle in question to Ricardo. Mill had complimented the latter for the manuscript of the chapter 'On Foreign

Trade' he received in November 1816, stating that 'the inquiry concerning foreign trade ... is like the rest, original, and sound, and excellently demonstrated'. He listed the proposition 'that it may be good for a country to import commodities from a country where the production of those same commodities costs more, than it would cost at home' among that chapter's 'new propositions of the highest importance, and which you fully prove' (letter by Mill in Ricardo, 1951d, p. 99). Thweatt's suggestion that James Mill was responsible for Ricardo's three paragraphs on comparative advantage would be more compelling if a manuscript of Mill containing the essence of the principle and dated before 1817 is ever discovered. To date no such 'smoking gun' has materialized. We are left with the thoughtful reflection of Gomes (1987, p. 144) that 'perhaps what we have here is simply a case of multiple discovery, evidently fairly common in science. Like the other famous multiple discovery made about this time – diminishing returns – it emerged simultaneously in the minds of different thinkers under the pressure of relentless debate over urgent policy matters'.

4.2 Dynamic and static aspects of Ricardo's international trade theory

The vast influence that the principle of comparative advantage has had over the theory of international trade stands in sharp contrast not only with the small amount of space which its elaboration occupies in chapter 7 of Ricardo's *Principles*, but with the fact that this principle never appears in any of the other numerous references to trade in his book. These almost invariably involve trade in 'corn', the wage good *par excellence* of the classical economists (Maneschi, 1992). Several economists have stressed that the principal role of international trade for Ricardo was to achieve the dynamic benefits associated with a rise in the rate of profit rather than the static gains from resource reallocation according to comparative advantage.[8] In his pioneering article which combined Ricardian trade theory with the Ricardian theory of rent, Findlay (1974, p. 10) observed that 'while the theory of comparative advantage is perhaps Ricardo's most famous single contribution to economic analysis and the repeal of the Corn Laws the policy objective most closely associated with his name, it is a curious fact that Ricardo always used different models in his consideration of these problems'. The model of Ricardian trade presented in section 4.4 shows that in fact comparative advantage can be readily integrated with a dynamic analysis of trade.[9] Hence even if we grant Findlay's contention that Ricardo used two different models to analyze the static and dynamic dimensions of foreign trade, there was no logical necessity to proceed in this fashion.

To set the stage for an integrated Ricardian model, it is important to note the two distinct types of gain from trade that Ricardo described in chapter 7 of his *Principles*:

> It is quite as important to the happiness of mankind, that our enjoyments should be increased by the better distribution of labour, by each country producing those commodities for which by its situation, its climate, and its other natural or artificial advantages, it is adapted, and by their exchanging them for the commodities of other countries, as that they should be augmented by a rise in the rate of profits. It has been my endeavour to shew throughout this work, that the rate of profits can never be increased but by a fall in wages, and that there can be no permanent fall of wages but in consequence of a fall of the necessaries on which wages are expended. If, therefore, by the extension of foreign trade, or by improvements in machinery, the food and necessaries of the labourer can be brought to market at a reduced price, profits will rise. (Ricardo, 1951a, p. 132)

The first of these gains from trade derives from the reallocation of the labor force according to comparative advantage, the other from the rise in the profit rate which results if (and only if) the commodities imported are 'necessaries'. Their availability at a lower world price causes wages to fall and, by the fundamental theorem of Ricardian economics, the profit rate to rise. Since capital accumulation varies directly with the profit rate, this restores dynamism to an economy where diminishing returns to an expanding labor force on a fixed amount of land have led to a rise in the price of corn and of the wage rate, and consequent declines in the profit rate and the rate of capital accumulation. Trade thus serves to temporarily reverse an economy's march towards the stationary state. It should come as no surprise that the principal 'case study' to which Ricardo applied his analysis of the gains from trade should be linked to his theory of rent, or that the dynamic benefits of trade (as evidenced by the frequency with which they are mentioned throughout the *Principles*) should far outweigh in his mind the static ones attributable to 'the better distribution of labour'. These contentions are documented in section 4.3. The principal policy implication of both the *Essay on Profits* (1951b) and the *Principles*, and an important aim of Ricardo's parliamentary career, was the repeal of Britain's Corn Laws which prevented free trade in corn.[10]

This linkage of Ricardo's trade theory to the analysis of diminishing returns in the agricultural sector sheds light on another feature of chapter 7 of his *Principles* which appears as an anomaly to believers in a Ricardian trade model based on constant costs. In a long footnote he appended to the last of his three paragraphs on comparative advantage, Ricardo stated that a country possessing very considerable advantages in machinery and skill, and which may therefore be enabled to manufacture commodities with much less labour than her neighbours, may, in return for such commodities, import a portion of the corn required for its consumption, even if its land were more fertile, and corn could be grown with less labour than in the country from which it was imported. (Ricardo, 1951a, p. 136)

A country's importation of a *portion* of the corn which it consumes clearly implies incomplete rather than complete specialization (Viner, 1937, p. 452).[11] This casts doubt on the textbook version of the Ricardian trade model. As all students of international economics know, the latter postulates that returns to the labor input (the sole factor of production considered) are constant in all sectors. Transformation curves are thereby linearized, and trade causes one or both trading partners to become fully specialized in their export commodities.[12] Ricardo clearly never intended a 'landed nation' (to use Adam Smith's expression) with a comparative advantage in manufactures to become fully specialized in them, or believed that one which tended to specialize in corn could do so without undergoing diminishing returns in that commodity. This suggests that the economy's production possibility schedule is not a straight line, but rather a curve reflecting diminishing returns to labor in the agricultural sector of the economy. The simple 'Ricardian' trade model outlined in section 4.4 allows for the incomplete specialization of both trading partners owing to diminishing returns in their agricultural sectors. In contrast to the textbook Ricardian version, this model attempts to portray the type of trade primarily discussed throughout the *Principles* together with the associated dynamic gains. These are illustrated by the passages quoted in the next section.

4.3 Foreign trade in the other chapters of Ricardo's *Principles*[13]

Besides Ricardo's allusion to a country's incomplete specialization in corn, the footnote in chapter 7 of his *Principles* quoted above is significant because it specifically mentions machinery, skill and land as factors of production. Even if attention is limited to that chapter, it is hard to escape the conclusion that the Ricardian trade model is a multifactor one, with circulating capital an indispensable concomitant of the employment of labor, and the production of agricultural goods such as corn involving land. The latter is subject to diminishing returns to labor, as Ricardo had elaborated and illustrated with numerical examples in chapters 2, 5 and 6 of his *Principles*.

Although chapter 7 devoted to foreign trade is the last of the seven theoretical chapters of the *Principles*, Ricardo referred frequently and at some length to foreign trade in the remaining chapters. These references provide a useful cross-check on the type of model that is most consonant with his thinking on trade issues. The first impression which strikes one is the pride of place which Ricardo accords to the importation of corn in most of his examples relating to foreign trade, to the point that it appears almost an obsession. His advocacy of the repeal of the Corn Laws was the motivating force behind his *Essay on Profits*.[14] The *Principles* grew out of what had initially been a plan simply to write an expanded version of the *Essay*.[15] Although the *Principles* developed in far greater depth certain themes (such as the theory of value) found only in embryonic form in the *Essay*, it is natural that the leitmotiv of the *Essay*, writ large, reappeared in the *Principles*.

Without attempting an exhaustive catalog of the references to foreign trade in the *Principles*, some of the more significant ones will be mentioned. Chapter 19, entitled 'On Sudden Changes in the Channels of Trade', reflects the unsettled condition of England in the aftermath of the Napoleonic Wars. The price of grains had been maintained artificially high because of these wars, and there was obvious concern about the consequences of suddenly allowing cheap foreign grains to enter the country. Ricardo disagreed with those who contended that such importation should be prevented, on the ground that it would imply the annihilation of the fixed capital currently employed in agriculture.[16] His justification for this is reminiscent of the maxim 'let bygones be bygones': given that capital expenditures were incurred in the past, there is no reason to maintain this capital if conditions have changed. Ricardo pointed out that 'those who deplore the loss of capital in this case, are for sacrificing the end to the means' (1951a, p. 269). The inability to withdraw capital from the land was no reason to prevent the importation of cheap corn. Of those who think otherwise, Ricardo stated:

> They do not see that the end of all commerce is to increase production, and that by increasing production, though you may occasion partial loss, you increase the general happiness. To be consistent, they should endeavour to arrest all improvements in agriculture and manufactures, and all inventions of machinery; for though these contribute to general abundance, and therefore to the general happiness, they never fail, at the moment of their introduction, to deteriorate or annihilate the value of a part of the existing capital of farmers and manufacturers. (Ricardo, 1951a, p. 271)

Ricardo stressed the distributional implications of his trade theory as follows:

> But there is this advantage always resulting from a relatively low price of corn,– that the division of the actual production is more likely to increase the fund for the maintenance of labour, inasmuch as more will be allotted, under the name of

profit, to the productive class, and less under the name rent, to the unproductive class. (Ricardo, 1951a, p. 270)

At the same time, Ricardo did not advocate immediate free trade in corn at the end of a war which had interfered with it, but showed himself conscious of what are nowadays known as the 'adjustment costs' which this would impose: 'the best policy of the State would be, to lay a tax, decreasing in amount from time to time, on the importation of foreign corn, for a limited number of years, in order to afford to the home-grower an opportunity to withdraw his capital gradually from the land' (1951a, pp. 266–7). Otherwise, farmers would insist on a risk premium in times of emergency to compensate them for the drastic fall in price expected at the end of the emergency, and this would raise the price of corn to consumers even more.

In chapter 22, entitled 'Bounties on Exportation, and Prohibitions of Importation', Ricardo stated that 'perhaps in no part of Adam Smith's justly celebrated work, are his conclusions more liable to objection, than in the chapter on bounties'. In contrast to Adam Smith, he concluded that 'landlords have a most decided interest in the rise of the natural price of corn; for the rise of rent is the inevitable consequence of the difficulty of producing raw produce, without which its natural price could not rise'. However, the home country, as well as the world as a whole, would be hurt by the bounty. In what must surely be one of the earliest descriptions of the deadweight loss of a tax, Ricardo stated that it is 'the worst species of taxation, for it does not give to the foreign country all that it takes away from the home country, the balance of loss being made up by the less advantageous distribution of the general capital' (1951a, pp. 304, 313–4). He was all the keener to rectify Smith's mistake since Smith had alleged that the agricultural classes and laborers had borne the full brunt of British protectionism:

> In the present day the authority of Adam Smith is quoted by country gentlemen, for imposing similar high duties on the importation of foreign corn. Because the cost of production, and, therefore, the prices of various manufactured commodities, are raised to the consumer by one error in legislation, the country has been called upon, on the plea of justice, quietly to submit to fresh exactions. Because we all pay an additional price for our linen, muslin, and cottons, it is thought just that we should pay also an additional price for our corn.... It would be much wiser to acknowledge the errors which a mistaken policy has induced us to adopt, and immediately to commence a gradual recurrence to the sound principles of an universally free trade. (Ricardo, 1951a, pp. 317–8)

Once more, Ricardo stressed the policy implications of agricultural protectionism, as regards the natural price of corn and the share of national income accruing to the landlord class, all of which are vital components of the *Essay on Profits* as well as of the discussion of trade issues in the *Principles*. Ricardo's hostility towards the landlords, evident from this passage as well as that quoted earlier where they are referred to as the 'unproductive' class, turned into a veritable tirade in chapter 24, entitled 'Doctrine of Adam Smith Concerning the Rent of Land'. The following passage gives its flavor:

> The interest of the landlord is always opposed to that of the consumer and manufacturer. Corn can be permanently at an advanced price, only because additional labour is necessary to produce it; because its cost of production is increased. The same cause invariably raises rent, it is therefore for the interest of the landlord that the cost attending the production of corn should be increased. This, however, is not the interest of the consumer.... Neither is it the interest of the manufacturer.... All classes, therefore, except the landlords, will be injured by the increase in the price of corn. The dealings between the landlord and the public are not like dealings in trade, whereby both the seller and buyer may equally be said to gain, but the loss is wholly on one side, and the gain wholly on the other; and if corn could by importation be procured cheaper, the loss in consequence of not importing is far greater on one side, than the gain is on the other. (Ricardo, 1951a, pp. 335–6)

Ricardo (p. 336) then berated Adam Smith for believing that 'the interest of the landlord is not opposed to that of the rest of the community', and pointed out that a rise in the price of corn not only gives the landlord a higher rent in terms of corn but an even greater command over other commodities, which have fallen in price compared to corn.

The same theme was taken up in chapter 28, 'On the Comparative Value of Gold, Corn, and Labour, in Rich and Poor Countries'. The difficulty of producing food in a rich country raises its price, and leads to its being imported unless the landlords intervene with the legislature to prevent this. Ricardo (1951a, p. 374) thus contradicted Adam Smith's contention that the price of corn is lower in rich than in poor countries, arguing that it is the 'natural price' of corn 'which governs its market price, and which determines the expediency of exporting it to foreign countries'. In the course of the same paragraph, Ricardo presented an example of trade in corn between England and France which comes much closer than anything found in chapter 7 to explaining how the terms of trade between two trading countries are determined. It demonstrates his awareness of the considerations underlying this determination on both the demand- and supply-side:

> If the importation of corn were prohibited in England, its natural price might rise to 6*l.* per quarter in England, whilst it was only at half that price in France. If at this time, the prohibition of importation were removed, corn would fall in the

English market, not to a price between 6*l.* and 3*l.*, but ultimately and permanently to the natural price of France, the price at which it could be furnished to the English market, and afford the usual and ordinary profits of stock in France; and it would remain at this price, whether England consumed a hundred thousand, or a million of quarters. *If the demand of England were for the latter quantity, it is probable that, owing to the necessity under which France would be, of having recourse to land of a worse quality, to furnish this large supply, the natural price would rise in France; and this would of course affect also the price of corn in England.* All that I contend for is, that it is the natural price of commodities in the exporting country, which ultimately regulates the prices at which they shall be sold, if they are not the objects of monopoly, in the importing country. (Ricardo, 1951a, pp. 374–5; emphasis added)

The italicized sentence in that paragraph shows that the natural price of corn in the exporting country, France, depends on the effect of the size of the English demand on the difficulty of producing French corn. An increase in this demand due to a lifting of restrictions on corn imports would induce France to bring inferior lands into cultivation, causing an increase in the natural price of corn. Expressing this price in terms of manufactured goods, and using modern parlance, one could say that the point of intersection between France's upward-sloping supply curve of corn exports and England's downward-sloping demand curve for corn imports denotes the initial equilibrium volume of corn traded and the terms of trade. A rise in the English demand for corn engendered by freer trade would cause the import demand curve to shift to the right, and intersect the export supply curve at a higher relative price of corn, implying an improvement in France's terms of trade.

Even the new chapter 31 'On Machinery' in the third edition of the *Principles*, which Sraffa (1951, p. lvii) called 'the most revolutionary change' of that edition, has implications for foreign trade despite its primarily domestic focus. Machinery (and its attendant short-term deterioration in the condition of the workers) is more likely to be introduced in a country where wages are rising because of the increasing cost of food:

In America and many other countries, where the food of man is easily provided, there is not nearly such great temptation to employ machinery as in England, where food is high, and costs much labour for its production. The same cause that raises labour, does not raise the value of machines, and, therefore, with every augmentation of capital, a greater proportion of it is employed on machinery. The demand for labour will continue to increase with an increase of capital, but not in proportion to its increase; the ratio will necessarily be a diminishing ratio. (Ricardo, 1951a, p. 395)

In spite of this effect, Ricardo warned against the false inference some might draw that machinery should not be encouraged. First, he noted that machinery is likely to be introduced gradually rather than suddenly. Secondly, he expressed the concern that a policy inimical to its introduction is likely to backfire because of the resulting capital outflow:

> The employment of machinery could never be safely discouraged in a State, for if a capital is not allowed to get the greatest net revenue that the use of machinery will afford here, it will be carried abroad, and this must be a much more serious discouragement to the demand for labour, than the most extensive employment of machinery; for while a capital is employed in this country, it must create a demand for some labour; machinery cannot be worked without the assistance of men, it cannot be made but with the contribution of their labour. By investing part of a capital in improved machinery, there will be a diminution in the progressive demand for labour; by exporting it to another country, the demand will be wholly annihilated. (Ricardo, 1951a, pp. 396–7)

Ricardo concluded the chapter by arguing that if a country rejects the use of machinery which is then adopted elsewhere, it ends up exporting goods which have a higher embodied labor content than the exports which other countries are now able to produce more cheaply. The final paragraphs of chapter 31 are of interest because Ricardo implied that capital, in contradiction to what he had said in chapter 7 regarding 'the difficulty with which capital moves from one country to another, to seek a more profitable employment' (1951a, pp. 135–6), is likely to move from a nation which discourages the adoption of machinery to one that does not. The price which the former nation would have to pay is the resulting 'disadvantageous exchange' of its exports for its imports. The static comparative advantage theory often associated with chapter 7 is here modified into one where dynamic comparative advantage plays a leading role.

Many more such passages from the *Principles* could be added, but the above suffice to establish the fact that the type of foreign trade that was uppermost in Ricardo's mind involved the import of corn in exchange for manufactured goods. Such trade would tend to occur in a prosperous country such as the England of his day since under autarky the margin of cultivation would be pushed further there, leading to a high natural price of corn and rent for the landowners. The consequence would be a lower rate of profit and hence of capital accumulation. Free trade in corn would have dynamic benefits in addition to the static efficiency ones identified by the theory of comparative costs. Ricardo's trade theory is thus intimately related to his theories of rent, profit rate determination and capital accumulation. A model which attempts to capture these features, and illustrate the dynamic gains from trade which are at the heart of his system, is set out in the next section.

4.4 A dynamic model of Ricardian trade

The following model extends that of Findlay (1974), which in turn was based on the closed-economy Ricardian model of Pasinetti (1960). A two-sector economy contains an agricultural ('corn') sector subject to diminishing returns to labor, and a manufacturing ('velvet') sector subject to constant returns. C and V are the outputs of corn and velvet, and L_c and L_v the labor employed in those sectors. Velvet is the numeraire commodity and $p = P_c/P_v$ the relative price of corn in terms of velvet.

If α is the constant productivity of labor in velvet, the output of velvet is given by

$$V = \alpha L_v. \tag{4.1}$$

The corn production function is

$$C = F(T, L_c) = f(L_c), \tag{4.2}$$

since T, the amount of agricultural land, is constant. The period of production is the same in both sectors. The natural wage rate is fixed at w in terms of corn, the only wage good, and is advanced to workers in both sectors. Denoting by $f'(L_c)$ (or f' for short) the marginal product of labor in the corn sector, the corn profit rate r_c, defined at the no-rent margin and earned on this advanced wage, is

$$r_c = (pf' - pw)/pw = (f' - w)/w = (f'/w) - 1. \tag{4.3}$$

Since this profit rate is earned on the advances to workers in the corn sector, wL_c, total profits in that sector are $P_c = (f' - w)L_c$. Wages are $W_c = wL_c$ and rent claims the residual share, $R = f(L_c) - f'.L_c$.

Similarly, the profit rate in the velvet sector is

$$r_v = (\alpha - pw)/pw = (\alpha/pw) - 1. \tag{4.4}$$

Competition ensures a uniform profit rate r in both sectors, so that

$$r = r_c = (f'/w) - 1 = r_v = (\alpha/pw) - 1. \tag{4.5}$$

Hence

$$f' = \alpha/p, \qquad (4.6)$$

which shows that the values of the marginal product of labor are likewise equated in the two sectors. (4.6) can be rewritten as

$$p = \alpha/f', \qquad (4.7)$$

so that the relative price of corn varies directly (inversely) with the marginal velvet (corn) product of labor. Since the ratio of the marginal products of labor in the two sectors is equal to the marginal rate of transformation of velvet into corn, the latter also coincides with the relative price of corn. This price is therefore bounded by the slopes (evaluated with respect to the vertical axis) of the transformation curve PQ at P and Q in panel (a) of Figure 4.1. A movement from P to Q implies that the supply of corn changes from zero to OQ, yielding the supply curve of corn SS shown in panel (b).

Assume that wages are spent entirely on corn, that capitalist-farmers reinvest all their profits, and that landlords spend their corn rent entirely on velvet. If $L = L_c + L_v$ is the total labor force, which is assumed to be identical to the population, the wage fund equals wL and constitutes the economy's circulating capital stock, K. Since total profits, rK in terms of corn, are reinvested in the corn sector, K grows at the absolute rate $dK/dt = rK$, so that its relative growth rate is[17]

$$(dK/dt)/K = r. \qquad (4.8)$$

The total demand for corn is thus $D_c = wL + rK = wL(1 + r)$. Substituting from (4.5) and (4.6), this can be written

$$D_c = w(1 + r)L = f'.L = \alpha L/p. \qquad (4.9)$$

For a given value of L, the demand curve for corn is represented by the rectangular hyperbola DD in panel (b) of Figure 4.1. Its intersection A with SS yields the equilibrium price and output of corn, p_1 and C_1, corresponding to point E on the transformation curve PQ.

If the labor force grows over time, the transformation curve PQ shifts out to P'Q'. At the price ratio p_1, given by the slopes of PQ and P'Q' at E and E', the output of velvet increases while that of corn remains unchanged (Findlay, 1974, p. 5). According to (4.9), the demand for corn rises in proportion to L, as shown by D'D' in Figure 4.1 (b), while the supply curve is unchanged. As the equilibrium point moves from A to B, the price of corn rises from p_1 to p_2.

Figure 4.1 Labor force growth in a closed Ricardian system

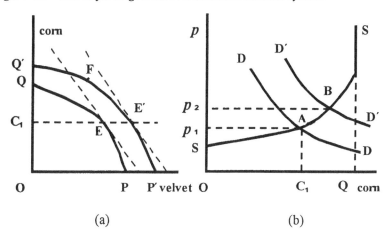

(a)   (b)

The corresponding equilibrium point on $P'Q'$ in Figure 4.1 (a) is F, lying above and to the left of E'. From (4.5) and (4.6), the rise in p is associated with decreases in the marginal corn product of labor and in the rate of profit. From (4.8) the growth rate of the capital stock also falls. So does the growth rate of the labor force, if the labor force is infinitely elastic at the natural wage rate w, so that $(dN/dt)/N = (dK/dt)/K$.[18] Hence the economy decelerates as it heads towards the stationary state.

These trends are illustrated in Figure 4.2. Setting the demand for corn given by (4.9) equal to its supply given by (4.2), we obtain

$$f'(L_c).L = f(L_c), \tag{4.10}$$

or

$$f'(L_c) = f(L_c)/L. \tag{4.10a}$$

Curve AB plots $f'(L_c)$ against L_c, and curve OC_1 plots per capita corn output $f(L_c)/L$ for the value $L = L_1$. The equilibrium value of L_c is OF_1, given by the intersection D_1 of AB and OC_1. If D_1F_1 is a vertical line through D_1, and E_1 its intersection with the horizontal line wH whose height is w, we see from (4.5) that the profit rate r_1 is given by D_1E_1/E_1F_1. Corn output is given by the area AD_1F_1O, profits are $G_1D_1E_1w$ and the wage bill is wE_1F_1O. Rent income R_1 in terms of corn is given by the residual area $AD_1F_1O - G_1D_1F_1O = AD_1G_1$, equal to $f(L_c) - f'.L_c$ when $L_c = OF_1$.

As L grows over time, the per capita corn output curve takes the successive positions OC_2, OC_3, ... , so that the labor force in the corn sector grows from OF_1 to OF_2, OF_3, ..., and the profit rate falls from r_1 to $r_2 = D_2E_2/E_2F_2$, $r_3 =$

Figure 4.2   Effects of labor force growth on profits and rental income

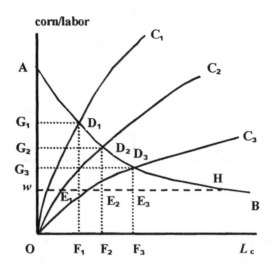

D_3E_3/E_3F_3, ... Eventually the per capita corn output curve intersects AB at point H, where $f' = w$ and $r = 0$. The growth rates of capital and labor fall to zero as the economy enters the stationary state. Rental income in terms of corn grows over time from AG_1D_1 to AG_2D_2, AG_3D_3, ... Since the price of corn also increases over time with the decline in $f'(L_c)$, the purchasing power of rent in terms of velvet grows even faster than shown by these 'triangular' areas.

In a passage quoted above, Ricardo stated that 'if ... by the extension of foreign trade, or by improvements in machinery, the food and necessaries of the labourer can be brought to market at a reduced price, profits will rise'. This two-part proposition can be illustrated as follows. If technical change were to occur in a Hicks-neutral way in the corn sector, the part of Ricardo's contention relating to 'improvements in machinery' is illustrated in Figure 4.3 by proportional upward shifts in the AB and OC curves (which are similar to those in Figure 4.2) to A'B' and OC'. As shown by (4.7), the relative price of corn falls in that proportion. Rental income in terms of corn rises in the same proportion, from ADG to A'D'G', and the profit rate rises from DE/EF to D'E/EF. Both the agricultural labor force, and rental income in terms of velvet, remain unchanged.[19]

To confirm the part of Ricardo's contention relating to foreign trade, consider the introduction of trade in a Ricardian economy. To find out which commodity it exports, the autarky (no-trade) price ratio, p_a, must be compared

Figure 4.3   Technical progress in the corn sector raises the profit rate

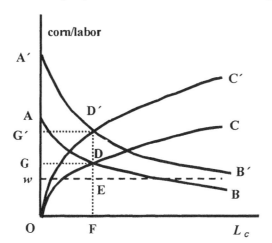

to the international terms of trade, p_t. If $p_t < p_a$, as shown in panel (a) of Figure 4.4, corn is imported in exchange for velvet. On the assumption that p_t is not so low that the economy becomes specialized in velvet production, corn imports equal the difference QR between demand and supply. In panel (b), which is similar to Figure 4.2, autarky equilibrium in the corn sector is shown by point D, the intersection of AB and OC, where $f' = DF = \alpha/p_a$. Since corn is now imported at the price $p_t < p_a$, equilibrium in the corn sector moves to point H on AB, where $HJ = \alpha/p_t$, and to point M on OC. The opening to trade thus increases the marginal corn product. Corn imports M_c are equal to the difference between corn demand D_c, given by (4.9), and corn supply given by (4.2). Hence per capita corn imports are

$$M_c/L = f'(L_c) - f(L_c)/L, \qquad (4.11)$$

given by the vertical distance HM between the curves AB and OC corresponding to $L_c = OJ$. It is also equal to QR in Figure 4.4 (a) divided by L. If there is no change in the wage rate, the opportunity to import cheap corn raises the profit rate from DE/EF in the closed economy to HI/IJ in the open one. An enhanced rate of capital accumulation accompanies the increase in r. While capitalists gain from trade, landlords suffer a 'double whammy': on the one hand, their corn rent declines from ADG to AHK; on the other hand, the purchasing power of this rent declines even more because of the fall in the price of corn in terms of velvet.

Figure 4.4   Corn imports raise the profit rate

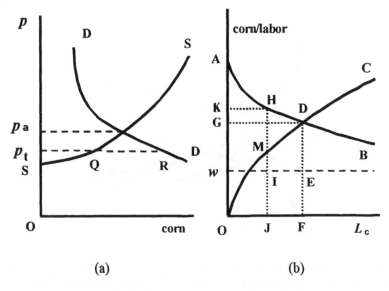

(a)   (b)

Hence both parts of Ricardo's statement are confirmed. We also note parenthetically that technical progress in the velvet sector, symbolized by a higher value of α, leads to a proportional increase in the price of corn but leaves the marginal corn product and profit rate unchanged. Rental income in terms of corn is also unchanged, but it can buy more velvet in proportion to the increases in p and α. The economy's march towards the stationary state is not affected at all by technical progress in the 'manufacturing' sector of the economy (velvet being a 'non-basic' good in Sraffian terminology, rather than a 'basic' good like corn),[20] and landlords are the sole beneficiaries. Similarly, if trade were to make velvet cheaper rather than corn, so that p_t is higher instead of lower than p_a in Figure 4.4 (a), the economy would export corn instead of importing it. The open-economy equilibrium in Figure 4.4 (b) would be located to the right (instead of left) of point D, leading to a decline in the rate of profit and corresponding loss of dynamism.

We conclude that the economy's drift towards the stationary state can be arrested either by technical progress in the corn sector, or by taking advantage of the opportunity to purchase cheap corn imports. Whether the boost to the economy's growth rate is temporary or permanent depends on whether agricultural improvements can occur more or less continuously in the first case (a decidedly unclassical assumption), or on whether foreign countries can continue to supply cheap corn for the indefinite future in the second case. That Ricardo himself was not pessimistic, on the basis of one or the other of these contingencies, about Britain's medium-term prospects is shown by his characterizing the stationary state as one 'from which I trust we are yet far distant' (1951a, p. 109).

4.5 Comparative advantage in the short run and the long run

In the Ricardian trade-and-growth model outlined in the last section, the transition from a closed to an open economy can have a drastic impact on the allocation of labor and on the trajectories followed by variables such as capital accumulation and the profit rate in the two trading partners. While trade has clear dynamic implications, its direction still depends on the comparative advantage ruling at the moment the economy opens to trade and at every point thereafter. There is certainly no logical impediment to the integration of the traditional textbook Ricardian model of comparative advantage with a Pasinetti–Findlay model featuring diminishing returns in the agricultural sector. Several such attempts at integration (starting with Findlay, 1974) have in fact been made. While it is true that two Nobel prize winners, among other economists, have maintained that Ricardo's trade-and-growth model was motivated by absolute rather than comparative advantage,[21] this would imply a denial of what is often regarded as Ricardo's main claim to fame, the principle of comparative advantage.

Comparative advantage in fact plays a fundamental role in the two-sector trade model sketched in the previous section. The direction of trade depends on a comparison between a country's autarky price ratio p_a and the terms of trade p_t, or alternatively between the two countries' autarky price ratios, since the terms of trade must lie between them. If we denote the variables and parameters relating to the 'home' country by lower-case letters and those relating to the 'foreign' country by upper-case ones, the initial direction of trade according to (4.7) depends on the autarky values of α/f and A/F' in the home and foreign countries.[22] The home country is more likely to import corn the higher its value of p_a, that is, the higher its productivity in the velvet sector and the lower its marginal product of labor in the corn sector, compared to the corresponding values in the foreign country. The agricultural production functions can differ internationally and, for a given production function, the value of the marginal corn product of labor is lower, the higher the ratio of labor (L_c) to land (T). The direction of trade, however, is determined not just by the values of f' and F' in autarky, but by the *ratio* α/f' compared to the *ratio* A/F', that is, by comparative and not absolute advantage. As in Ricardo's cloth–wine example, it is possible that $\alpha > A$ and $f' > F'$, so that the home country has an absolute advantage in both goods. However, as long as $\alpha/f' \neq$

A/F', each country has an incentive to trade and to reap the static benefits from doing so. Of equal or greater importance are the dynamic benefits from trade accruing to the corn-importing country. Since Ricardo's attention was focused on Britain, he did not mention the corresponding dynamic losses that the corn-exporting country incurs, unless a ready availability of fertile land (as was perhaps the case in North America at that time) allows it to produce corn at a practically constant cost.

What are the asymptotic implications of the dynamic Ricardian trade model as both trading partners head towards the stationary state? It is clear that the trajectories they follow can be highly complex, involving one or more reversals of comparative advantage. For simplicity's sake, assume that trade opens between them when they have already reached their stationary states. In that case, $f' = w$, $F' = W$, and their profit rates as well as their growth rates of capital and labor are zero. The direction of trade then depends on a comparison between α/w and A/W. The only viable pattern of specialization can be shown to be such that one country fully specializes in corn while the other produces both goods (Maneschi, 1993a). With the labor force endogenous in both countries, it increases in the incompletely specialized country (say the home country) and decreases in the corn-producing one. Since the price ratio α/w remains unchanged in the home country as it passes from autarky to trade, its corn production is also unchanged, and its growing labor force flows to the velvet sector to produce exports to be exchanged for the corn needed to support it. The foreign country's labor force declines in the course of its becoming fully specialized in corn. Since its comparative advantage in corn causes it to extend the margin of cultivation, its profit and growth rates (which were zero in autarky) turn negative, causing the loss of population.

These changes in the countries' factor endowments must be counted as an additional gain or loss from trade, to be added to the dynamic benefits or losses accruing to each country *en route* to the stationary state, and to the static gains which they enjoy at all points of time. The outcome is diametrically opposed to the Heckscher–Ohlin model, since trade determines long-run factor endowments instead of being determined by them. These endowment changes have non-economic implications for a country's standing in the hierarchy of nations, and must be placed in a very different category from the static and dynamic welfare implications of trade mentioned above.

Ricardian comparative advantage marked the beginnings of the new subfield of international economics, and was hailed as a major insight throughout the nineteenth and early part of the twentieth century. Its generalizations, and the role it played in associated issues such as the determination of the terms of trade, are discussed in Chapter 6. The modifications (and, in one case, rejection) which the concept met at the hands of the neoclassical economists are examined in Chapters 7 and 8. Aside from the Pasinetti–Findlay model discussed in the present chapter, several other models carry a neo-Ricardian label and will be briefly considered in section 10.4 as modern descendants of the Ricardian system. Chapter 5 provides an interlude in the saga of the formal development of the concept of comparative advantage by examining a trio of heterodox thinkers and men of action who believed that, in a developing nation, comparative advantage need not be accepted as given, but can actually be created.

Notes

1. Chipman (1965a, p. 482) pointed out that, in the third and subsequent editions of his *Essay on the External Corn Trade*, Torrens changed the phrases 'excess of profit' in this statement to the more appropriate 'excess of produce'.
2. As Schumpeter (1954, pp. 607–8) commented, 'Ricardo and his immediate followers ... glibly assumed that the advantage would be halved – which may have spelled error but also may have been merely carelessness'.
3. While absolute advantage is not needed to decide which commodity a country exports, it influences how wealthy a country is compared to its trading partner. If it holds an absolute advantage in every commodity, its per capita income must exceed its trading partner's, regardless of the terms of trade.
4. As Chipman (1965a, p. 481) noted, Ricardo 'described the work in a letter to Malthus shortly after its appearance as "on the whole a very able performance" ([Ricardo, 1951c], p. 188)'.
5. According to Blaug (1990, p. x), who finds his theory persuasive, 'William Thweatt's essay on James Mill and comparative advantage must rank as one of the greatest surprise stories in the entire history of economic thought'.
6. John R. Hicks should also be added to this list, as Gomes (1987, p. 142) has pointed out. The three references in question are Stigler (1965, p. 274), Shoup (1960, p. 169) and Hicks (1983, p. 61).
7. Ricardo's surprising assumption that Portugal is superior to England in both industries has been explained in a number of ways. Samuelson (1969, p. 5) argued that 'probably, Ricardo regarded his reader as one who was tempted by the protectionist argument of the mercantilists, and in need of being reassured that another country could not undersell him in everything even if it were *more* productive in everything'. Gomes (1987, p. 140) maintained that 'the very implausibility of the particular example chosen to illustrate the principle ... only served to highlight the economic logic of the argument'.
8. Aside from the references by Stigler, Hicks and Shoup mentioned in endnote 6, see Robinson (1974), Thweatt (1976), Walsh (1979), Blaug (1987), Gomes (1987), Maneschi (1992, 1993a).
9. For other attempts at integrating these two models, see Maneschi (1983) and Burgstaller (1986).
10. Similarly, the paramount concern of Torrens's *Essay on the External Corn Trade*, as its title suggests, was free trade in corn rather than free trade in general.
11. Although Ricardo's comparative cost example was in terms of wine and cloth (both of which allegedly undergo 'manufacture'), it is interesting that in this footnote he resorted to an example similar to that used by Torrens two years earlier in his *Essay on the External Corn Trade*, which implied that Britain has an absolute advantage but a comparative disadvantage in corn *vis-à-vis* Poland.

12. Viner challenged Pareto's allegation that full specialization was implied by Ricardo because of his statement, which completes the footnote in question, that if two men make both shoes and hats, and one is superior to the other in both occupations, he should 'employ himself exclusively' in the manufacture of that good in which his comparative advantage is greater. As Viner (1937, p. 452) pointed out, 'Ricardo's statement that it would be to the interest of two *individuals* to specialize completely if each had a comparative advantage in the production of one of the commodities seems an inadequate basis, moreover, upon which to convict him of the belief that complete specialization would necessarily be profitable to each of two *countries* if they had comparative differences in costs of production'.

13. This section is based on Maneschi (1992).

14. As Hilton argues in his entry 'Corn Laws' in *The New Palgrave Dictionary*, except for Ricardo most classical economists were at times ambiguous towards Corn Law repeal. In fact, 'probably only Ricardo placed hostility to the Corn Laws at the centre of his system. His corn model postulated that without access to cheap supplies of foreign grain, population pressure would either force domestic farmers onto more marginal land or else would compel them to cultivate the old land more intensively. In either case prices would rise, profits would decline, and the economy would move towards a stationary state' (Hilton, 1987, p. 670). O'Brien (1975, p. 41) also maintains that 'the corn model is quite clearly the fundamental concern of Ricardo's *Principles*'. Similarly, Gomes (1987, pp. 180, 189) contends that for Ricardo 'foreign trade provided the means of escape from the consequences of diminishing returns and a falling rate of profit' and that 'the significant contribution of trade to national economic development lay in its impact on agricultural prices. When he thought of free trade it was always in terms of a manufacturing country being able to obtain cheap food and raw materials from other countries better endowed with natural resources'.

15. As Sraffa (1951, p. xiii) explains, 'At first Ricardo's intention (at James Mill's suggestion) had been merely to produce an enlarged version of the *Essay* .... Mill, however, as he tells Ricardo in the same month [August 1815], is determined to give him no rest till he is 'plunged over head and ears in political economy'. Six weeks later (on 10 October) the large book is already being treated by Mill as a definite commitment'.

16. This example, incidentally, suggests that a full-blown Ricardian trade model should allow for the existence of fixed capital in agriculture as well as in manufacturing.

17. The model can readily be modified so as to allow for the reinvestment of a fraction γ of profits, the balance $(1 - \gamma)$ being spent on velvet. For the effects of this on the economy's equilibrium, see Maneschi (1983).

18. If the market wage rate is allowed to deviate from the subsistence wage rate w, as in Casarosa (1978) and Maneschi (1983), the growth rate of the population can be functionally related to the difference between the market and the subsistence wage rates. The dynamic features of this model are more complex, although the economy's eventual approach to the stationary state is not affected.

19. This analysis, and that discussed below which relates to technical progress in the velvet sector, follow those of Findlay (1974, pp. 7–8).

20. On the distinction between basic and non-basic commodities, see Sraffa (1960).

21. See endnote 6 above.

22. A is the upper-case letter corresponding to α.

5. Creators of Comparative Advantage: Alexander Hamilton, John Rae and Friedrich List

Although Ricardo and Torrens developed the concept of comparative advantage and their followers popularized it, the classical school offered few suggestions for the reasons why Torrens's 'territorial division of labor' should assume any particular pattern, or why Ricardo's four magic numbers should take particular values. Such theorizing had to await another century for Eli Heckscher and Bertil Ohlin. But even if certain statesmen and economists of the early classical era had been familiar with these theories, they would have rejected them by alleging that they were not relevant to what John Stuart Mill referred to as 'a young and rising nation'. Their main concern was to foster industrialization in such countries via the promotion of what Friedrich List, by analogy with Alexander Hamilton's 'American system', called a 'national system of political economy'. Since Adam Smith had a clearly negative attitude towards this argument and yet was the acknowledged founder of the nascent field of political economy, these writers needed to challenge his authority by undertaking some of the earliest critiques of the sacred book of the new creed, the *Wealth of Nations*. Though they did not use the term 'comparative advantage', their thesis can be summarized in the statement that comparative advantage in the manufacturing sector is not given by Providence, but can be created with the assistance of appropriate public policy.

This chapter does not aim to carry out a comprehensive survey of the numerous national economists who appeared in several countries and, in word and deed, affected both political economy and the development of their economies. Their legacy to mainstream economics has been the legitimization of the infant-industry argument for protection. Attention will be limited to the three economists who were pre-eminent in this field, Alexander Hamilton, John Rae and Friedrich List. Though none of them was born in the US, they all resided there for longer or shorter periods of time. The founder of the school of national economists is Hamilton, whose influence on the other two

75

is unmistakable. We therefore begin by examining Hamilton's influential *Report on Manufactures*.

5.1 Alexander Hamilton's *Report on Manufactures*

'It is one of the most impressive pieces of writing in political economy (i.e. economics applied to statecraft) in our literature. It has, curiously enough, more to say to us today than it did to its readers in 1791' (Hacker, 1957, p. 184). That was how one scholar characterized the *Report on the Subject of Manufactures*, the last of four major reports on the American economy which Alexander Hamilton, Secretary of the Treasury to George Washington, submitted to Congress on December 5, 1791. Ironically, this epoch-making document, which the House of Representatives had commissioned almost two years earlier, was his only major report which Congress failed to adopt.

Much has been written about the background, originality and significance of Hamilton's *Report*. Given the focus of this book, this section will explore only those aspects relating to the subject of free trade and protectionism, and how public policy can modify the structure of a country's comparative advantage in order to exploit fully its economic potential. As the editors of the *Papers of Alexander Hamilton* have said of the *Report*, 'it contains few, if any, specific proposals that even the most enthusiastic supporters of Hamilton could maintain were original. In this sense, the Report is as much a product of its times as the creation of its author' (Syrett et al., 1966, p. 1). Given the audience to which it was addressed, it was designed as a policy document. But it turned out to be a significant scholarly contribution for the impact it had on subsequent thinkers and national economists.

Hamilton's mandate was clear from the instructions he received from the House of Representatives in January 1790: to 'prepare a proper plan ... for the encouragement and promotion of such manufactories as will tend to render the United States independent of other nations for essential, particularly for military supplies' (*Journal of the House of Representatives of the United States* of 1826, as cited in Cooke, 1982, p. 98). In drawing up his *Report*, Hamilton benefitted from the expertise and advice of an enthusiastic advocate of manufactures, Tench Coxe, who became Assistant Secretary of the Treasury in May 1790 after being secretary of the Pennsylvania Society for the Encouragement of Manufactures. Hamilton decided to broaden his mandate, and 'going far beyond what Congress had explicitly requested ... presented a long and cogent essay on the imperativeness of manufactures for a newly independent, overwhelmingly agricultural, and still undeveloped country' (Cooke, 1982, p. 99). This broader focus converted the *Report* from a document of interest mainly to American policymakers to a plan of economic development whose appeal, both in the US and overseas, would extend well beyond the realm of government affairs.

In light of the instructions he had received, it is not surprising that Hamilton's advocacy of the establishment of manufactures was based in part on non-economic arguments, particularly those relating to national security and to self-sufficiency in certain strategic commodities. He argued for a diversified economy by noting that

> not only the wealth; but the independence and security of a Country, appear to be materially connected with the prosperity of manufactures. Every nation, with a view to those great objects, ought to endeavour to possess within itself all the essentials of national supply. These comprise the means of *Subsistence habitation clothing* and *defence.* (Hamilton, 1966, p. 291)

He pointed to the 'extreme embarrassments of the United States during the late War, from an incapacity of supplying themselves' (ibid.) as a topical illustration of the importance of this national security objective. Hamilton thus focused attention on the nation-state as an agent in international affairs, and on national interest as a legitimate policy goal. This refrain was taken up later by John Rae and to an even greater extent by Friedrich List, who were both familiar with the *Report*.[1]

Of greater interest here are the economic arguments which Hamilton skillfully used to support the introduction of manufactures in the US. In advancing them, he found it necessary to confront Adam Smith on his own ground. Hence, 'keenly aware of Smith's intellectual spell, Hamilton carried on a running debate with the distinguished Scottish philosopher' (Cooke, 1982, p. 99). His intimate familiarity with Smith's *Wealth of Nations* is evident from the language of his *Report*.[2] But curiously enough he never mentioned Smith by name, even though parts of the *Report* paraphrase him, at times using his very words and expressions. There is even a lengthy passage from the *Wealth of Nations*, though devoid of attribution.[3]

Opinions differ widely on whether Hamilton was Smithian or anti-Smithian. According to Hacker (1957, p. 12), 'he follows Adam Smith so plainly and completely that one can only express wonder that the Hamilton text has been misunderstood for so long'. As stated above, Cooke disputed this view:

> The notion that Hamilton was Smith's disciple dies hard.... The persistent view that Hamilton was intellectually the Scotsman's American twin needs, in sum, no refutation except a close reading of the *Report on Manufactures.* True, Hamilton did endorse some of Smith's ideas – among several of them, the benefits of a division of labor and the use of machinery – but for the most part he set forth economic doctrines that Smith's *Wealth*

of Nations was designed to topple. Mercantilism, not laissez-faire, was Hamilton's creed, if, that is, a label must be affixed to his ideas. (Cooke, 1982, pp. 99–100)

Hamilton's attitude is comparable to that of other critics of Smith, including Rae and List, who wholeheartedly endorsed some of the teachings of the *Wealth of Nations*, while highlighting their differences from it in other fundamental respects. Certain passages of the *Report* could indeed lead one to conclude that Hamilton was a Smithian economist, while others just as easily lead to the opposite conclusion. But Cooke is correct in maintaining that Hamilton's claim to fame rests on theories and related policy implications which clearly differed from Smith's.

Hamilton's rhetorical skills are revealed by his adeptness at using parts of Smithian doctrine to contradict or cast doubt on others. For example, after rejecting Smith's expressed view that agriculture is inherently more productive than manufacturing and suggesting instead that they are equally productive, Hamilton went on to list seven reasons which favor the establishment of manufactures in a country which lacks them. He derived the first two reasons ('the division of labor' and 'an extension of the use of machinery') from the *Wealth of Nations*. Following Adam Smith, Hamilton (1966, p. 252) asserted that 'manufacturing pursuits are susceptible in a greater degree of the application of machinery, than those of Agriculture'. Since the division of labor can be carried out further in manufacturing than in agriculture, the former has a greater productive potential than the latter.[4]

Hamilton complemented his advocacy of manufacturing by anticipating and disposing of some potential objections to the encouragement of manufactures in the US. One of these was that specialization in agriculture 'at least secures the great advantage of a division of labour, leaving the farmer free to pursue exclusively the culture of his land, and enabling him to procure with its products the manufactured supplies requisite either to his wants or to his enjoyments' (Hamilton, 1966, pp. 261–2). Hamilton recognized the force of this argument and the merits of specialization, but only in a 'system of perfect liberty'. This was another of Adam Smith's favorite expressions which Hamilton borrowed without acknowledgment from the *Wealth of Nations*:

> If the system of perfect liberty to industry and commerce were the prevailing system of nations – the arguments which dissuade a country in the predicament of the United States, from the zealous pursuit of manufactures would doubtless have great force. In such a state of things, each country would have the full benefit of its peculiar advantages to compensate for its deficiencies or disadvantages. If one nation were in condition to supply manufactured articles on better terms than another, that other might find an abundant indemnification in a superior capacity to furnish the produce of the soil. (Hamilton, 1966, p. 262)

Even though nations which are 'merely agricultural' would not be as wealthy as those which combine agriculture with manufacturing, they would be compensated by the progressive improvement of their lands. This and similar passages have led Hacker (1957, p. 172) to conclude that 'thus Hamilton, ever reasonable, presented the position of a world system where the rule of comparative costs is generally recognized, and there are neither impediments to universal free trade nor national necessities to interfere with it'. But Hamilton went on to argue that

> the system which has been mentioned, is far from characterising the general policy of Nations. The prevalent one has been regulated by an opposite spirit. The consequence of it is, that the United States are to a certain extent in the situation of a country precluded from foreign Commerce. (Hamilton, 1966, pp. 262–3)

The reason for this lay on the export rather than the import side. While the US was free to import manufactures, it faced difficulties in exporting its 'principal staples'. Because of the policies pursued by other countries, specialization in accordance with Smithian principles would

> expose [the United States] to a state of impoverishment, compared with the opulence to which their political and natural advantages authorise them to aspire. Remarks of this kind are not made in a spirit of complaint. 'Tis for the nations, whose regulations are alluded to, to judge for themselves, whether, by aiming at too much they do not lose more than they gain. 'Tis for the United States to consider by what means they can render themselves least dependent, on the combinations, right or wrong of foreign policy.... If Europe will not take from us the products of our soil, upon terms consistent with our interest, the natural remedy is to contract as fast as possible our wants of her. (Hamilton, 1966, pp. 263–5)

Hamilton here introduced considerations of commercial policy designed to qualify or even overturn Smith's advocacy of free trade.[5] Since Europe's commercial policy had interfered with American exports, a retaliatory policy was called for.[6]

Hamilton's ideas about the place of the US in the territorial division of labor resulted from an objective examination of the American economy as it actually was at that time, as well as from its perceived potential. The juxtaposition of actuality and potentiality led to the formulation of commercial policies to expedite the transition from the present to the future. While present-day textbooks of international economics separate the positive theory of international trade from the normative one of commercial policy, such a dichotomy did not characterize Hamilton's views any more than it did Adam Smith's, who described the gains from trade in Book IV of the *Wealth of Nations* devoted to the policies underlying mercantilism and other 'systems of political economy'. Hamilton's realization that the 'system of perfect liberty', whose theoretical advantages he recognized, did not prevail at that time suggested a move away from free trade based on the prevailing pattern of comparative advantage. Cooke (1964, p. xxiii) maintains that 'the Report on Manufactures, in fact, entitles Hamilton to be called our first national planner'. Hamilton was mainly preoccupied with the strategy of economic development in a new nation such as the US rather than with the welfare implications of trade based on a given structure of output. His statement that 'it is the interest of nations to diversify the industrious pursuits of the individuals, who compose them' (Hamilton, 1966, p. 260) was inspired by both economic and non-economic considerations.

Development economists and international trade theorists use different criteria when they theorize about a country's optimal pattern of output.[7] In the 1960s Ragnar Nurkse left a mark on the emerging field of development economics by advocating balanced growth, in contrast to the pattern of unbalanced growth occurring in an economy which specializes according to comparative advantage. Both Adam Smith and Hamilton (probably, once again, influenced by Smith) had anticipated this approach by arguing that manufactures should be encouraged not only for their own sake, but for that of the agricultural sector itself. The latter would benefit from a steady and reliable demand for its output coming from the urban sector of the economy, instead of having to rely on an uncertain and fluctuating foreign demand.[8] Hamilton conceded that fostering manufactures would cause a smaller amount of land to be cultivated, but noted the tradeoff between extensive and intensive cultivation resulting from the fact that land productivity would be enhanced by a 'more steady and vigorous cultivation'.

Hamilton went on to debunk Smith's argument that investors who set out to maximize their own returns end up choosing investments which are socially optimal. Smith had made this argument memorable with his well-known metaphor of the 'invisible hand' (the only such reference in the *Wealth of Nations*). Hamilton presented several reasons why Smith's argument was not relevant to new ventures:

> These have relation to – the strong influence of habit and the spirit of imitation – the fear of want of success in untried enterprises – the intrinsic difficulties incident to first essays towards a competition with those who have previously attained to perfection in the business to be attempted – the bounties premiums and other artificial encouragements, with which foreign nations second the exertions of their own Citizens in the branches, in which they are to be rivalled. (Hamilton, 1966, p. 266)

It is difficult to improve on Hamilton's rationale for infant industry protection.[9] He went on to discuss at some length each of the above points, which he ranked in increasing order of importance. To overcome the first obstacle, the reluctance to abandon long-established productive activities, may 'require the incitement and patronage of government' (p. 267), and similarly for the remaining obstacles; indeed, 'the extraordinary aid and protection of government' (p. 268) is needed to allow a new industry to compete against the superior establishments of other nations. When foreign governments subsidize their own exporters, they add artificial obstacles to new domestic undertakings on top of the natural ones already referred to. According to Robbins (1968, p. 113), 'the alleged necessity of government encouragement to offset the inertia of habit and the "fear of want of success in untried enterprises" goes to the root of the matter. As a practical down-to-earth plea for government intervention in such connections, Hamilton's advocacy could hardly be bettered'.

Hamilton went on to examine, and then rebut, the allegations circulating at that time that the US did not possess a comparative advantage in manufactures because of (1) scarcity of hands, (2) dearness of labor, and (3) want of capital.[10] Although the scarcity of hands was a widely recognized phenomenon, Hamilton did not believe it disqualified the country from establishing its own manufactures, and this for several reasons. First, manufacturing allows the employment of part-time labor or of people otherwise excluded from the labor force, such as women and children. Secondly, Hamilton (1966, p. 270) looked to 'the vast extension given by late improvements to the employment of Machines, which substituting the Agency of fire and water, has prodigiously lessened the necessity for manual labour'. Thirdly, the very dearness of labor encouraged its immigration from abroad, as shown by the 'large proportion of ingenious and valuable workmen, in different arts and trades, who, by expatriating from Europe, have improved their own condition, and added to the industry and wealth of the United States' (ibid.). Foreign workers would migrate in even greater numbers when they realized that the US was seriously intent on establishing manufactures.

Hamilton recognized that the second factor allegedly militating against manufactures, the dearness of labor, is related to the first, being an alternative way of expressing it.[11] But labor was dear not only because it was scarce, but because high profits stimulated high wages. And according to Hamilton, 'the Undertaker can afford to pay the price' (p. 272), thanks to the natural and artificial protection enjoyed by fabrics (typifying manufactures) in the US. Not only were raw materials cheaper there, but foreign fabrics were disadvantaged by being subject to transport costs, trade taxes and other fees.

The third point, the want of capital, also did not trouble Hamilton since he believed that any domestic shortage of capital would be made good by foreign capital flowing from Europe to seek a higher rate of return. He dismissed Adam Smith's point (later reiterated by Ricardo) that people prefer to invest their capital at home rather than abroad, by pointing out that this can be counteracted by a lack of investment opportunities or by low returns at home, as well as by the enticing prospect of a booming market such as the American one. The US would prove to be an attractive haven for foreign capital since 'little more is now necessary, than to foster industry, and cultivate order and tranquility, at home and abroad' (p. 275). Hamilton took strong exception to

persons disposed to look with a jealous eye on the introduction of foreign Capital, as if it were an instrument to deprive our own citizens of the profits of our own industry. Instead of being viewed as a rival, it ought to be Considered as a most valuable auxiliary; conducing to put in Motion a greater Quantity of productive labour, and a greater portion of useful enterprise than could exist without it. (Hamilton, 1966, p. 276)

He cited instances of foreign capital being attracted not only to agriculture, but to manufacturing and infrastructural projects such as canals, bridges and river navigation.

In sum, Hamilton did not regard the pattern of specialization in an economy such as the American one as predetermined, for two main reasons. The first was that factor endowments themselves were not exogenously given, à la Heckscher–Ohlin, but endogenous since foreign capital, labor and enterprise could supplement domestic endowments. Secondly, again contrary to Heckscher–Ohlin assumptions, technology was not given, but could change with innovations or the introduction of machinery. Hamilton showed how machinery could substitute for high-cost labor, and even provided a rudimentary numerical example designed to show how such substitution could halve the labor cost of production (p. 272).

Since neither technology nor factor endowments were given in the burgeoning American economy, their fluid nature favored the establishment of manufactures. Moreover, the human resources found in the US, marked by a diversity of talents and mechanical aptitudes, could be matched with the diversity of employments which only manufacturing could offer:

If there be anything in a remark often to be met with – namely that there is, in the genius of the people of this country, a peculiar aptitude for mechanic improvements, it would operate as a forcible reason for giving opportunities to the exercise of that species of talent, by the propagation of manufactures. (Hamilton, 1966, p. 256)

The existence of diverse industrial activities, in turn, would foster exertion, resourcefulness and a spirit of enterprise:

> To cherish and stimulate the activity of the human mind, by multiplying the objects of enterprise, is not among the least considerable of the expedients, by which the wealth of a nation may be promoted. Even things in themselves not positively advantageous, sometimes become so, by their tendency to provoke exertion. Every new scene, which is opened to the busy nature of man to rouse and exert itself, is the addition of a new energy to the general stock of effort. The spirit of enterprise, useful and prolific as it is, must necessarily be contracted or expanded in proportion to the simplicity or variety of the occupations and productions, which are to be found in a Society. It must be less in a nation of mere cultivators, than in a nation of cultivators and merchants; less in a nation of cultivators and merchants, than in a nation of cultivators, artificers and merchants. (Hamilton, 1966, p. 256)

Hamilton's subtle reference to 'the wealth of a nation' can be viewed as an indirect critique of Adam Smith, who had not stressed this important stimulus to economic development in the *Wealth of Nations*. Hamilton held out the prospect of a feedback process whereby the availability of a variety of manufacturing activities promotes in workers the very aptitudes which are needed to further such activities. In order to convey the message that a more complex economy is a more dynamic one, he followed Smith in articulating a sequence of stages through which an economy passes. A somewhat different sequence was enunciated later by Friedrich List.

The protection of infant industries smacked of mercantilism to Adam Smith, and he dismissed it in Book IV of the *Wealth of Nations* as a policy which is at best useless and at worst counterproductive, his main objection being that it promotes monopoly. Hamilton was at pains to show that while protection can raise the price of a commodity, this effect is only short-lived:

> It is universally true, that the contrary is the ultimate effect with every successful manufacture. When a domestic manufacture has attained to perfection, and has engaged in the prosecution of it a competent number of Persons, it invariably becomes cheaper. It ... seldom or never fails to be sold Cheaper, in process of time, than was the foreign Article for which it is a substitute. The internal competition, which takes place, soon does away [with] every thing like Monopoly, and by degrees reduces the price of the Article to the *minimum* of a reasonable profit on the Capital employed. (Hamilton, 1966, p. 286)

After establishing the desirability of promoting the manufacturing sector, Hamilton discussed in detail the appropriate policy measures. He expressed a decided preference for 'pecuniary bounties' (that is, subsidies) over protective duties and prohibitions of rival articles, and went on to provide several justifications for his view that a bounty 'has been found one of the most efficacious means of encouraging manufactures, and it is in some views, the best' (Hamilton, 1966, p. 298). Four of the rationales he provided are surprisingly consistent with the modern theory of commercial policy. The first is the direct nature of the encouragement of new enterprises provided by subsidies. This is an example of what is sometimes referred to as the 'specificity rule', which postulates that 'it is more efficient to use policy tools that are closest to the sources of the distortions separating private and social benefits and costs. Intervene at the source' (Lindert, 1986, p. 149). Secondly, Hamilton (1966, p. 296) noted that duties 'evidently amount to a virtual bounty on the domestic fabrics since by enhancing the charges on foreign Articles, they enable the National Manufacturers to undersell all their foreign Competitors'. However, they lead to a 'temporary augmentation of price', the 'inconvenience' of which is avoided by a bounty (p. 299).[12] Hamilton thus perceived, with remarkable clarity, that duties combine a subsidy on production with a tax on consumption, as is clear to present-day economists. Thirdly, since subsidies, unlike duties, do not lead to an increase in price, they do not discourage imports 'by interfering with the profits to be expected from the sale of the [foreign] article' (p. 300). Import substitution, while it may be a by-product of infant-industry protection, was clearly not one of Hamilton's policy goals. Fourthly, he noted that while a duty grants protection in the home market, it does nothing to promote the exportation of the article. The truth of this observation became painfully clear to countries which practiced extensive import substitution after the end of World War Two. The associated inefficiencies and their failure to gain export markets eventually led some to abandon this policy in favor of export promotion.

In addition to duties and bounties, Hamilton listed nine other policies designed to encourage manufactures, two of which may have caught John Rae's attention. One of these was premiums, which

> serve to reward some particular excellence or superiority, some extraordinary exertion or skill, and are dispensed only in a small number of cases. But their effect is to stimulate general effort. Contrived so as to be both honorary and lucrative, they address themselves to different passions; touching the chords as well of emulation as of Interest. They are accordingly a very economical means of exciting the enterprise of a Whole Community. (Hamilton, 1966, p. 304)

Another policy was 'the encouragement of new inventions and discoveries, at home, and of the introduction into the United States of such as may have been made in other countries; particularly those which relate to machinery'. Hamilton added that 'this is among the most useful and unexceptionable of the aids, which can be given to manufactures. The usual means of that encouragement are pecuniary rewards, and, for a time, exclusive privileges'. Moreover, one should 'extend the same benefit to Introducers, as well as Authors and Inventors' (Hamilton, pp. 307–8); in other words, innovators (to use Schumpeter's term) as well as inventors should be rewarded.[13]

Hamilton believed that infant industry protection should be temporary in nature:

> As often as a duty upon a foreign article makes an addition to its price, it causes an extra expence to the Community, for the benefit of the domestic manufacturer. A bounty does no more: But it is the Interest of the society in each case, to submit to a *temporary* expence, which is more than compensated, by an increase of industry and Wealth, by an augmentation of resources and independence; & by the circumstance of eventual cheapness. (Hamilton, 1966, p. 302; emphasis added)

The fact that protection need only be temporary was implied by Hamilton's prediction, mentioned above, that the ultimate impact of a successful domestic manufacture is that 'it invariably becomes cheaper' than its previous import price because of domestic competition. Even more explicit was his statement that 'the continuance of bounties on manufactures long established must almost always be of questionable policy: Because a presumption would arise in every such Case, that there were natural and inherent impediments to success' (p. 301). The heart of the infant industry argument is thus that a *finite* lapse of time should be required for skills and expertise to develop in 'a new and useful branch of industry', and that the setting-up costs thereby incurred be more than offset by the long-run benefit to society. These insights of Hamilton were developed further by Rae and List.

Hamilton's *Report* was a precursor of development economics and of national planning for economic development. In the aftermath of the Smithian revolution, it restored a role for economic policy in furthering the aims of the nation-state. It was a source of inspiration for the national economists who followed Hamilton. More importantly for our purposes, it planted the seeds of the argument that comparative advantage can be created through policy actions and need not be accepted as determined by factors beyond a nation's control.

5.2 John Rae's *New Principles of Political Economy*

John Rae, a Scottish economist who migrated to Canada and later to the US, is the next important figure who helped to conceptualize infant industry protection and the creation of comparative advantage. In 1834 he published in Boston a book with a lengthy title: *Statement of Some New Principles on the Subject of Political Economy, Exposing the Fallacies of the System of Free*

Trade, and of Some Other Doctrines Maintained in the 'Wealth of Nations'. With few exceptions, it remained unknown (or, if known, unappreciated) in both Britain and the US for the rest of the century. Potential readers may have been antagonized by its title, which suggested a diatribe against Adam Smith and the principle of free trade.[14] Its publication in a former colony of Britain rather than the mother country may also have prevented it from gaining its proper recognition. The *New Principles* was eventually championed by Nassau Senior, who brought it to the attention of John Stuart Mill. Mill quoted it at some length in chapter 11 (entitled 'Of the Law of the Increase of Capital') of Book One of his *Principles of Political Economy* of 1848, and placed Rae's analysis of the forces leading to the accumulation of capital on a level with Malthus's principle of population growth (Mill, 1920, p. 165). As noted in Chapter 6, he also referred to Rae in two chapters of Book Five of the *Principles*, the second of which contains his well-known paragraph advocating infant industry protection. Thanks to Mill's eloquent defense, inspired by Rae's book, this argument thereafter entered mainstream economics.[15]

Rae's *New Principles* contains a pioneering formulation of capital theory, anticipating the much later ones of Eugen Böhm-Bawerk and Irving Fisher, and articulates the important role of invention and of the growth of knowledge in a country's economic development. Rae defined the quickness of returns (or 'order') of a capital instrument by the period of time it takes for a given outlay to yield a return double in value. The shorter this period, the higher the instrument's productivity or rate of return.[16] He represented the more quickly returning orders by the letters A, B, C, ... and the more slowly returning ones by Z, a, b, c, ... An important factor affecting the rate of capital formation is the strength of what he called the 'effective desire of accumulation', which corresponds to Irving Fisher's 'rate of time preference' or 'degree of impatience'. This is in part determined by altruistic feelings towards future generations, which Rae named the 'social and benevolent affections'.

That Rae was acquainted with Hamilton's *Report on Manufactures* is apparent from a quotation from it in the *New Principles*, and these two publications are similar in several respects. Both authors advocated the promotion of manufactures in developing economies such as those of Canada and the US, and both critiqued Smith's *Wealth of Nations*. The full title of Rae's book advertised it as a critique of free trade and of the *Wealth of Nations*. This critique was much more profound than Hamilton's, in part because it was presented at book length rather than in a government document, in part thanks to Rae's willingness to actually quote from the *Wealth of Nations* in order to rebut its arguments. His critique was also notable because of his capital-theoretic frame of reference, and his consequent alertness to the needs of futurity in the formulation of public policy.

Both Hamilton and Rae accepted most of the teachings of the *Wealth of Nations*, and skillfully used them to advance their own theses where these conflicted with Smith's. Rae quoted from Book IV of the *Wealth of Nations* several passages set out above in section 3.5. He pointed out that Smith had implicitly postulated a series of 'axioms' such as (i) wealth can increase only via capital accumulation, and (ii) capital accumulation depends on saving out of current revenue. Since he assumed that government regulations turn industry into a less advantageous direction, Smith had deduced that they must also reduce income and hence saving, capital accumulation and future welfare. This led to his hostility towards the promotion of infant industries:

> By means of such regulations, indeed, a particular manufacture may sometimes be acquired sooner than it could have been otherwise, and after a certain time may be made at home as cheap or cheaper than in the foreign country. But though the industry of the society may be thus carried with advantage into a particular channel sooner than it could have been otherwise, it will by no means follow that the sum total, either of its industry, or of its revenue, can ever be augmented by any such regulation. The industry of the society can augment only in proportion as its capital augments, and its capital can augment only in proportion to what can be gradually saved out of its revenue. But the immediate effect of every such regulation is to diminish its revenue, and what diminishes its revenue, is certainly not very likely to augment its capital faster than it would have augmented of its own accord, had both capital and industry been left to find out their natural employments. (Smith, 1976, p. 458)

Rae believed that the Smithian 'axioms' underlying the creation of national wealth are unwarranted. Instead, he held that a nation's wealth depends primarily on knowledge and skills, which can often be transferred from other countries through legislative efforts.[17] To Smith's contentions that 'the natural advantages which one country has over another in producing particular commodities are sometimes so great, that it is acknowledged by all the world to be in vain to struggle with them' and that 'whether the advantages which one country has over another, be natural or acquired, is in this respect of no consequence' (ibid.), Rae protested that

> on the contrary, in my opinion, it is of the greatest consequence. Now natural advantages cannot be procured by any expenditure of revenue or capital. But one country can often with ease, and at a trifling expense, acquire the practical skill and the knowledge of particular arts and manufactures which another possesses, and, by doing so, gain the advantage of procuring for itself the products of this skill and knowledge at home, instead of having to go abroad for them. (Rae, 1834, pp. 71–2)

A country's 'actual productions' should never be characterized as its 'natural productions':

The products of different regions are spoken of by political economists, as bestowed on them by nature, are termed natural productions, and the attempt to transfer them to other sites, is held to be a procedure in opposition to the designs of providence, whose intentions, it is asserted, in giving them these productions, were, that the inhabitants of different countries should exchange the products of their several territories with one another.... Because one country alone now produces particular commodities, we are by no means warranted to conclude that nature intended they should be produced only there. On the contrary ... these arts [of production] should be advanced from their first rough simplicity, and carried to greater and greater excellence, by passing from one region and people to another. (Rae, 1834, pp. 257–8)

Later Rae traced the ultimate consequence of the transfer of technology by noting that technical progress in society B can allow it to acquire a competitive advantage which it did not initially enjoy, to the disadvantage of its trading partner, society A:

As there are no limits to the inventive faculty, so no community can assure itself that any commodity which it now produces and exports to some other community, may not come to be produced in that community, and so be no longer exported there. But while in the society B, the effects of the progress of invention would be thus beneficial, in A they might operate prejudicially. (Rae, 1834, pp. 304–5)

An import-biased innovation in B thus deteriorates A's terms of trade, leading to declines in A's income and rate of capital formation. The facility with which technology can be transferred internationally prompted Rae (1834, p. 258) to ask the rhetorical question: 'who can positively say what fifty years hence will be the productions of any country?' In addition, 'Rae listed cases in which the transfer between countries of productive modes had altered comparative cost relationships' (Goodwin, 1961, p. 126).

Rae pointed out that Adam Smith himself had insisted that 'the revenue of a trading and manufacturing country must, other things being equal, always be much greater than that of one without trade or manufactures', since 'a small quantity of manufactured produce purchases a great quantity of rude produce' (Smith, 1976, p. 677).[18] In analyzing the transfer of a manufacturing process from abroad, Rae provided a very early definition of a public good when he stated that 'the necessary first cost of the scheme should be borne by the whole community' (Rae, 1834, p. 53). This requires the direct assistance of policymakers:

The difficulty is, to discover a method of inducing an individual to incur an unavoidable outlay, the returns from which, although very beneficial to the whole society, are no more so to him who lays out a great deal, than to others who lay out nothing. The whole society, or rather the legislator, the power acting for the whole society, might do so, and in similar cases has done so, and, to judge of the measure by the events consequent on it, with the happiest success. Why, then, should he not? (Rae, 1834, pp. 55–6)

Like Hamilton, Rae based his argument for the promotion of infant industries on the desirability of a manufacturing base for a country's economic development and on the difficulties faced by individuals trying to set up a new establishment. These difficulties include the cost of importing special machinery and of attracting specialized workmen from abroad, the large financial outlay required, the need to modify an imported technology because of differences in climate, materials and factor prices, and the trial and error inevitably associated with a new venture (1834, pp. 46–56).

Rae (again, like Hamilton) was cautious in recommending candidates for infant industry protection. The calculation to be made by policymakers in selecting such industries should resemble that made in appraising any investment project:

We know indeed that we must expend something, but we think that in the long run we shall be better repaid for this expenditure, by this undertaking, than by any other in which we could employ our funds.... The question to be determined in every such case, would then be similar to that which an individual determines when deliberating on any scheme for the augmentation of his private capital, and would resolve itself into an inquiry, whether or not the probable returns from the proposed measure, be likely to be a sufficient remuneration for the expense of carrying it into effect. (Rae, 1834, pp. 60, 67)

Rae urged policymakers to establish 'rules determining when the passage of any art is practicable, and when the benefits derived from it will exceed, or fall short of the necessary expense of effecting the passage', the criterion for success being that 'the commodity, the product of the art in question, comes to be made at the same cost in the country to which its manufacture is transferred, as in that from which it comes, or at less cost than there' (1834, p. 364). In addition to the direct benefits of a project, this calculation should include indirect ones such as the saving of transport costs and the assurance that supply would not be interrupted in the case of wars or other disturbances. Rae was thus applying a form of benefit-cost analysis which takes into account risk factors as well as the more conventional economic outputs and inputs. If the transfer of a technology is desirable, the legislator can effect it 'by premiums for successful individual imitations of the foreign article', in order to ascertain its viability. If further encouragement is then warranted, this should be followed 'by general bounties on the home manufacture; or by duties on that imported from abroad' (p. 368). These are some of the same protective measures advocated by Hamilton, but Rae (since he was not writing a policy document) did not elaborate on them in the same detail.

Rae's powerful advocacy of the promotion of infant industries and the full title of his book suggest that he was opposed to free trade. But chapter 12 of Book Two, 'Of exchanges between different communities', describes (without however using the term 'free trade') the benefits resulting from such exchanges. Like most economists of the classical period, Rae focused more on the benefits of foreign trade than on the sources of comparative advantage. To appraise these benefits, he classified commodities into 'utilities' and 'luxuries'. The abstract of chapter 11 in the 'Table of Contents and Summary of Principles' of the *New Principles* defines them as follows: 'In so far as any commodity, when compared with another, excels it only in the gratification it affords to vanity, it is to be considered a luxury, in so far as it compares with others in the capacity which its physical qualities give it to gratify real wants, it is considered as a utility' (1834, p. xv).[19]

A 'utility' (in Rae's sense) is imported in exchange for exports if people 'can procure it for less labor than the substitute they already possess', after allowing for the cost of transport (p. 302). This is a classic instance of Jacob Viner's 'eighteenth-century rule' discussed in Chapter 3. But Rae argued that trade in utilities not only lowers the amount of labor needed to provide a community with these commodities, but also carries its capital instruments to more quickly returning orders, thus stimulating capital formation. He thereby provided a new definition of gains from trade, different from that of other classical writers or of the neoclassical economists who followed them:

> The revolution effected might nearly compare to an improvement in both societies. Like other improvements, they would not be confined in their operation to the particular branches of industry in which they had place, but would be diffused equally over both societies, carrying the whole instruments in each towards the more quickly returning orders. Profits would rise equally in all employments. The absolute capital of both communities would be increased in proportion to the augmented provision made for their future wants. (Rae, 1834, p. 303)

Just as free trade yields dynamic benefits of this type, trade restrictions imply a less dynamic economy:

> The fewer obstructions, therefore, that stood in the way of such transfers [of commodities between different societies], the farther, in these cases, would the stock of instruments in those societies be carried towards the order A, as any obstruction that might occur would, on the contrary, have the effect of checking the progress towards the more quickly returning orders, and keeping them nearer the order Z. (Rae, 1834, p. 304)

The quickening of the orders of the society's entire range of capital instruments and consequent rise in the profit rate stimulated by trade were the same conclusions which Rae had derived in the case of an invention, or of an improvement such as that in the art of bread baking described in a previous chapter of his book. Like an invention, a trade-induced fall in the price of 'utilities' increases the ratio between the 'capacity' (or productivity) of instruments and their cost, carrying them to an order of quicker return.

When Rae analyzed trade in luxuries in chapter 12 of his book, his conclusions had the same negative tone as those he had reached for luxuries in a closed economy in chapter 11, where he had shown that an increase of productivity in the manufacture of luxuries can be socially deleterious. By enabling poorer people to purchase them, their rarity and hence their value in the eyes of their former customers are diminished, so that instruments are carried to slower orders of return. Trade in luxuries has similarly negative implications, though Rae did note that exporters of luxuries can sometimes gain from technical progress. If trade is subject to obstructions or if the importing country has a large demand for this commodity, technical progress acts as 'a sort of factitious improvement ... which, while it lasts, is sometimes nearly equivalent to a real improvement' (p. 308). Rae also pointed out that some commodities combine the features of utilities and luxuries: 'there is beneath almost every luxury a substratum of utility of greater or less depth' (p. 310). The closer commodities are to the luxury side of the spectrum, the farther does an innovation in the instruments which produce them carry them towards more slowly returning orders.

Was Rae inconsistent in simultaneously supporting policies of free trade and of infant industry protection?[20] His theory of capital is the key to clarifying this apparent contradiction. Both policies have the potential of increasing the profit rate by raising the ratio between the capacity of instruments and their cost, and hence of carrying instruments to more speedily returning orders. By focusing on situations involving changes in technical knowledge or learning by doing, where the time required for a new technique of production to become profitable is an integral part of the analysis, the infant-industry argument can be justified as an application of capital theory rather than trade theory. As has been many times remarked, it is not inconsistent with a free trade philosophy.[21] Free trade is optimal for a country with no monopoly power in trade only if the static assumptions customarily made in international trade theory are satisfied. These include a given technology, given factors of production and a frictionless and timeless movement along the production possibility surface, and are therefore not relevant to an analysis of infant industries which focuses on changes in technology over time. The promotion of an industry is socially beneficial if it meets the criterion that the resulting increase in output will more than compensate for the resource cost which its introduction entails.[22] Rae came close to expressing this criterion in a form that has become known as the Mill–Bastable test, to be described in Chapter 6.

The legitimacy of infant industry protection under appropriate conditions leaves the door open for changes in comparative advantage stimulated by government policy. In light of Rae's lively awareness of the potential for such changes, his lack of interest in investigating the sources of comparative advantage, whether derived from factor endowments or other exogenous country characteristics, is not surprising. When explanations of trade along Heckscher–Ohlin lines were formulated a century later, as discussed in Chapter 8, differences in factor endowments among countries were coupled with the assumption that technology is identical everywhere. Rae would have rejected the latter assumption out of hand, since technological knowledge in the developing countries with which he was familiar was unavailable or very rudimentary. Such asymmetry in technological *savoir-faire* called for legislative efforts to transfer technologies from abroad. Rae was confident, as was Hamilton, that the manufacturing sector offered many such candidates for promotion by the government. Moreover, technology is never simply transferred unaltered from its country of origin, but is actually 'carried to greater and greater excellence, by passing from one region and people to another' (1834, p. 258). If a technique of production is confined to a particular community, the presumption is that it is still in its infancy, and that it will advance towards maturity only as it gets diffused to other countries. Rae argued that the international diffusion of technology makes it very hard to predict the future international division of labor, or to characterize the current pattern of outputs as 'natural productions'. Like Hamilton, Rae was an important forerunner of present-day theories of the creation of comparative advantage.

5.3 Friedrich List's *National System of Political Economy*

It may seem strange to associate the name of Friedrich List with international trade and comparative advantage, since he is often remembered as an advocate of protection and of a national development policy. If List was aware of the discovery of the concept of comparative advantage by Robert Torrens and David Ricardo, he was clearly not impressed by it because he never mentioned it.[23] His primary interest was the economics of development rather than of international trade, and he has in fact been eulogized in some developing countries as a patron saint of a nationalist path to industrialization and economic development.[24] List tended to view trade through the prism of its potential for assisting or impeding development. For countries in the temperate zone, first and foremost his native Germany, he condemned a trade-induced specialization in agricultural commodities since he regarded agriculture as a country's most backward sector, both economically and culturally. For such countries, List recommended a balanced and harmonious growth of both agriculture and manufacturing, a concept he may well have derived from Alexander Hamilton or even, as pointed out above, from Adam Smith. He captured this ideal with the following memorable metaphor:

> A nation which exchanges agricultural products for foreign manufactured goods is an individual with *one* arm, which is supported by a foreign arm ... an agricultural-manufacturing nation is an individual who has *two* arms *of his own* always at his disposal. (List, 1885, p. 180)

Echoing Hamilton's argument, manufacturing was to be encouraged not only for its own sake, but because it assisted the progress of agriculture by providing the market demand, tools, skills and incentives needed to raise agricultural productivity. Since 'the whole social state of a nation will be chiefly *determined by the principle of the variety and division of occupations and the co-operation of its productive powers*', it should not aim to specialize, but rather to seek 'the *balance* or the *harmony of the productive powers*' (1885, pp. 159–60).[25]

List is generally regarded as a precursor of the German Historical School. His attitude towards free trade was highly relativistic, since he believed free trade and protection to have different different welfare implications for a nation according to its current stage of development.[26] A backward economy based on agriculture should practice free trade, exchanging its primary goods for manufactures. List also favored free trade within a nation or between states which were eventually destined to merge into a single nation, as was the case for the Zollverein in his native Germany, whose realization was one of his lifelong goals.[27] But countries in the temperate zone where manufacturing was in its early stages needed a 'system of protection' in order to overcome the natural and artificial advantages of countries – mainly England – which had a head start in manufacturing. At first 'the protective duties must be very moderate, they must only rise gradually with the increase of the mental and material capital, of the technical abilities and spirit of enterprise of the nation' (1885, p. 179). List was resolutely opposed to protection of agriculture at any stage of a country's development.[28] He also argued that after an industry has become established, protection should be gradually reduced so as to expose it to the beneficent effects of competition. He even prescribed this medicine to his German compatriots, maintaining that 'under all circumstances partial but carefully limited foreign competition is really beneficial to their own manufacturing progress' (p. 188). Protection was thus time-specific as well as country-specific. In sum, List's prescription for the level of protection in an initially agricultural country with a manufacturing potential takes the form of an inverted U, rising gradually from zero to a maximum before being reduced or eliminated.

List's justification for protection is at first reminiscent of the infant industry argument. Although Schumpeter claimed for this argument the authority of J. S. Mill, who had accepted it 'evidently realizing that it ran within the free-trade logic', he also realized that it fell well short of doing justice to List's 'vision', a capacity with which he regarded him as being well endowed: 'even as a scientific economist ... List had one of the elements of greatness, namely, the grand vision of a national situation, which, though not in itself a scientific achievement, is a prerequisite for a certain type of scientific achievement'.[29] The end-product of List's vision, for which protection would act as a midwife, was the creation of a modern, urbanized society with the associated cultural and geopolitical characteristics.[30] When protection was warranted, List prescribed moderate rates of duty:

It may in general be assumed that where any technical industry cannot be established by means of an original protection of forty to sixty per cent. and cannot continue to maintain itself under a continued protection of twenty to thirty per cent. the fundamental conditions of manufacturing power are lacking. (List, 1885, p. 313)

Protection was designed to promote basic, machinery-intensive sectors, and much less or not at all the finer manufactures. Even in the case of the US, a country where List resided for a few years and for whose manufactures he generally advocated protection from British imports, he made the following interesting exception:

As long as wages are disproportionately higher there than in the older civilised States, [the United States] can best promote the development of their productive powers, their civilisation and political power, by allowing the free import as much as possible of those manufactured articles in the cost of which wages are a principal element, provided that other countries admit their agricultural products and raw materials. (List, 1885, pp. 188–9)

List's call for industrialization was motivated by the cultural and 'civilizing' attributes of an urban way of life, such as the stimuli to inventiveness and resourcefulness which this promotes and are noticeably absent in rural settings: 'manufactures are at once the offspring, and at the same time the supporters and the nurses, of science and the arts' (1885, p. 200). The main aim of protection was the generation and harnessing of a nation's 'productive forces':

> [List] realized ... that emphasis upon the national future modifies welfare considerations *ex visu* of the present. This he expressed by his doctrine of 'productive forces' (*Produktionskräfte*) that in his system hold place of honor as compared with the consumers' goods that can be made available at a given level of the productive forces – not unfelicitous [sic], this, as an educational device but not much more than a label for an unsolved problem. (Schumpeter, 1954, p. 505)

The development of 'productive forces', the concept which Schumpeter found so intriguing, is a logical expression of this grand vision.[31] This term had been used before by the French economist Charles Dupin, with whose writings List was acquainted.[32] But List gave this expression a broader interpretation, which 'included political, administrative, and social institutions, natural and human resources, industrial establishments, and public works' (Henderson, 1983, pp. 159–60). The blossoming of a country's productive forces required not only a period of protection, but the infrastructural investments which only the government was equipped to make.

List had well-defined but sadly mistaken ideas about the prospective evolution of the territorial division of labor, affected both by a country's stage of development and its geographical location. There was much scope for mutually profitable trade between the temperate zone and the tropical (or 'hot', or 'torrid') zone, the former exporting manufactures to the latter in exchange for 'colonial products'. List regarded this as a climatically and culturally determined division of labor. It is synthetically described in the introduction to his *National System*:[33]

> Agriculture and manufacturing industry are subjected by nature to special conditions. The countries of the temperate zone are especially fit for the development of manufacturing industry; for the temperate zone is the region of intellectual and physical effort. If the countries of the torrid zone are little favored in reference to manufactures, they possess, on the other hand, the natural monopoly of many precious commodities which the inhabitants of the temperate climates greatly prize. The exchange of the manufactured products of the one for the commodities of the other, constitutes a division of labor and co-operation of the productive power throughout the chief commercial nations, and mainly constitutes the great international trade of the world. *A country of the torrid zone would make a very fatal mistake, should it try to become a manufacturing country. Having received no invitation to that vocation from nature, it will progress more rapidly in riches and civilization if it continues to exchange its agricultural productions for the manufactured products of the temperate zone.* (List, 1856, p. 75; emphasis added)

List justified this division of labor by arguing that 'countries with a temperate climate are (almost without exception) adapted for factories and manufacturing industry. The moderate temperature of the air promotes the development and exertion of power far more than a hot temperature' (1885, p. 212). He went on to assert that 'in comparison with this exchange of the manufactured products of the temperate, for the agricultural productions of the torrid zone, other international trade is of a secondary importance, if we but except the trade in a few special articles; wine, for instance' (1856, p. 76). List would have been surprised to hear that the lion's share of world trade a century and a half later would take place among the temperate-zone countries, rather than that between them and the tropical countries. In the first half of the nineteenth century, intraindustry trade had not yet made its début on the world stage. Far from seeing much scope for trade between countries in the temperate zone, List was concerned about the potential damage which a prematurely introduced free trade could wreak in the late industrializers. In the absence of protection, the latter would continue to export primary products in exchange for manufactures, condemning them to remain in a state of perpetual inferiority with respect to Great Britain.

Although the international division of labor, which he believed would be fostered by free trade, appears to be climatically determined, List extended its scope to countries that can hardly be called tropical:

> The theory of free trade will then find admission into Spain, Portugal, Naples, Turkey, Egypt, and all barbarous and half-civilised or hot countries. In such countries as these the foolish idea will not be held any longer, of wanting to establish (in their present state of culture) a manufacturing power of their own by means of the system of protection. (List, 1885, p. 189)

The destruction of the previously flourishing manufacturing sectors of Spain and Portugal, allegedly resulting from their acquiescence in trade liberalization with England, was described by List in some detail in Chapter 5 of Book One of the *National System*. Because of past defective policymaking and a backward social structure, these countries no longer met the cultural preconditions for a manufacturing sector, and a policy of protection would have been counterproductive. Elsewhere in his book, however, List placed the primary weight on climatic rather than cultural preconditions for industrialization. He stated that 'both *international* and *national division of labour* are chiefly determined by climate and by Nature herself' (1885, p. 161), and that a temperate country was 'most favoured by nature' because its 'climate is most conducive to bodily and mental exertion' (p. 162). Such a country was thereby enabled to make the countries of tropical climates and of inferior civilisation tributary in a certain measure to itself. The countries of the temperate zone therefore are above all others called upon to bring their own national division of labour to the highest perfection, and to use the international division of labour for their enrichment. (List, 1885, p. 162)

Referring to this exchange as 'the great commerce of the world', List (1885, p. 266) predicted that trade between the two zones would greatly expand in the future.[34]

In view of these and similar statements, it is perhaps surprising that List, as mentioned earlier, has been praised in developing countries such as India as a precursor of a nationalist path to economic development. As Gomes (1987, p. 270) has commented, 'those who see List as a champion of industrialisation in underdeveloped countries forget that he saw no future for many of these countries along that road'. In her magnificently detailed study of how List and his writings were received in France, Coustillac (1996) reported that, in a monograph on List entitled *A Development Economist in the 19th Century: Friedrich List*, Anson-Meyer (1982) rejected the international division of labor which List endorsed, and attributed it to List's support of a German colonial policy designed to emulate that of the other European powers. List extended his intended division of labor not only to countries in the tropical zone but to those in South-eastern Europe, which he regarded as potential suppliers of raw materials and future markets for German manufactures. He resembled Ricardo to the extent that he adapted his system of thought and policy prescriptions to what he perceived to be the interests of his own country.

List realized that the international division of labor, which he held to be determined by nature, would make the tropical countries dependent on those of the temperate zone. But he argued that this dependence would be reduced by competition between the temperate-zone countries, which would oblige them to sell their manufactures for low prices and prevent any one of them from monopolizing this trade. His favored territorial division of labor would be encouraged by a policy of free trade. By admitting primary goods duty-free into their markets, temperate-zone countries would obtain inputs for their manufactures at the cheapest price, allowing them to maintain their competitiveness.

Although List (1885, p. 267) recognized that 'through machinery and new inventions the imperfect manufacturing industry of the East has been destroyed for the benefit of the European manufacturing power, and the latter enabled to supply the countries of the torrid zone with large quantities of fabrics at the cheapest prices', it is unfortunate that he did not see fit to protest against this tragic consequence of colonialism. Indeed, he believed that the temperate-zone countries are uniquely fitted to colonize and bring civilization to those in the torrid zone, while exchanging manufactures for the latter's 'colonial goods'. He argued that 'this exchange ... is based upon natural causes, and will be so for all time' (p. 270). He viewed with equanimity, bordering on insensitivity to the welfare of the indigenous peoples of Asia, the fact that 'India has given up her manufacturing power with her independence to England' and that 'all Asiatic countries of the torrid zone will pass gradually under the dominion of the manufacturing commercial nations of the temperate zone' (ibid.). List's favorable attitude towards colonialism was a natural consequence of his nationalist outlook. Contrary to the opinion of Adam Smith, to whom colonialism was a manifestation of the mercantilism he detested, List's views were in this respect similar to those of the British politician E. G. Wakefield, who favored 'systematic colonization', and of his disciple Robert Torrens, advocate of a British 'imperial Zollverein'.

5.4 The promotion of infant industries and of infant economies

Hamilton, Rae and List contributed in different ways to the formulation of the infant-industry argument. Schumpeter (1954, p. 6) defined the 'Filiation of Scientific Ideas' as 'the process by which men's efforts to understand economic phenomena produce, improve, and pull down analytic structures in an unending sequence', and offered several such sequences in the history of economic thought, for example, Petty–Cantillon–Quesnay. While there is no straightforward filiation of ideas on the promotion of infant industries, a policy with antecedents stretching back well into mercantilist times, one can discern a stream starting with Hamilton and bifurcating into a Rae–Mill branch and a List branch. Although Rae was acquainted with Hamilton's *Report*, and List almost certainly was, there is no indication that Rae and List knew of each other's existence. They shared a common adversarial attitude, probably inherited from Hamilton, toward some of the teachings of Adam Smith and his school, but then went off in very different directions. Rae's irritation with Smith caused him, oyster-like, to create a pearl consisting of the theory of capital, a precious gift to the economics profession since its field of application extends well beyond the analysis of infant industries. It is difficult to articulate rigorously a policy toward infant industries in the absence of a capital-theoretic perspective.

List's world view was at the same time broader and narrower than Rae's. It was narrower in the sense that, being a less able theoretician, List was unable to think in terms of a model such as Rae's, which pitched a society's rate of time preference against the productivity of its capital instruments, leading him to advocate a policy of government assistance to overcome the reluctance of investors to start a new enterprise. But List had an all-encompassing vision of the development of an economy from infant to adult status via the harnessing of its productive forces. This vision went well beyond the economic dimension, to include political, cultural, sociological and even religious aspects. Like Hamilton, and to a greater extent than Rae, List had the welfare of an entire nation at heart, and fought with great passion against policies implemented by the dominant powers which he perceived as inhibiting the maturation of a nation's economic status. It is for this reason that List, to a far greater extent than Hamilton or Rae, has been revered by economists and policymakers in many countries, witness the dozen translations made of the *National System of Political Economy*. In fact, this book has been translated more often than the work of any German economist other than Karl Marx. With his argument that economic policies such as free trade are specific to time and place rather than universally valid, List can also be credited with being a precursor of the German Historical School. The same specificity of time and place characterizes the infant-industry argument for protection, whose validity depends on an accurate assessment of the viability of an industry and of the benefits and costs involved in launching it.

We return to the infant-industry argument in section 6.5 of the next chapter devoted to John Stuart Mill. It is fitting to conclude this chapter by recalling the earlier observation that a common element uniting Hamilton, Rae and List was that they all spent parts of their lives in the US. The infant-industry argument was embraced by several American economists contemporaneous with our trio or coming after them, including Daniel Raymond and especially Henry C. Carey. The latter founded a school that called itself 'nationalist' and advocated protectionism so extreme that Schumpeter (1954, p. 516) referred to Carey as 'the man who could conceive of the United States as a world unto itself, with all this implies economically, morally, culturally'. A much more balanced view was held by the dean of American economists of the next generation, Frank Taussig. According to Schumpeter (1954, p. 870), 'he was the country's great authority on international trade and especially the tariff ... [and] a master of the art of welding factual and theoretical analysis'. Calling him 'one of the foremost US economists for half a century', Samuels (1987, p. 596) commented that 'in the field of international trade, in which he was the principal US figure for decades, his major concerns were the complexities of comparative advantage ... and the history and analysis of protection'. Taussig greatly admired Marshall, and the similarities between them led Schumpeter to call him the 'American Marshall'. Like Marshall, he leaned towards free trade but respected the infant industry argument. Regarding his first book written when he was only 23, *Protection to Young Industries as Applied in the United States*, which doubled as a Ph.D. thesis, Schumpeter commented:

As much on grounds of political morality as on grounds of economic expediency, Taussig never was in sympathy with the tariff legislation of this country. He was far indeed from being a protectionist in the ordinary sense of the term. But he was not a free trader either. He frankly recognized whatever seemed to him tenable in the protectionist arguments – particularly, but not exclusively, the infant industry argument – and never tried to minimize it as economists who sympathize with free trade are in the habit of doing. (Schumpeter, 1951, p. 197)

Taussig's *Principles of Economics* and his later *International Trade* (1927) became classic textbooks. In the latter, he included a chapter entitled 'Comparative advantage and protection in the United States' synthesizing material published in his previous books. Confirming Schumpeter's and Samuels's comments quoted above, this chapter contains a superb mixture of theoretical insights about the nature of comparative advantage and factual observations on how the latter molded the structure of the American economy. Taussig noted that protection appeared to have promoted the growth of certain industries but not others, and that 'the principle of comparative advantage applies more fully and unequivocally to the United States than to any country whose conditions are known to me' (1927, p. 179). He divided the reasons for comparative advantage into 'physical causes ... the consequences of climate, soil, the stores of mineral in different parts of the earth's crust' and 'human causes – man's ways of doing things' (pp. 180–81). The 'inventiveness and ingenuity' of its labor force led the US to become 'the great country of agricultural machinery', with the consequence that 'in agriculture as practiced in the United States the guiding and controlling mind tells more than in the agriculture of any other country' (pp. 181–2). Taussig analyzed agricultural industries such as beet sugar, and explained the failure to adopt the cultivation of the latter in certain parts of the country not to their climate, but to alternative crops in which they held a higher degree of comparative advantage.

With regard to 'the more advanced manufactures of iron and steel ... natural resources become a minor element in explaining the industrial achievements; human factors count most. The comparative advantage is found to rest chiefly on the national character and national aptitude, factors elusive of explanation yet persistent in effect' (p. 190). Taussig noted the two-way trade in many manufactures, with the US exporting those benefitting from economies of scale: 'where ingeniously perfected machinery can be applied in large-scale operations, the American is likely to hold his own, but not where a handicraft skill is needed for a special article' (p. 191). Though he never mentioned Hamilton, Taussig echoed Hamilton's view that Americans had developed traits that made them specially apt in applying machinery, but he could not explain why this had happened, or why other nationalities had developed a superiority in other lines of activity. Such issues 'bear on important matters of economic policy, and indeed focus on the fundamental question of the weight and influence of the various political and legislative steps by which a people's economic development can be promoted. The familiar doctrine of protection to young industries is but one among the obvious aspects of this large group of problems' (p. 196). To a greater extent than the advocates of national systems considered in this chapter, Taussig carefully related a country's success in creating new industries to its underlying comparative advantage, and attributed the latter to the complex interplay of natural and human factors.

Notes

1. Four years earlier, in No. 11 of *The Federalist*, Hamilton spoke of an 'American system' when he urged: 'Let the thirteen States, bound together in a strict and indissoluble Union, concur in erecting one great American system superior to the control of all transatlantic force or influence and able to dictate the terms of the connection between the old and the new world!'
    In his *Outlines of American Political Economy* published in a series of letters and then in book form in 1827, Friedrich List mentioned the 'American System' repeatedly, comparing it favorably to 'Adam Smith's system'. The very title of his subsequent major work, *The National System of Political Economy*, was designed to direct attention to the nation-state as the focus of economic policy.
2. Hamilton was acquainted with the writings of several political economists, statesmen and philosophers: 'there is ample evidence ... that for several years before he joined the new government Hamilton had studied the writings of such leading political and economic theorists as Jacques Necker, David Hume, Malachy Postlethwayt, Adam Smith, and Sir James Steuart' (Syrett et al., 1966, p. 1).
3. Both Bourne (1894) and Rabbeno (1895) compared the *Report on Manufactures* and the *Wealth of Nations* in some detail. Bourne (1894, p. 329) presented lists of related passages from both sources in parallel columns. Regarding Hamilton's failure to mention Adam Smith by name, Bourne asked: 'Why should he have concealed the source of such valuable elements in his report? The answer, I think, is a simple one,– political expediency. The citation of an English writer on Political Economy would have weakened rather than strengthened his case'.
    In their editions of the *Report*, both Hacker (1957) and Syrett et al. (1966) added footnotes pointing out analogous passages from the *Wealth of Nations*. The passage from the *Wealth of Nations* found in the *Report* (Syrett et al., 1966, p. 311), for which no source was given, concerned the pre-eminence of good roads, canals and navigable rivers over all other improvements. In the third draft of the *Report*, Hamilton had inserted '(Smith W of Nations 1 Vol P 219)', but then crossed it out (Syrett et al., 1966, p. 116).
4. The view that agriculture is the *only* productive sector of an economy was the centerpiece of physiocratic doctrine. In chap. 9 of Book IV of the *Wealth of Nations*, Smith had criticized this and other parts of this doctrine, which he named the 'agricultural system of political economy', but (perhaps to acknowledge some truth in the physiocratic argument) he maintained that agriculture was the economy's *most* productive sector.
5. Smith, however, allowed for some exceptions to his free trade philosophy. For example, he approved of Britain's Navigation Acts ('as defence ... is of much more importance than opulence, the act of navigation is, perhaps, the wisest of all the commercial regulations of England'), as well as of retaliatory duties designed to induce other countries to lower their trade barriers (1976, pp. 463–72).

6. The question of reciprocity in foreign trade concessions was to be vigorously debated among classical economists in the nineteenth century, the chief advocate of reciprocity being Robert Torrens. The steps whereby Torrens 'eventually became the leading intellectual opponent of unilateral free trade and supporter of the policy of reciprocity' (Robbins, 1958, p. 187) are chronicled by Robbins (1958, chapter 7).

7. See, for example, Chenery (1961).

8. Smith stressed the advantages of complementarity between production in the town and in the countryside in Book III of the *Wealth of Nations*.

9. As noted in Chapter 3, this argument has a long history stretching back to mercantilist times. Viner (1937, pp. 71–2) lists numerous seventeenth and eighteenth century examples.

10. Hamilton, of course, did not use the term 'comparative advantage', but spoke of reasons used to raise 'objections to the pursuit of manufactures in the United States' (Hamilton, 1966, p. 269).

11. As pointed out in Chapter 9, this argument is reminiscent of the two forms in which the Heckscher–Ohlin theorem can be expressed, one based on quantities of factor endowments, the other on factor prices.

12. Hamilton described two ways to finance a subsidy, either by a duty levied on another type of article, or by a duty on the equivalent (or a similar) foreign article. In the latter case the price rises by less than if a pure protective duty is levied, since the bounty cheapens the domestic manufacture. Hamilton argued that a bounty can even lead to a decline in the price of the commodity because of enhanced competition.

13. As noted below, Rae elevated inventions to be the motive force of economic development.

14. Rae's book pleased neither the admirers of Adam Smith, for whom 'it was almost a matter of religious faith to deny the validity of Rae's attack on the dogmas of free trade' (James, 1965c, p. 162), nor the protectionist group in Boston which had sponsored its publication and had trouble understanding it.

15. In comparing Rae's articulation of the infant-industry argument to previous such attempts, Lionel Robbins (1968, p. 113) has argued that 'if we are looking for pure excellence of intellectual analysis, the palm must clearly go to John Rae'.

16. James (1965b, p. 149) expressed this relation by means of the formula $(1+r)^x = 2$, where x is the order of the instrument in terms of years and r is the internal rate of return.

17. Rae noted that the process of growing rich differs between individuals and nations, since 'as individuals seem generally to grow rich by grasping a larger and larger portion of the wealth already in existence, nations do so by the production of wealth that did not previously exist. The two processes differ in this, that the one is an *acquisition*, the other a *creation*' (Rae, 1834, p. 12).

18. As we saw above, Hamilton had also argued in favor of the establishment of manufactures, using Smith's arguments without mentioning his name.

19. Rae and Ricardo used the term 'luxury' goods in very different senses. In Ricardo's case, these are goods which are not 'necessaries', and any improvement in their production (or freer trade in them) leads to greater 'enjoyments' for those who can afford them, but has no effect on the profit rate. On the other hand, Rae believed that luxury goods cater to people's vanity, their effect on economic welfare being negative.

20. See Maneschi (1998b) for further thoughts on this issue.

21. As James (1965b, pp. 158–9) has argued, 'Rae's comments are a thoughtful and sophisticated statement of what came to be known later as the "infant industry" argument for protection. It is, in fact, difficult to discover anything in Rae's detailed argument that is objectionable. Any reasonable person, no matter how ardent his free-trade convictions, would be compelled to agree with the justice of Rae's contentions'.

22. According to Goodwin (1961, p. 202), 'John Rae, writing in Canada but unappreciated, was the only contemporary theorist who explained clearly the distinction and the possible conflict between short run optimum allocation and long run growth'.

23. List did not refer to Torrens in his *National System of Political Economy*, and his only two references (both highly critical) to Ricardo in that book relate to his rent theory. The second reference contains a garbled quotation from Ricardo's *Principles* to the effect that 'the chief object of political economy is to determine the laws by which the produce of the soil ought to be shared between the landowner, the farmer, and the labourer' (List, 1885, p. 361).

24. As Coustillac (1996) pointed out, since the late 1950s French economists such as François Perroux stressed List's role as a precursor of development economics. Among the justifications they offered for this view is List's focus on the role of the nation-state in harnessing a country's productive forces to launch a process of economic development.

25. Hirst (1909, pp. 115, 117, 157, 210) has convincingly documented her assertions that '[Hamilton's] Report ... must surely have been read by List, although he does not mention it either in the "Outlines" [of American Political Economy (List, 1827)] or in the "National System." It is difficult to avoid the conclusion that Hamilton, [Daniel] Raymond, and [Matthew] Carey had a strong positive, and [Thomas] Cooper a strong negative influence upon List's later work'.

26. On List's conception of the sequence of stages in economic development, see Hoselitz (1960, pp. 195–204).

27. According to List (1885, p. 177), the Zollverein should include not only Austria but such countries as Holland and Denmark, which he regarded as belonging to the 'German nationality'.

28. This stance of List was conveniently forgotten by latter-day arch-protectionists who invoked his name, but felt that 'fairness' demanded that protection should be evenly bestowed upon all sectors.

29. Schumpeter (1954, pp. 504–5). Gomes (1987, p. 276) has also argued that List's rationale for protection extends well beyond the infant-industry argument.

30. According to Jacob Viner (1958, p. 390), 'List stresses the importance of urbanization as a product of industrial development, and of high productive capacity in general as a product of urbanization, and his plea for manufactures, and the development through them of the "productive forces," is really a plea for urbanization'. The latter is associated with external economies. The economist who brought these to the center of analytical attention, Alfred Marshall, had respect for 'the brilliant genius and national enthusiasm of List' and understood the irritation of German economists with 'what they have regarded as the insular narrowness and self-confidence of the Ricardian school' (Marshall, 1920, p. 767).

31. Schumpeter made the penetrating observation that 'List saw a nation that struggled in the fetters imposed by a miserable immediate past, but he also saw all its economic potentialities. The national future, therefore, was the real object of his thought, the present was nothing but a state of transition' (ibid.).

32. Adam Smith himself could have inspired the use of this term by referring to the 'productive powers of labour' in the first sentence of chapter 1 of Book One of the *Wealth of Nations*. Aside from Dupin, List's nationalist economic orientation was shaped by other French economists such as J. A. Chaptal and Louis Say, a critic of his more famous brother J. B. Say (Coustillac, 1996). J. B. Say was singled out by List for censure and sarcasm in his *National System*.

33. This introduction appears in the 1856 translation of the *National System* (List, 1856) but not in the 1885 translation. Hirst (1909) contains another English translation of the introduction.

34. List denied that trade would benefit the temperate-zone countries at the expense of the tropical ones: 'the system of protection ... aims at developing *the manufacturing power of the whole temperate zone*, for the benefit of *the agriculture of the whole torrid zone*'. This would lead to 'the progress of civilisation and production in the countries of the torrid zone' (1885, pp. 193, 263).

6. John Stuart Mill: Comparative Advantage and the Terms of Trade

With the few exceptions noted below, little progress was made in the nineteenth century in exploring the reasons why countries have a comparative advantage in specific types of commodities. Insofar as comparative advantage was attributed to technology, the classical economists were aware that this is subject to change in a given country and to diffusion among countries. A role was recognized for comparative advantage in setting limits within which the terms of trade can vary. Within these limits, their location and the associated division of the gains from trade between the trading countries was made to depend on reciprocal demand. The co-discoverer of the concept of comparative advantage, Robert Torrens, was also one of the pioneers in establishing the theoretical importance of reciprocal demand for the law of international values. Progress was slowly made in extending the Ricardian model to more than two commodities by comparing the absolute advantages in commodity production of two trading countries to their relative wage rates. The theory of commercial policy, with its implications for free trade or protection, was also explored. Torrens again used his insights into reciprocal demand to become a staunch advocate of reciprocity in tariff concessions.

After section 6.1 examines some anticipations of the relationship between reciprocal demand, comparative advantage and the terms of trade, section 6.2 turns to the first satisfactory analysis offered by John Stuart Mill in his *Essays on Some Unsettled Questions of Political Economy* of 1844. Section 6.3 is devoted to what will be referred to as the Mill–Whewell law of international values, because of the strong presumption that the last three sections of the 'great chapter' 18 of Mill's *Principles of Political Economy* were inspired by Whewell (1850). After presenting Mill's solution for the equilibrium terms of trade, it is shown that it can be derived as a special case of the general mathematical solution which Whewell had constructed when he translated Mill's theory of international trade into mathematics. Section 6.4 describes the vast range of benefits, some non-economic in nature, that Mill expected international trade to confer on a country, and section 6.5 outlines his famous infant-industry argument for protection. The latter synthesized the conditions for the creation of comparative advantage that Hamilton and Rae had formulated, as described in Chapter 5. Section 6.6 analyzes some early generalizations of the theory of comparative advantage to many commodities, and section 6.7 explores how Ricardian comparative advantage based on the labor theory of value began to be modified towards the end of the classical era because of the increasing realization that the labor force was not homogeneous, but consisted of non-competing groups of labor. That final section of the chapter is a natural bridge to Chapters 7 and 8, which discuss neoclassical trade models based on theories of value differing significantly from those of the classical economists.

6.1 Reciprocal demand and the terms of trade

As noted in Chapter 4, Ricardo assumed that the terms of trade between England and Portugal settled roughly halfway between their autarky price ratios. Since he provided no justification for this assumption, his trade theory remained incomplete. Ricardo neither accounted for the equilibrium value of the terms of trade, nor did he state that comparative advantage set the limits within which they would settle. As Robbins noted,

> it was to resolve this difficulty that recourse was had to the notion of Reciprocal Demand. And here a great deal of the credit for discovery, if not for influence, must go to Torrens. The germs of the theory are to be found in Ricardo. But it is in Torrens, in his *Letters on Commercial Policy* and in *The Budget* series, that it begins to be worked out in any detail. (Robbins, 1958, p. 242)[1]

This awareness of the role of demand in determining the terms of trade underlay Torrens's transformation from a free trader to 'the leading intellectual opponent of unilateral free trade and supporter of the policy of reciprocity' in tariff concessions (Robbins, 1958, p. 187). Robbins granted, however, that 'John Stuart Mill's constructions, invented at about the same time but published later, are greatly superior' to other economists' speculations about the role of reciprocal demand, since 'Torrens was enormously hampered by the absence of the idea of a demand schedule and the continual assumption of constant outlay conditions' (ibid.). Torrens's assumption of a unitary elasticity of demand may have influenced Mill to make a similar working assumption in most of the numerical examples he constructed in his *Principles of Political Economy*.

In the last of the four lectures published as *Three Lectures on Commerce and One on Absenteeism* and delivered at the University of Dublin in 1834,

Mountifort Longfield, Ireland's first professor of political economy, related Ireland's terms of trade to the remittance of rents to Irish landlords residing in England, arguing that these affected the demand for Irish exports. The issue was 'whether exportation takes place in consequence of a diminished demand at home, or an increased demand abroad'. The latter would occur only if the landlords spent their income on Irish goods. The former possibility was far more likely, and 'if the home market is destroyed or diminished, more goods are forced into the foreign markets by a reduction of price' (Longfield, 1835, p. 82). A modern reader can recognize this as an early example of whether a transfer payment such as the remittance of rents would be associated with the secondary burden of a deterioration in the terms of trade. As Moss noted, 'Longfield recognized the relationship that exists between shifts in international demand and the terms of trade, though he was evidently unable to accept the fact that international demand determines the equilibrium terms of trade in the first place' (Moss, 1976, p. 136).[2]

Further progress in analyzing reciprocal demand and the relationship of the terms of trade to countries' comparative advantage was made by James Pennington. According to Viner (1937, p. 447), 'Pennington ... seems to have been the first explicitly to point out in print that the comparative costs set maximum and minimum rates for the terms of trade, and that within these limits the operation of reciprocal demand could fix the terms of trade at any point'. In his *Letter to Kirkman Finlay, Esq., on the Importation of Foreign Corn*, after presenting hypothetical figures for the prices of corn and cloth in England and Poland before trade, Pennington added:

> the question is, at what point the barter of cloth for corn, and the prices accommodated to that barter, will settle on the opening of the trade. I apprehend that the point will depend on this circumstance, namely, whether the demand in England for corn is so strong as to raise the price of corn in Poland ... or the demand in Poland for cloth so strong as to raise the price of cloth in England.... The probability is, that the barter point would shift and vary between the extremes above mentioned. (Pennington, 1840, pp. 40–41)

Though the last sentence is misleading and Pennington made some arithmetic slips in the numerical example (here omitted) that he inserted in the same passage, these do not invalidate his basic contention.

6.2 Mill's *Essays* and the first statement of the law of international values

Although Longfield (1835) and Pennington (1840) appeared earlier than John Stuart Mill's *Essays on Some Unsettled Questions of Political Economy*

(1844), according to Mill the *Essays* were in fact written in 1829–30. The title of the first of the *Essays*, 'Of the Laws of Interchange between Nations; and the Distribution of the Gains of Commerce among the Countries of the Commercial World', announced the positive goal of determining the terms of trade, which Mill called the 'rate [or terms] of interchange', and the more important normative goal of assessing how the gains from trade are divided between the trading countries: 'It is the purpose of the present essay to inquire, in what proportion the increase of produce, arising from the saving of labour, is divided between the two countries' (Mill, 1844, p. 5). Many passages from this first essay were reproduced verbatim in the *Principles* of 1848, where the analysis of reciprocal demand was further elaborated. As Viner (1937, p. 447) argued, 'it was from [Mill's] exposition in the *Essays*, repeated and developed later in the *Principles*, and not from Longfield, Torrens, or Pennington, that later economists took over the doctrine'.

After extolling Ricardo and the 'chapter on Foreign Trade, of his immortal *Principles of Political Economy and Taxation*' (1844, p. 1), Mill qualified this praise when he added the following reservation:

> Mr. Ricardo, while intending to go no further into the question of the advantage of foreign trade than to show what it consisted of, and under what circumstances it arose, unguardedly expressed himself as if each of the two countries making the exchange separately gained the whole of the difference between the comparative costs of the two commodities in one country and in the other. This, which was not an error, but a mere oversight of Mr. Ricardo, arising from his having left the question of the division of the advantage entirely unnoticed, was first corrected in the third edition of Mr. Mill's *Elements of Political Economy*. (Mill, 1844, pp. 5–7)

And thereby hangs a tale. Einaudi (1929), accepting Mill's word for Ricardo's alleged mistake, wondered on the basis of a statement by Torrens in 1857 whether the credit for the 'early correction of Ricardo' should go to James Mill or to James Pennington. Sraffa (1930) responded to Einaudi's query by pointing out that Ricardo never committed the error he was charged with, but that such an error did appear in the first edition of James Mill's *Elements of Political Economy* of 1821. A numerical example involving trade between England and Poland in cloth and corn implied that the entire gains from trade went to both countries. This error was removed only in the third edition of the *Elements* of 1826, where the gains from trade were split evenly between the two countries. In his *Letter to Kirkman Finlay* of 1840, Pennington also noted Mill's error, but as he based himself on the second edition of 1824, he was unaware that the error had been corrected 14 years earlier. Pennington's notice of the error, however, may have motivated him to find the explanation outlined above for the terms of trade and the consequent division of the gains from trade.

Sraffa ascribed the correction of James Mill's error to his son John Stuart, who in his autobiography reported that he used to meet with a study group at George Grote's house after 1825 to discuss issues relating to political economy. They used James Mill's *Elements* as a focus of discussion, and tried to clarify some contentious points which arose. John's new theory of international values began to take shape as a result of these meetings, but found its way into his *Essays* rather than into his father's *Elements*, which he was helping to revise. Sraffa (1930, p. 544) concluded from these events that 'the account given by J. S. Mill in the Essay of 1844, according to which James Mill made the correction but not the error, must be exactly reversed'.

There the matter rested until Thweatt (1986) sought to defend James Mill from Sraffa's charge that he had a defective understanding of the concept of comparative advantage. As discussed in Chapter 4, Thweatt (1976) had previously attributed this concept to him, and he now suggested that the author of the mistake in James Mill's *Elements* was John Stuart himself! John, at the tender age of 13, had been given the task of writing the first draft of the *Elements*, on the basis of his father's exposition of its chapters on the long walks they took together. It would not be surprising if he had made the mistake regarding the division of the gains from trade in the first edition, repeating it in the second edition of 1824. Part of the evidence for John's collaboration on the second edition was the insertion of a new numerical example involving trade in cloth and linen between England and Germany. These are the very commodities and countries which J. S. Mill utilized in the *Essays* and again in the *Principles*, but which his father never used in any of his other writings. In this new example, the entire gains from trade were attributed to both England and Germany. It is therefore likely that it was James Mill himself who finally, in the third edition of the *Elements*, corrected the error made by his son in the first two editions.[3]

The first of Mill's *Essays* contained his first statement of what he named in the *Principles* 'the Equation of International Demand' and the 'law of International Values':

> It may be considered, therefore, as established, that when two countries trade together in two commodities, the exchangeable value of these commodities relatively to each other will adjust itself to the inclinations and circumstances of the consumers on both sides, in such manner that the quantities required by each country, of the article which it imports from its neighbour, shall be exactly sufficient to pay for one another. (Mill, 1844, p. 12)

Compared to his later additions to chapter 18 of the *Principles*, the location of the terms of trade within the limits set by the countries' autarky price ratios still sounded rather tentative:

> As the inclinations and circumstances of consumers cannot be reduced to any rule, so neither can the proportions in which the two commodities will be interchanged. We know that the limits within which the variation is confined are the ratio between the costs of production in the one country, and the ratio between their costs of production in the other. The ratios, therefore, in which the advantage of the trade may be divided between the two nations, are various. The circumstances on which the proportionate share of each country more remotely depends, admit only of a very general indication. (Mill, 1844, pp. 12–3)

6.3 The Mill–Whewell law of international values

The above passage from the *Essays* was reproduced, with many others, in chapter 18 of Book III of Mill's *Principles*. The law of international values was stated more succinctly a few pages later in a paragraph where Mill used the term 'reciprocal demand':[4]

> The produce of a country exchanges for the produce of other countries, at such values as are required in order that the whole of her exports may exactly pay for the whole of her imports.... So that supply and demand are but another expression for reciprocal demand: and to say that value will adjust itself so as to equalize demand with supply, is in fact to say that it will adjust itself so as to equalize the demand on one side with the demand on the other. (Mill, 1920, pp. 592–3)

Beginning with the third edition of 1852, Mill added three new sections (6–8) to chapter 18 which have been the subject of much controversy. After calling chapter 18 'great' and 'stupendous', Francis Y. Edgeworth (1894, p. 609) went on to criticize the three new sections: 'The splendid edifice of theory constructed in the first five sections is not improved by the superstructure of later date which forms the latter part of the chapter. This second story does not carry us much higher'.[5] He followed up on this pun by claiming that the material found in the 'superstructure' was already contained in the previous sections, and quoted Bastable's comment that it was 'laborious and confusing'. This negative verdict was echoed by economists such as Marshall, Nicholson, Viner, Elliott, Metzler and Mundell (cited by Chipman, 1965a, and Appleyard and Ingram, 1979). Before 1965 only Schumpeter (1954) approved, albeit mildly, of the new sections. In the first part of his classic survey of the theory of international trade, Chipman denounced this 'monotonous chorus' of disapproval and argued that it is time to reverse Edgeworth's judgment: for §7 of the "great chapter" contains a convincing proof (admittedly for a special case) of the existence of equilibrium; not only that, it does so in terms of what can today be recognized as an ingenious and correct solution of a problem in nonlinear programming.... In its astonishing simplicity, [Mill's Law of International Values] must stand as one of the great achievements of the human intellect; and yet it has passed practically unnoticed for over a hundred years, if only because it was so advanced for its time. (Chipman, 1965a, pp. 484, 486)

Was Mill truly able to solve in his head a problem in nonlinear programming a century before this technique had been developed? When he constructed a nonlinear programming formulation of Mill's law, Chipman made several simplifying assumptions. He translated Mill's statements that 'the influence of cheapness on demand conforms to some simple law, common to both countries and to both commodities' and that 'in both countries any given increase of cheapness produces an exactly proportional increase of consumption' (1920, p. 598) to mean not only that the price elasticity of demand is unitary, but that consumers spend half of their income on each good. Chipman assumed that both countries have the Cobb–Douglas utility function $U = xy$, where x and y are the quantities consumed of the two commodities, and maximized it subject to their linear production possibility frontiers (PPFs). He illustrated the solution graphically with a piecewise linear world PPF and a map of community indifference curves common to both countries, and showed that full specialization in both of them requires that the ratio of the maximum outputs of each country's commodity of comparative advantage (cloth in England and linen in Germany) should lie between the slopes of the two PPFs. Chipman (1965a, p. 487) described this condition with the curious statement that both countries specialize 'if and only if each country has actually an absolute advantage, rather than just a comparative advantage, in the production of one of the commodities'. In that statement he departed from the standard definition of 'absolute advantage', using that term in the special sense that each country's maximum output of the commodity in which it has a comparative advantage exceeds the other country's maximum output of the same commodity.

Appleyard and Ingram (1979) questioned Chipman's assumptions and his high opinion of the superstructure added to Mill's chapter 18. They pointed out that Mill did not explicitly assume that half of consumers' income would be spent on each good in each country, and did not derive the inequalities derived by Chipman to guarantee full specialization in both countries. Moreover, neither Mill nor subsequent economists used the term 'absolute advantage' in Chipman's sense. They contended that Mill, in his new sections, had intended to resolve the problem that 'several different rates of international value may all equally fulfil the conditions of this law [the equation of international demand]' (1920, pp. 596–7). But in fact he had only proved the existence of equilibrium for the special case of unitary elasticities of demand adopted in the previous sections of the chapter, where the issue of multiple equilibrium points does not even arise. He had thus failed to accomplish the intention announced for his new sections.

In his response, Chipman (1979) agreed that his initial formulation of the utility function was unnecessarily restrictive, and could be generalized along the lines suggested by Melvin (1969), Harwitz (1972), and Appleyard and Ingram (1979). Any constant proportion between 0 and 1 can be spent on each good, and these proportions need not be the same in both countries. Chipman himself reformulated his model along these lines, and 'as part of the retraction referred to, I withdraw my statement (1965, p. 484) that Mill's method of proof constituted a solution of a problem in non-linear programming. This problem can be posed only in the case of identical tastes ..., and in any case this did indeed read more into Mill's reasoning than was there' (Chipman, 1979, p. 483).[6] He also granted that he had used the term 'absolute advantage' in a peculiar sense. But he remained adamant that Mill's great accomplishment in the new sections was his proof of the existence of equilibrium in the two-commodity case, given his special assumptions regarding consumer preferences and production possibilities. While admitting that Appleyard and Ingram 'have sown dark suspicions in my mind as to what Mill thought he had accomplished in section §7', Chipman (1979, p. 499) maintained that 'my original assessment of Mill's superstructure remains fully justified, whether it accomplished his announced purposes or not'.

In the first paragraph of section 6, Mill (1920, p. 596) stated that 'intelligent criticisms (chiefly those of my friend Mr. William Thornton), and subsequent further investigation, have shown that the doctrine stated in the preceding pages, though correct as far as it goes, is not yet the complete theory of the subject matter'. The words in parentheses were inserted only in the sixth edition of the *Principles* of 1865, and remain a mystery to this day since Thornton's writings did not relate to the theory of international trade.[7] One of the controversies surrounding the added sections of chapter 18 is whether the 'intelligent criticisms' which Mill received were not instead inspired by a memoir authored by the Cambridge philosopher William Whewell, his second memoir on economic subjects entitled *Mathematical Exposition of Some Doctrines of Political Economy* (Whewell, 1850). This was privately distributed by him before it was published in the *Transactions of the Cambridge Philosophical Society* in 1856. Although their significance has been questioned by some commentators,[8] Whewell's memoirs, which include the first mathematical version of the Ricardian model dated 1831, rank among the earliest contributions to mathematical economics.

Whewell's explicit aim was to render Mill's trade model in mathematical form, and explore its implications for the terms of trade and the gains from trade. There seems little doubt that Whewell was the source of Mill's inspiration for the new sections that he added to chapter 18 of his *Principles*. After quoting Viner's (1937, p. 450) statement that 'since [Whewell's 1850 memoir] was primarily a criticism of Mill's doctrines, Mill may have been acquainted with it', Chipman added that 'it is scarcely conceivable that he was not, for the memoir is devoted entirely to Mill's first essay (1844) and is an honest attempt to translate Mill's argument into mathematical language' (Chipman, 1965a, p. 492).[9] Other adherents to this view include Henderson (1985), Gherity (1988) and Creedy (1989, 1992).[10] Creedy (1992, p. 85) has inferred a strong probability of two-way trade between Mill and Whewell: 'instead of Whewell being judged as simply translating Mill into mathematics, it seems that Mill translated Whewell's extensions back into English (though it is relevant that this is the only place in the *Principles* where Mill felt the need to introduce some mathematical notation)'. If this is correct, Mill's translation of Whewell's memoir from mathematics into English was a pedagogically effective exercise. The likelihood of mutual influence of Mill and Whewell on each other suggests the desirability of renaming Mill's law the Mill–Whewell law of international values.[11]

Before showing that Mill's solution for an international equilibrium in section 7 of his 'great chapter' can be derived from Whewell's, it is first presented algebraically using as far as possible Mill's own notation, and illustrated graphically. After he had provided several numerical examples involving the trade of cloth and linen between England and Germany, Mill offered an algebraic version of his model. As Henderson and Creedy have pointed out, this was the only occasion on which Mill used algebraic symbols in his *Principles*, and is again suggestive of the influence that Whewell's memoir may have had upon him. Let the pre-trade relative prices of cloth in terms of linen be p in Germany and q in England. Since Mill assumed that $p > q$, England has a comparative advantage in cloth. She exports a quantity n of cloth utilizing the resources with which she produced linen for her own consumption before trade. If m was the cloth produced in Germany before trade, she will export pm of linen produced with the resources previously devoted to cloth production. Since England exchanges n of cloth for pm of linen, her terms of trade are

$$t = pm/n \qquad (6.1)$$

units of linen per unit of cloth.[12] Since t is proportional to p for given values

Figure 6.1 Mill's international equilibrium

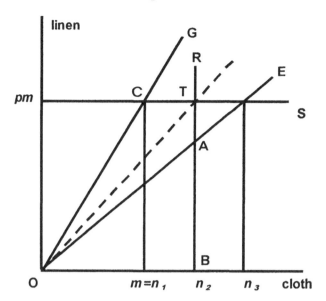

of m and n, England's terms of trade are more favorable to her the higher the value of p, that is, the higher the autarky price of cloth in Germany.[13]

Mill's equilibrium is shown in Figure 6.1, which is similar to the offer curve diagrams presented by Edgeworth (1894, pp. 610–13). The vertical and horizontal axes represent quantities of linen and cloth, and the rays OG and OE, whose slopes are p and q, the relative production costs in Germany and England. German linen exports of pm are matched with three alternative values of cloth exports from England. If n takes the value n_2, the terms of trade t are given by the slope of the ray OT, pm/n_2, where T is the intersection of the vertical line representing n_2 cloth exports with the horizontal line representing pm linen exports. The English and German offer curves are given by OAR and OCS, because of Mill's assumption that the price elasticities of demand are unitary in each country.

Mill noted that full specialization in each country requires n to have the lower and upper bounds

$$m \le n \le (p/q)m. \tag{6.2}$$

Since in his previous numerical examples he had assumed that $p = 2$ and $q = 1$, the corresponding lower and upper bounds for n were m and $2m$. Mill observed that the location of n within this interval defines the international division of the gains from trade:

> If $n = m$, the whole advantage will be on the side of England. If $n = 2m$, the whole advantage will be on the side of Germany. If n be greater than m, but less than $2m$, the two countries will share the advantage; England getting $2m$ of linen where she before got only n; Germany getting n of cloth where she before got only m. (Mill, 1920, p. 600)

The lower and upper limits of n are shown in Figure 6.1 by $n = n_1$ and $n = n_3$. At the lower limit, the terms of trade coincide with Germany's autarky price ratio; at the upper limit, with England's.

In a footnote Mill explored what would happen if n were either lower than m or higher than $2m$. If $n < m$, he noted that England could not supply sufficient cloth to satisfy Germany's previous demand, so that Germany must continue to produce cloth in addition to linen. Moreover, 'this portion of the supply [of cloth] would regulate the price of the whole'. By trading at the German cost of production, England 'would gain the whole advantage of the trade, Germany being no better off than before' (1920, p. 601n). Unfortunately, Mill devoted the rest of his lengthy footnote to the argument that 'n is always, practically speaking, confined within these limits' (that is, those set by (6.2)), and that incomplete specialization on the part of Germany 'would not be the practical result' (p. 601). As Edgeworth and, following him, Chipman (1965a, p. 488n) have noted, 'here Mill changed his premises in the middle of the argument' by assuming that Germany must have other commodities besides linen which England would want to import, allowing her to produce all the cloth required by Germany so that 'this augmented n will now be equal to m ... And so with every other case which can be supposed' (Mill, 1920, p. 601n). In this respect, Whewell was much shrewder than Mill when he noted that it was very likely that trade would occur at one of the limiting ratios.[14]

A more general way of writing the inequalities (6.2) was derived by Melvin (1969, p. 111).[15] Let (a', b') and (a'', b'') be the maximum amounts of cloth (C) and linen (L) producible in Germany (country I) and England (country II), so that $p = b'/a'$ and $q = b''/a''$. Let the German and English utility functions be $U' = C^{\alpha'} L^{\beta'}$ and $U'' = C^{\alpha''} L^{\beta''}$, where $\alpha' + \beta' = \alpha'' + \beta'' = 1$. Since α' is the fraction of income spent on cloth in Germany and β'' the fraction of income spent on linen in England, it follows that $m = \alpha' a'$ and $n = \beta'' b''/q = \beta'' a''$. Substituting these values into (6.2), we obtain

$$a'/b' \leq \beta'' a''/\alpha' b' \leq a''/b''. \tag{6.3}$$

According to Chipman's (1965a) original interpretation (which he modified in Chipman, 1979), $\alpha' = \beta'' = 0.5$. (6.3) then reduces to the pair of inequalities $a'' \geq a'$ and $b' \geq b''$, which Chipman (1965a) had defined as each country having an 'absolute advantage' in its export commodity.

Although the above formulation allows each country to spend different fractions of its income on cloth and linen (that is, $\alpha' \neq \alpha''$), the postulated Cobb–Douglas utility functions continue to carry the implication that the price elasticities of demand are unitary in each country. In section 8, Mill relaxed this 'purely arbitrary hypothesis respecting the relation between demand and cheapness' (1920, p. 601), and allowed for unitary demand elasticities in England combined with (i) price inelastic, then (ii) price elastic demands in Germany, noting that England's terms of trade would be more favorable in case (ii) than in case (i). He next assumed that demand elasticities deviate from unity in each country, and in the same direction, so that both are either elastic or inelastic. He observed that it could then accidentally happen that the terms of trade are the same as in the case of unit elastic demands; but that in the inelastic case, the volume of trade would be reduced. He summarized the results reached to that point as follows:

> The only general law, then, which can be laid down, is this. The values at which a country exchanges its produce with foreign countries depend on two things: first, on the amount and extensibility of their demand for its commodities, compared with its demand for theirs; and secondly, on the capital which it has to spare from the production of domestic commodities for its own consumption. The more the foreign demand for its commodities exceeds its demand for foreign commodities, and the less capital it can spare to produce for foreign markets, compared with what foreigners spare to produce for its markets, the more favorable to it will be the terms of interchange: that is, the more it will obtain of foreign commodities in return for a given quantity of its own. But these two influencing circumstances are in reality reducible to one: for the capital which a country has to spare from the production of domestic commodities for its own use is in proportion to its own demand for foreign commodities: whatever proportion of its collective income it expends in purchases from abroad, that same proportion of its capital is left without a home market for its productions. (Mill, 1920, pp. 603–4)

At the beginning of section 7, Mill had anticipated the 'two things' on which the terms of trade depend: 'we must take into consideration not only ... the quantities demanded in each country of the imported commodities; but also the extent of the means of supplying that demand which are set at liberty in each country by the change in the direction of its industry' (1920, p. 597). He referred to the second factor as 'some other element not yet taken into account. In order to isolate this unknown element, it will be necessary to make some definite and invariable supposition in regard to the known element' (p. 598), which was his assumption of unitary elasticities.

The two factors to which Mill referred appear in the formulas derived by Whewell for the proportional changes in the two countries' price ratios brought about by the opening of trade. Whewell denoted by x and X the proportional declines in the relative prices of the imported commodities of England and Germany in the trade equilibrium compared to autarky. Post-trade prices are equated in the two countries, thanks to what is now known as the law of one price, which he called (1850, p. 11) the 'equation of uniformity of international prices'. The terms of trade, expressed as the relative price of cloth, are therefore given by

$$t = \frac{q}{(1 - x)} = p(1 - X). \qquad (6.4)$$

Whewell solved the latter for the proportional decline in Germany's relative price of cloth, X, in terms of the proportional decline in England's relative price of linen, x, obtaining

$$X = \frac{k - x}{1 - x}, \qquad (6.5)$$

where $k = (p - q)/p$ is the relative difference between the two countries' autarky price ratios, and thus an index of the difference in comparative advantage between them. He substituted (6.5) into what he called 'the equation of import and export', expressing Mill's law that each country's exports must pay for its imports, and obtained (1850, p. 12) the following expression for x:[16]

$$x = \frac{r(1 - Sk) - 1}{r(1 - S) - s}. \qquad (6.6)$$

In addition to k, this expression contains the parameters $r = pm/qn$, the ratio of the pre-trade value of German cloth consumption in terms of linen to England's pre-trade linen consumption; and S and s, the 'susceptibilities' of German and English demands. Susceptibility was defined by Whewell (1850, p. 2) as the relative change in the expenditure on a commodity divided by the relative change in its price, and has been shown to be equal to one minus the absolute value of the price elasticity of demand (Chipman, 1965a, p. 492; Creedy, 1989, 1992).[17]

In Mill's numerical examples where the price elasticity of demand is unitary in each country, $s = S = 0$ (since expenditure does not change with price) and (6.6) simplifies to

$$x = \frac{r - 1}{r}. \qquad (6.7)$$

Although Whewell did not derive this special case of his formula (6.6), and Mill never referred to Whewell's equations, (6.7) shows that in Mill's case the terms of trade depend solely on the parameter r. Moreover, x varies positively with r, and is positive if and only if r exceeds 1. Given that x, $X < 1$, (6.5) and (6.7) show that X is positive if and only if $x < k$, or $r < 1/(1 - k) = p/q$. If the value of x given by (6.7) is substituted into (6.4), and r is replaced by pm/qn, we obtain

$$t = pm/n, \qquad (6.8)$$

the value found by Mill and given by (6.1). This shows that Mill's solution can be obtained as a (very) special case of Whewell's general formula.

Mill's algebraic formulation of the law of international values appears rather rudimentary compared to Whewell's. Up to section 8 of chapter 18, the main case which Mill considered, and the only one for which he provided a proof for the existence of equilibrium, was that of unitary elasticities of demand. The great advantage of Whewell's formulas is that they yield the terms of trade for any values of the countries' elasticities of demand, the first of the two factors influencing the terms of trade described by Mill in the passage quoted above. They also clearly identify the second of these factors, the dimensionless parameter r, which equals the ratio of the amount of linen that Germany can produce with the resources released from cloth production, pm, to the amount of linen output qn that England converts into cloth output. It can be interpreted as the ratio of the German demand for cloth imports (in terms of linen) to the English demand for linen imports at each country's pre-trade prices. The ratio r is illustrated by TB/AB in Figure 6.1, which confirms that the terms of trade are more favorable to England the higher the value of r.

(6.4)–(6.6) show that, besides the susceptibilities of demand and the ratio r, a third factor entering the expression for the terms of trade is k, the relative gap between the two countries' autarky price ratios. By considering only the case of zero susceptibilities, Mill overlooked the importance of this third factor, which does not appear in (6.7). Whewell's derivation of these expressions should be sufficient to absolve him of Schumpeter's charge that he was not engaging in a genuine example of mathematical economics.[18]

In the numerical examples he presented in section 7, Mill varied the ratio of m to n in order to illustrate the cases where the gains from trade go entirely to one of the countries, or are shared between them. As an alternative to this, one can vary Whewell's ratio r. The entire gain goes to England if $r \geq p/q >$ 1. The entire gain goes to Germany if $r \leq 1$, and the gain is shared by both countries if $1 < r < p/q$. It is immaterial whether the change in r occurs because one of the countries changes in size, which according to Chipman (1965a, 1979) was Mill's intended thought experiment, or because of a change in tastes, as argued by Appleyard and Ingram (1979). Either type of change leads to a change in the ratio r, Mill's 'unknown element' which appears as a parameter in Whewell's formulas.[19]

Country size, however, is definitely involved in what Edgeworth (1899) called 'Mill's paradox'. In Mill's words, this is that 'the richest countries, *ceteris paribus*, gain the least by a given amount of foreign commerce: since, having a greater demand for commodities generally, they are likely to have a greater demand for foreign commodities, and thus modify the terms of interchange to their own disadvantage' (Mill, 1920, p. 604). This 'paradox', however, is readily clarified by the above analysis, since an increase in a country's domestic product can be expected to affect the ratio r so as to deteriorate its terms of trade.

Since Mill never acknowledged Whewell's memoir, we will never know if he carried out the exercise sketched out above of specializing Whewell's formulas for x and X to the case where $s = S = 0$. This is the simplest of all possible cases to analyze, and the one that Mill himself focused on. If Mill did verify his results in this way, he must have been comforted by the fact that they were consistent with those obtained with the aid of Whewell's formulas. While Mill's own model lacked the generality it could so easily have had if he had explicitly adopted Whewell's analysis, this would have been oddly inconsistent with the literary style and the pedagogical orientation of his *Principles*, and might have alienated the vast majority of his readers. Given the state of political economy in the middle of the nineteenth century, we should give Mill credit for (in Creedy's words) 'translat[ing] Whewell's extensions back into English' and making the principle of reciprocal demand easily accessible to his readers.

Henderson (1989) referred to Whewell's formulas as his 'solution to the reciprocal demand riddle' and argued (p. 667) that 'Whewell's mathematically explicit statement of Mill's Equation of International Demand ... was the key to unlocking the theory of international trade'. Although these formulas may strike the modern reader as inelegant, they represent a remarkable achievement and a significant contribution to mathematical economics when considered in the light of the early date of Whewell's memoir. Mill's determination of the terms of trade in function of the trading partners' reciprocal demands for each other's products has been called by Jacob Viner (1937, p. 535) 'his chief claim to originality in the field of economics'. Given the strong probability that

Whewell's memoir assisted Mill in arriving at the complete derivation of his model, it seems appropriate for Mill to share the distinction of formulating the law of international values with Whewell, in spite of the fact that Mill (for reasons related to the earlier methodological dispute between them) failed to give him any of the credit.

6.4 Foreign trade as 'a sort of industrial revolution'

In the chapter immediately preceding the 'great chapter' of his *Principles*, Mill explored the nature of the gains from trade. After outlining the efficiency gains consisting of the increase in the quantities of commodities that trade makes available to the trading countries, he went on to criticize the 'vulgar theory' that preceded Ricardo's, in particular Adam Smith's vent-for-surplus theory, which he called 'a surviving relic of the Mercantile Theory' and dismissed as an example of what he called 'the fallacy of general over-production'.[20] He then went beyond 'the direct economical advantage of foreign trade' to enumerate its 'indirect effects, which must be counted as benefits of a high order', including 'the tendency of every extension of the market to improve the processes of production' (1920, pp. 579–81). The latter was referred to in Chapter 3 as the 'productivity theory' of trade of Adam Smith. It is surprising that Mill, having just criticized Smith, did not take this opportunity to soften this criticism by linking this theory to Smith. He went on to discuss the demonstration effect of trade in inducing people in an economy in the early stages of development to work harder, so they can import new commodities from abroad:

> The opening of a foreign trade, by making them acquainted with new objects, or tempting them by the easier acquisition of things which they had not previously thought attainable, sometimes works a sort of industrial revolution in a country whose resources were previously undeveloped for want of energy and ambition in the people: inducing those who were satisfied with scanty comforts and little work, to work harder for the gratification of their new tastes, and even to save, and accumulate capital, for the still more complete satisfaction of those tastes at a future time. (Mill, 1920, p. 581)

This is a benefit of trade which is ignored in neoclassical trade theory, which assumes that tastes are given and not altered in any way when an isolated society becomes open to trade. Mill made this point with his customary eloquence, and his phrase that trade 'sometimes works a sort of industrial revolution' is a memorable one. It would have been appropriate, however, for Mill to observe that Hume had made a similar point almost a century earlier, as was remarked in Chapter 3. Mill went on to outline other benefits of a non-economic nature which he believed to be even more important than the creation of new tastes and of a zeal for hard work:

> But the economical advantages of commerce are surpassed in importance by those of its effects which are intellectual and moral. It is hardly possible to overrate the value, in the present low state of human improvement, of placing human beings in contact with persons dissimilar to themselves, and with modes of thought and action unlike those with which they are familiar. Commerce is now what war once was, the principal source of this contact.... There is no nation which does not need to borrow from others, not merely particular arts or practices, but essential points of character in which its own type is inferior. Finally, commerce first taught nations to see with good will the wealth and prosperity of one another.... It is commerce which is rapidly rendering war obsolete, by strengthening and multiplying the personal interests which are in natural opposition to it. And it may be said without exaggeration that the great extent and rapid increase of international trade, in being the principal guarantee of the peace of the world, is the great permanent security for the uninterrupted progress of the ideas, the institutions, and the character of the human race. (Mill, 1920, pp. 581–2)

Mill's observation that contact with foreigners provides important external benefits in the form of skills, and even 'points of character', which any nation can profitably borrow from them, was well taken but hardly novel in 1848. Part of the above passage is reminiscent not only of Rae's *New Principles* but also of Hume's essay 'Of the Jealousy of Trade', which stressed that Britain's prosperity was fostered rather than endangered by that of her neighbors. The second part is notable for its optimistic forecast, alas disproved by subsequent events, that closer trade ties were making war 'obsolete'.

6.5 The infant-industry argument for protection

Mill's advocacy of infant-industry protection (which he called 'naturalizing a foreign industry') was instrumental in making this policy respectable in principle among economists and policymakers after 1848. The famous paragraph supporting it in prescribed circumstances is found in Book V of the *Principles*, devoted to the role of government. Acknowledging his indebtedness to John Rae, Mill made a clear distinction between actual and potential comparative advantage, and argued for policies designed to bring them closer together:

> The superiority of one country over another in a branch of production often arises only from having begun it sooner. There may be no inherent advantage on one part, or disadvantage on the other, but only a present superiority of acquired skill and experience. A country which has this skill and experience yet to acquire, may in other respects be better adapted to the production than those which were earlier in the field: and besides, it

is a just remark of Mr. Rae, that nothing has a greater tendency to promote improvements in any branch of production than its trial under a new set of conditions.... A protecting duty, continued for a reasonable time, might sometimes be the least inconvenient mode in which the nation can tax itself for the support of such an experiment. But it is essential that the protection should be confined to cases in which there is good ground of assurance that the industry which it fosters will after a time be able to dispense with it; nor should the domestic producers ever be allowed to expect that it will be continued to them beyond the time necessary for a fair trial of what they are capable of accomplishing. (Mill, 1920, p. 922)

What has come to be known as the 'Mill test' for infant-industry protection is that the industry should eventually be able to produce at internationally competitive costs, as implied by the condition that the industry should 'after a time be able to dispense with it', or that the country 'may in other respects be *better* adapted to the production than those which were earlier in the field' (emphasis added). As noted in Chapter 5, Hamilton and Rae had similar criteria for the successful promotion of new industries. It was subsequently pointed out by Bastable (1903, p. 140) that the Mill test, while necessary, is not sufficient. The industry should also meet what Kemp (1960, p. 65; 1964, p. 186) termed in his honor the 'Bastable test', which stipulates that eventually the community should be compensated with a sufficiently high return for the sacrifice entailed by protection, given the social discount rate.[21]

After Mill had anointed the infant-industry argument with respectability in his *Principles*, it has had a checkered career. Mill himself had second thoughts about his argument after he heard reports that it had been abused by policymakers in Australia and the US. He added a further paragraph in the sixth edition of 1865 intimating that the protecting duty 'be strictly limited in point of time, and provision be made that during the latter part of its existence it be on a gradually decreasing scale' (1920, p. 923).[22] He also modified some of the language of the original paragraph in the seventh edition of 1871. But Mill never renounced his belief in the legitimacy of such protection under well defined conditions. The classical and neoclassical economists who followed him had sharply divided views on the validity of this argument, but it was sanctioned by notable ones such as Marshall and Taussig. It is only in recent times that economists have provided rigorous criteria for protection (such as particular types of market failure) and the form protection should take.[23]

6.6 An early generalization of comparative advantage to many commodities

Mill's generalization of the law of comparative costs to more than two commodities and more than two countries was deceptively simple: 'Trade among any number of countries, and in any number of commodities, must take place on the same essential principles as trade between two countries and in two commodities' (1920, p. 588). He disregarded the multicommodity generalization of the Ricardian model pioneered by Mountifort Longfield. As is often true of pioneering attempts, Longfield's was not fully satisfactory, as both Viner (1937, pp. 454–6) and Moss (1976, pp. 127–30) have noted, but still came close to the mark.[24]

After presenting some numerical examples in the third of his *Three Lectures on Commerce and One on Absenteeism*, Longfield observed that

> the proportion which the general rate of wages in one country bears to the general rate of wages in another country, depends upon the proportion which the general productiveness of labour in the former bears to the general productiveness of labour in the other, and the course of trade is quite independent of this proportion. *That kind of labour will succeed in each country which is more productive in proportion to its price....* Neither high wages, nor low productiveness of labour, can render commerce disadvantageous to a country, or can place its industry in need of protection. Commerce will flow according as the proportion in particular trades is below or above the average proportion. (Longfield, 1835, pp. 55–6; emphasis added)

As will be described in Chapter 7, Longfield gave the correct solution for the direction of trade in a multicommodity Ricardian model, a commodity being exported by a country if and only if the productivity of the labor producing it, relative to the other country's, exceeds its relative wage rate. Towards the end of this lecture, Longfield noted the corollary that the higher a country's wage rate, the smaller the range of commodities it can export:

> But if a nation enjoyed an immense superiority in the production of two or three articles of very general demand, the wages of her labourers might be, in consequence, so high that she could not compete with the rest of the world in any other manufacture, under a system of free trade. (Longfield, 1835, p. 69)

This passage relates the high wages earned by a country's workers to a high foreign demand for articles in which they are able to specialize, and absolves Longfield to some extent of Viner's charge that 'where he failed ... was in not providing a satisfactory explanation of the mode of determination of the ratio between wages in the two countries' (Viner, 1937, pp. 455–6).[25]

Another of Longfield's innovations was his recognition of what 140 years later was called the 'Dutch disease', a name derived from the adverse effects of the development of natural gas in The Netherlands in the 1970s on its traditional export sectors. He presented an example where England is twice as efficient as other countries in shipbuilding and navigation, and then improves her capital and skills so as to become three times as efficient in manufacturing.

Her navigation would then decline, and that of other nations increase, since she lost her comparative advantage in it, even though she retains an absolute advantage.[26]

6.7 Modifications of Ricardian comparative advantage

Aside from the relative productivities and relative wages of labor, Longfield (1835, p. 56) noted that 'the next circumstance which gives direction to the stream of commerce, is, that the relative wages of labour in one country may vary by a different law from that which is observed in another'. Labor may be divided into what Cairnes (1874) later called 'non-competing groups'. Referring to the passage in Longfield (1835, p. 69) quoted above, Viner (1937, p. 494) noted that Longfield saw clearly 'that the course of trade under free trade will be governed by wage costs (i.e., labor–quantity costs times wage rates) and not, as posited by Ricardo, by comparative labor–quantity costs'. Moss (1976, pp. 129–30) cited an example of this drawn from Longfield's *Lectures on Political Economy*. Two countries in the West Indies are identical except that in one the inhabitants are all free, while in the other the laborers are enslaved. In consequence 'the commerce between those countries will necessarily consist of exchange of the products of harsh disagreeable labour from the country of slaves, for the results of skilled and educated labour from the land of freemen'. But if the slaves were to be suddenly emancipated, 'it is highly probable that their exports would no longer consist principally of sugar' (Longfield, 1834, pp. 71–2) due to the rise in the cost of labor.

It is worth noting that Mill, without citing Longfield, presented two examples in chapter 25 of Book III of his *Principles* which qualify Ricardian comparative advantage based on the labor theory of value. He preceded these examples with the statement:

> If wages, in any of the departments of industry which supply exports, are kept, artificially, or by some accidental cause, below the general rate of wages in the country, this is a real advantage in the foreign market. It lessens the *comparative* cost of production of those articles, in relation to others; and has the same effect as if their production required so much less labour. (Mill, 1920, p. 682)

The first example, similar to Longfield's, related to the US prior to the civil war, producing cotton and tobacco exports cheaply by means of slave labor. After the slaves were emancipated, their wages tended to rise towards those of the formerly free laborers, erasing some of America's comparative advantage in these crops:

Accordingly, American cotton is now habitually at a much higher price than before the war. Its previous cheapness was partly an artificial cheapness, which may be compared to that produced by a bounty on production or on exportation: or, considering the means by which it was obtained, an apter comparison would be with the cheapness of stolen goods. (Mill, 1920, pp. 682–3)[27]

It is interesting to note that Bertil Ohlin (1933), in searching for anticipations of his factor endowment theory among the classical writers, found only two, Sismondi and Longfield, and referred to Longfield's example of trade involving the society with slave labor. He added in this connection that 'curiously enough, John Stuart Mill, although he must have been familiar with Longfield's writings, seems never to have touched upon this line of reasoning' (Ohlin, 1933, p. 32). Ohlin obviously overlooked chapter 25 of Mill's *Principles*. As noted in Chapter 8, he quoted only some passages of Longfield's *Lectures on Political Economy* as an example of anticipations of his own factor endowment theory, ignoring the equally or more significant Longfield (1835).

Although more could be said about the evolutionary changes which the concept of comparative advantage was undergoing towards the end of the classical era, we proceed in Chapter 7 to examine how the first generation of neoclassical economists, as represented by Alfred Marshall, Vilfredo Pareto and Enrico Barone, undertook some radical modifications of the theory of international trade which they inherited.

Notes

1. Robbins added that 'there are independent developments, which, however, do not seem to have attracted any very great attention in Longfield ... (1835) and Pennington ... (1840)' (ibid.).
2. In his monograph on Longfield, Moss (1976) analyzed in chapter 8 his theory of international trade and its implications for commercial policy.
3. Thweatt (1986, p. 40) concluded that 'consequently, Sraffa's statement that "James Mill made the correction but not the error must be exactly reversed" (1930, p. 544) must itself be "exactly reversed", since we have John's own words that his father corrected the third edition'. If Thweatt is correct, J. S. Mill's attribution of the mistake in the *Elements* to Ricardo was a ruse designed to deflect the blame for it from both Mills and place it on Ricardo's capable shoulders, while citing extenuating circumstances for a mere 'oversight' by a great man concerned with far weightier issues.
4. The first part of Viner's statement, that 'Mill does not seem to have used this term [reciprocal demands], whose first use is commonly attributed to Torrens' (Viner, 1937, p. 536n), is therefore incorrect.
5. Edgeworth, the Drummond Professor of Political Economy at Oxford, 'held an academic position in England which was regarded as second only to that of Alfred Marshall' (Creedy, 1986, p. 123).
6. Dalal (1979) showed that Mill's results can be obtained as the solution of a pair of nonlinear programming problems, one for each country. However, it cannot be deduced from this that Mill

himself, implicitly or explicitly, derived his law of international values from such an exercise.

7. William Thornton was a close friend of Mill and the author of *On Labour: Its Wrongful Claims and Rightful Dues, Its Actual Present and Possible Future* (1869). It was Mill's review of this book that precipitated his famous recantation of the wages fund theory.

8. Whewell was viewed with some reservations by Schumpeter (1954, p. 448, 449n), who praised his 'touch of originality by making an attempt that no commonplace mind would have made in his day, viz. to express mathematically a few propositions of the economic theory of his time'. But Schumpeter added that 'this effort does not go beyond stating in symbols what had already been stated in words and therefore does not really constitute mathematical economics (there is no mathematical *reasoning*)'. On Whewell's alleged role in the formulation of Mill's superstructure and his contributions to mathematical economics more generally, see Chipman (1965a), Theocharis (1968, 1983, 1993), Henderson (1985, 1989), Cochrane (1970, 1975), Rashid (1977), Gherity (1988), Creedy (1992), Peake (1994).

9. Whewell's translation of Mill into mathematics was similar to Marshall's attempt some years later to make a similar translation of parts of Mill's *Principles*. It is somewhat surprising that Marshall never referred to Whewell in his own *Principles*, in spite of their shared Cambridge background and affinity for a mathematical mode of expression.

10. Various explanations have been offered for why Mill failed to give Whewell the credit he deserved, and acknowledged Thornton instead. These include Mill's friendship for Thornton and his antagonism towards Whewell arising from previous disputes relating to scientific method and moral philosophy (Hollander, 1985, pp. 153–8 and 641–5). Chipman's view (1965a, p. 492) is that 'Mill's acknowledgement to Thornton seems like a curious afterthought – a bouquet to a close friend'.

11. Creedy (1992, chapter 8) outlines a model which he names the 'Mill/Whewell model'.

12. Chipman notes that Mill made an 'unfortunate slip' when he stated that 'then will n [of cloth], after the opening of the trade, exchange for $(p/q)m$ [of linen]', where (p/q) represents 'the advantage of Germany over England in linen as estimated in cloth, and (what is the same thing) of England over Germany in cloth as estimated in linen' (1920, pp. 600–601). According to Chipman (1979, pp. 481–2), 'The error resulted from the fact that he considered only the value $q = 1$ in his numerical examples. An examination of Mill's previous argument ... shows that England's cost ratio has nothing to do with the matter'. Mill's mistake was also noticed by Dalal (1979, p. 587), and it underlines the danger of relying on numerical examples, Mill's preferred method, in contrast to Whewell's algebraic approach.

13. Mill (1920, pp. 600–601) illustrated the dependence of t on p with several numerical examples.

14. Whewell (1850, p. 22) concluded that 'if there be a trade between any two countries, say Poland and England, Poland exporting, we will suppose, corn, and England, cloth, the case in which the trade is advantageous to both countries is (on the suppositions made) confined within narrow limits, namely, when the mutual demand is very nearly equal'. For a different set of reasons noted in Chapter 7, Graham (1923) also contended that trade was more likely to occur at one of the limiting ratios than between them. Viner (1937, pp. 448–53) traced the evolution of economists' views on the feasibility of trade at one of the limiting ratios and the partial specialization this implies.

15. See also Harwitz (1972, p. 186) and Appleyard and Ingram (1979, p. 472).

16. Since Mill used some of the same algebraic symbols as Whewell, but with different meanings, I changed most of Whewell's symbols as set out below:

Whewell's notation:	P	p	Q	q	M	m	n	$=$	PQ/q
My notation:		p	$1/q$	m	qn	S	s		$r = pm/qn$

Whewell's symbol k equals $1 - 1/Pp$ in his notation, and is given by $(p - q)/p$ in mine.

17. Whewell (1850, p. 5) chose the term 'susceptibility' because he noted that for positive and large values of s (very inelastic demands), 'a small increase in the quantity supplied ... will produce

a large diminution in the price ... In such cases we may say that the price is very susceptible of change ... by alteration of the supply'.

18. Creedy (1989, pp. 270, 272) agrees with this conclusion.

19. Chipman (1979, p. 495n) concurs with the eclectic interpretation advanced by a referee of his paper, approvingly quoting the referee's comment that 'Mill would have felt underrated by both Appleyard–Ingram and by Chipman' for maintaining that any changes must be attributable either to a change in size or to a change in tastes, but not both.

20. Williams ([1929] 1949, p. 265) found Mill's critique of Smith to be 'less true and more naive than "the surviving relic of the Mercantile Theory"'. Referring to England, he argued that through specialization for the world markets, her factors of production became committed to producing for export and would be hard put to serve the domestic market. The factors themselves have in a sense been created by international trade, their fortunes are tied to it, and they cannot be employed in other ways.

21. Kemp (ibid.) combined these two tests when he coined the term 'Mill–Bastable dogma'.

22. In correspondence (cited by Irwin, 1996, p. 129), Mill indicated that protection should last 'a certain limited number of years, say ten, or at the very most twenty'.

23. See the critiques of the infant industry argument by Baldwin (1969) and Irwin (1996, chapter 8).

24. Generalizations of the principle of comparative costs to many commodities and many countries during the classical period are discussed by Viner (1937, pp. 453–67).

25. Viner (1937, p. 456) was on firmer ground when criticizing the solutions that Longfield presented prior to this passage: 'His first two solutions are both obviously arbitrary and incorrect. Wages in the two countries would be proportional neither to the average productivities in all pretrade employments, not to the productivities in the two countries in the relatively most productive employment of *one* of the countries'.

26. Longfield discussed how innovations alter a country's comparative advantage, and with what frequency: 'as every year produces improvements in our manufactures, so every year may be expected to bring some alteration in our commerce. A machine is discontinued, not because it is found to be inefficient, but because another more efficient is discovered' (1835, pp. 62–3).

27. The second example offered by Mill was that of domestic manufactures in the Swiss Canton of Zurich, carried out by people who divide their time between them and agricultural employment subject to seasonal variation. Since the production of these manufactures is mainly regarded as a way of utilizing leisure time, their cost is very low and again not proportional to the quantity of labor time allocated to them.

7. Neoclassical Trade Theory: Alfred Marshall, Vilfredo Pareto and Enrico Barone

7.1 Alfred Marshall and his school

Alfred Marshall holds a pre-eminent place in the pantheon of neoclassical trade theorists because of his invention of reciprocal demand (or offer) curves which he used to analyze an international trade equilibrium, its stability, and how it changes in response to factors such as trade taxes or technical change. International trade theory held such interest for Marshall that he intended to write one of his first books on that subject. He abandoned this plan in favor of other projects when he realized that the manuscript would 'never make a comfortable book in its present shape' (cited in Whitaker, 1975, p. 62). Part II of this contemplated text was to be, in his words, 'a book on the method of diagrams applied to economic theory including foreign trade curves'. As a substitute for this text, Henry Sidgwick asked for and obtained Marshall's permission to print privately a selection of chapters from Part II. Two chapters that he chose became *The Pure Theory of Foreign Trade* (Marshall, 1879), while two others became *The Pure Theory of Domestic Values.*

Marshall's early interest in international trade was sparked by his study of J. S. Mill's *Principles* and led to his attempt to convert Mill's economics into mathematical form. In a letter to L. C. Colson, Marshall wrote: 'I read Mill's *Political Economy* in 1866 or '7, while I was teaching advanced mathematics; and, as I thought much more easily in mathematics at that time than in English, I tried to translate him into mathematics before forming an opinion as to the validity of his work'. In a letter to J. B. Clark, Marshall reported that 'in the next four years [after 1870] I worked a good deal at the mathematical theory of monopolies, and at the diagrammatic treatment of Mill's problem of international values' (cited in Whitaker, 1975, p. 37). By means of offer curves, Marshall was able to illustrate in a memorable way the general solution of the Mill–Whewell model of international equilibrium.[1] He noted and demonstrated graphically the possibility of multiple equilibrium points. In order to analyze their stability or instability, he went on to introduce the first phase diagrams used by economists.

Some authors have claimed that Marshall's role did not go beyond the graphical illustration of Mill's concepts. Both Viner and Schumpeter cited an excerpt from a letter which Marshall wrote to H. H. Cunynghame in 1904, in which he stated that 'as to international trade curves:– mine were set to a definite tune, that called by Mill'. According to Viner (1937, p. 541), 'Marshall's treatment of the relation of reciprocal demand to terms of trade is in the main an exposition and elaboration in geometrical form of Mill's analysis'. Schumpeter (1954, p. 609) was led to conclude that 'in this field Marshall did not do more than to polish and develop Mill's meaning'. However, Creedy has pointed out that this often cited excerpt from Marshall's letter has been misinterpreted, since Marshall's intention was to differentiate and express a preference for Mill's approach to international values rather than Cournot's. Hence 'Marshall is saying that he had good reasons for following the path of Mill rather than Cournot when considering international values, not that his diagrams do little more than restate Mill in another language' (Creedy, 1990, p. 102).

Although Marshall never wrote his intended book on international trade, much of what he wanted to say on the subject is found in *Money Credit and Commerce* (Marshall, 1923) published a year before his death. Fortunately many economists were given access to Marshall's 1879 book, and the profession did not have to wait until 1923 to be introduced to offer curves. They were skillfully used by Francis Y. Edgeworth (1894) to illustrate Mill's numerical examples, as discussed in Chapter 6.[2] Marshall even allowed Maffeo Pantaleoni to incorporate offer curve diagrams in an economics textbook published in Italian and then in an English translation (Pantaleoni, 1898).[3] Following the convention he had adopted in his *Principles of Economics*, Marshall relegated his offer curves (which he referred to simply as demand curves) to the back of his 1923 book in Appendix J. The material included in the latter was mainly a revised version of *The Pure Theory of Foreign Trade* written 44 years earlier. Among his revisions, Marshall now referred explicitly to such concepts as elasticity that he had meantime developed in his *Principles*. A more questionable innovation (discussed below) was the aggregation of exports and imports into 'representative bales'.

Figure 7.1   The Edgeworth–Viner offer curve diagram

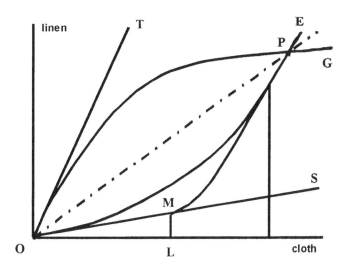

Marshall and comparative advantage

Viner (1937, pp. 546–7) pointed out an important difference between the ways in which Edgeworth and Marshall represented an international equilibrium by means of offer curves. While Marshall ignored the two countries' comparative advantage in his diagrams, Edgeworth tried to take it into account even though his diagram was incomplete. Edgeworth's diagram, in the form in which Viner revised it in his Chart XV, is shown in Figure 7.1, where the two axes measure the quantities of cloth exported by England and linen exported by Germany. Edgeworth drew the lines OS and OT tangential to OE and OG, the offer curves of England and Germany, in order to indicate the ratio of the costs of production of linen compared to cloth in the two countries under autarky. It is clear that the terms of trade given by OP, the ray joining the origin to the point of intersection of the offer curves, lies between the two autarky price ratios. The offer curve diagram is thus an effective way to illustrate Pennington's contention discussed in Chapter 6, as well as to represent the equilibrium terms of trade. Marshall and Edgeworth used it to analyze the stability of a trade equilibrium as well as the shifts in the terms of trade due to disturbances such as changes in demand, technical improvements or trade taxes.[4] As Edgeworth (1894, pp. 424–5) noted, the offer curve diagram does not fully reveal the workings of the model which underlies it, since 'a movement along a supply-and-demand [offer] curve of international trade should be considered attended with rearrangements of internal trade; as the movement of the hand of a clock corresponds to considerable unseen movements of the machinery'.

After presenting Edgeworth's diagram, Viner (1937, p. 547) went on to note that it was 'open to a criticism to which all the Marshallian diagrams as usually drawn are equally open, if they are supposed to represent two commodities or classes of commodities both of which are producible at home at constant costs'. The curve OE should not begin to rise immediately at the origin, but should initially follow the straight line segment OM, where the ordinate of point M, ML, represents the amount of linen which England produces and consumes in autarky. Thereafter the curve diverges from M as shown by the branch ME. A similar modification (not shown) should be made to the German offer curve.

While Edgeworth incorporated the two countries' comparative cost ratios in his offer curve diagram, Marshall disregarded them both in 1879 and 1923, and explained the shapes of the offer curves in the vicinity of the origin solely in terms of demand factors. Thus he argued that 'if E has some important exports which are nearly indispensable to G, while G has none which are nearly indispensable to E, then OG will be nearly vertical in the neighbourhood of O; but OE will not be nearly horizontal in the neighbourhood of O' (Marshall, 1923, p. 332). It is interesting to speculate on Marshall's reasons for not recognizing in 1923 the way in which comparative advantage affects the shapes of the offer curves, given that almost 30 years had elapsed since Edgeworth's 1894 articles. He simply borrowed Mill's assumption that England and Germany export cloth and linen respectively, but never attempted to justify it in terms of relative labor or other costs. The reasons for Marshall's failure to rigorously incorporate supply-side factors in his diagrams were probably his rejection of the Ricardian labor theory of value and his unwillingness to formulate an alternative theory.[5] Ohlin's comments on this are revealing:

> Marshall's analysis does not go back to the things behind supply schedules, i.e. to the relation between costs and supply prices.... Certainly there is one appalling thing [about Marshall, 1923], namely that significant parts of the classical doctrine are left out entirely. Marshall hardly makes any use of the real cost analysis in terms of days of labour or units of productive power.... He seems to have shrunk from tying his curve analysis of the play of international supply and demand down to a labour theory of value of the Ricardian type.... On the whole, he seems to have been content with dealing with international exchange in the most narrow sense without putting it in its organic connection with the general system of price and value. (Ohlin, 1933, pp. 567–8)

Rather than aiming at a comprehensive depiction of the supply and demand forces affecting international trade, Marshall had the rather different purpose of using offer curves to analyze stability issues and the impact of trade taxes.[6]

While Marshall ignored comparative advantage in his offer curve diagrams, possibly because it could not be integrated with his new concept of representative bales (as discussed below), he made numerous informal remarks on the nature of foreign trade in his last two books (Marshall, 1919, 1923). Some of his 'common-sense' remarks, however, turned out to be rather inaccurate forecasts of the contemporary trends in world trade. For example, he held that 'the percentage of the world's trade which is governed by differences in natural resources is increasing, while that which is governed by differences of industrial phase, and of aptitude for particular sorts and grades of manufacture, is less now than formerly' (Marshall, 1923, p. 105). In 1933 Ohlin pointed out that the figures of world trade then available (admittedly, a decade after Marshall had published his last book) lent no support to Marshall's contention since much of this trade was taking place between the leading manufacturing countries, the US, Great Britain, France and Germany. Of course this is even truer today than two-thirds of a century ago. Marshall's failure to predict this trend in world trade is all the more curious since he had a very clear understanding of what later came to be known as intraindustry trade. As he stated, 'a country often exports a commodity over one frontier, while she imports practically the same over another.... But, more commonly, the commodities which enter into trade of this kind differ a little from one another, though called by the same name' (Marshall, 1923, p. 104). Such trade now constitutes the bulk of the trade that advanced economies carry on with each other. After noting this phenomenon, Ohlin observed in 1933 that 'Marshall probably underestimated the importance of the fact that economies of large-scale production and specialization increase rapidly and that they make one country better adapted to manufacture certain goods, while other countries specialize in others' (Ohlin, 1967, p. 87).

Marshall's 'representative bales'

As mentioned above, one of Marshall's innovations in his 1923 book was his concept of 'representative bales' of tradable goods. Instead of following Mill in assuming that yards of cloth and linen exchange for each other, 'it seems better to suppose either country to make up her exports into representative "bales"; that is, bales each of which represents uniform aggregate investments of her labour (of various qualities) and of her capital' (Marshall, 1923, p. 157). He thereby attempted two difficult aggregation problems, of heterogeneous inputs as well as heterogeneous outputs. If outputs are produced at constant costs, the latter aggregation might suggest a Hicksian composite commodity, except that the composition of this commodity changes with shifts in demand. The aggregation of inputs had already been proposed by authors such as Cairnes, but was rejected by Pareto (as outlined in section 7.2) and Haberler. According to the latter, '[a bale's] "real cost" remains constant, whilst the individual goods which compose it may vary. We can readily follow Marshall so long as we keep to the Labour Theory of Value, with its assumption that homogeneous labour is the sole factor of production' (Haberler, 1936, p. 150). Haberler illustrated what he called 'Marshall's generalisation of the theory of international values' by means of the England–Germany offer curve diagram and a table on which it was based outlining the reciprocal demands and supplies of 'E-bales' and 'G-bales'. Since Haberler redefined a bale as the amount produced by a unit of labor, the only factor of production he considered, he assumed that the slope of a line joining the origin to the intersection of the offer curves equals both the commodity ('bale') terms of trade and the factoral terms of trade, or ratio of money wages. With E-bales shown on the horizontal axis, the steeper this line is, the more advantageous the terms of trade are to England.

The 'bale' which Marshall introduced in 1923 is an awkward device at best.[7] Even if we accept Haberler's (and implicitly Ohlin's) emendation that the outputs represented in a bale are produced at constant cost by labor only, the changeable composition of a country's output bundle makes it impossible to discuss the other country's demand for it and hence its derived demand for the underlying inputs. Consider again Figure 7.1 where we relabel the axes *à la* Haberler as E-bales and G-bales. It is shown below that as her terms of trade improve and the equilibrium point travels away from O and towards E, England produces fewer commodities. When the terms of trade reach their highest level, she produces and exports only one commodity and imports all the others. In Edgeworth's diagram, England's comparative advantage was indicated by the slope of the ray OS, equal to the opportunity cost of cloth in terms of linen in autarky, while that of Germany was given by the slope of OT. With the axes redefined as bales, the slope of OS now purportedly measures the number of G-bales per unit of E-bale produced under autarky. But this is a meaningless concept as no G-bales are, or can be, produced in England under autarky, since England then needs to produce the entire range of commodities she wishes to consume. A similar consideration applies to Germany's autarky price ratio given by the slope of OT. Hence it is impossible to reinterpret Edgeworth's diagram in Haberler's manner and argue that the terms of trade ray is located between the autarky price ratios. It is also absurd to argue that England has a comparative advantage in an unspecified bale of E-goods. Haberler's well-meaning attempt to adapt the offer curve diagram to reflect a multicommodity model, even if limited to a single factor, strains it to the point of breakdown.

Frank Graham criticized the Mill–Marshall model in several influential papers (Graham, 1923, 1932) culminating in a book (Graham, 1948). He argued that its two-commodity, two-country structure assigns an excessive weight to reciprocal demand in determining the terms of trade. If the model is generalized to several commodities as well as countries, the terms of trade are likely to coincide with the rate of transformation between two goods in one of the countries, instead of being what he called a 'limbo' price ratio. According to Graham, supply factors are much more important than demand factors in determining the terms of trade. He provided a large number of numerical examples to illustrate his contention, including some complex ones stretching to several countries as well as commodities. Graham was in turn criticized for giving excessive weight to supply factors at the expense of demand ones.[8] This dispute is somewhat reminiscent of the more general one in the theory of value regarding the role of demand versus supply determinants, and recalls the famous Marshallian metaphor of the scissors: 'we might as reasonably dispute whether it is the upper or the under blade of a pair of scissors that cuts a piece of paper, as whether value is governed by utility or cost of production' (Marshall, 1920, p. 348). While it is true that in a multicommodity model a given commodity may be produced by both trading countries, and that a shift in demand may cause a quantity adjustment rather than a change in prices, it is demand factors which initially determine the borderline commodity.

While Graham's conclusions should be qualified, his work had the great merit of attracting attention to the importance of introducing many countries and commodities into the Ricardo–Mill–Marshall model of comparative advantage and to point out the dangers of 'two-ness' in trade models. This is the term which Ronald Jones ([1977] 1979) used to illustrate the limited circumstances under which the properties of the Heckscher–Ohlin model formulated in a two-commodity, two-factor context transfer to a multicommodity, multifactor one. Much of the work of generalizing two-dimensional models in recent decades can be traced back to Graham's writings. In addition, Graham attracted attention to the issue of protection for increasing-returns industries, which has been a prominent part of the new trade theory examined in Chapter 9. We next turn attention to the multicommodity generalizations of the Ricardian model which followed Longfield's but preceded Graham's writings.

Figure 7.2   Edgeworth's multicommodity diagram

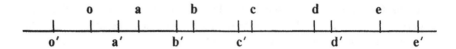

The multicommodity Ricardian model: Mangoldt and Edgeworth

Another major contribution of Edgeworth (1894) was his introducing the English-speaking world to the multicommodity generalization of the Ricardian model made by H. Mangoldt (1871) in a German work whose first edition dates from 1863 and has still not been translated into English. Edgeworth went beyond Mangoldt's numerical examples by portraying the trade equilibrium with the diagram shown in Figure 7.2. Five commodities A through E are traded between countries I and II, the logarithms of their costs of production being shown by a, b, c, ... in country I and a', b', c', ... in country II. The distances of these points from the origins o and o' measure the logarithms of the unit labor coefficients. The origins themselves measure the logarithms of the wage rates in I and II, so that $o'o$ equals the logarithm of the ratio w/w' of these wages. The distance of o to the right or left of o' depends on the strength of the reciprocal demand of each country for the other's goods. If ℓ_i (ℓ_i') is the unit labor coefficient of commodity i in country I (II), a point such as a measures $\log w + \log \ell_A = \log w\ell_A$, the logarithm of A's cost of production in country I. If $a > a'$, as shown in the diagram, then $w\ell_A > w'\ell_A'$. Commodity A is therefore produced in country II where it is cheaper and exported to country I. The diagram shows that A, B and C are produced in II and that D and E are produced in I, the country with the higher wage rate.

Following Mangoldt, Edgeworth (1894, p. 633) noted that the multicommodity case differs from the two-commodity one in that 'it is not in general possible to determine *a priori*, from a mere observation of the costs of production in the respective countries before the opening of the trade, which commodities will be imported and which produced at home. "Comparative cost" cannot be ascertained by simply comparing the costs of different articles in the two countries'. The impact of changes in reciprocal demand can be portrayed by assuming that the top row in Figure 7.2 is rigid while the bottom row is free to slide left or right. The costs of production of the commodities as well as the wage rate of country I then vary with respect to those of country II, so that some commodities which were a country's exports become imports or vice versa. Viner (1937, pp. 458–62) reproduced and elaborated on Edgeworth's diagram, and showed that the terms of trade between two commodities such as A and D, expressed as the relative price of D in terms of A, are given by (antilog od)/(antilog oa'). The same procedure of sliding one row of the diagram relative to the other shows that when a country's wage rate rises with respect to the other country's, the number of commodities it exports remains the same or shrinks as their cost of production now exceeds the other country's.

Edgeworth (1894, p. 634) quoted Mangoldt's observation that 'there come first into international trade those commodities of which the costs of production compared with the costs of production of other commodities in the same land differ most widely from each other, then those for which the difference is next greatest'. Edgeworth, however, did not follow up on this hint by constructing what later came to be known as a 'chain of comparative advantage', one link of which separates the commodities which the two countries produce and export. In discussing Edgeworth's diagram, Viner did not do this either, although he observed in a footnote that Haberler (1929, 1936) had 'another and in some respects more general method of dealing with this problem' (Viner, 1937, p. 461). Haberler's procedure was inspired by a seven-commodity numerical example found in Appendix H of Marshall (1923), in which commodities were ranked in decreasing order of the ratios of their labor coefficients in the two countries.[9] Haberler set up a chain of comparative advantage which, applied to Edgeworth's example, yields the following series of inequalities:

$$\ell_A/\ell_A' > \ell_B/\ell_B' > \dots > \ell_E/\ell_E'. \qquad (7.1)$$

These inequalities rank the commodities A, ... , E in order of increasing comparative advantage for country I. When the equilibrium ratio of money wages w'/w is inserted in the above chain, all commodities to the left of it are imported and those to the right exported by country I.

As an elaboration of the Edgeworth–Haberler model, it can be shown that the chain of comparative advantage given by (7.1) has implications for the spacing of points in Figure 7.2, which must be such that

$$a'b' > ab, \ b'c' > bc, \ \dots \ , \ d'e' > de. \qquad (7.2)$$

To prove this, note that the first inequality of (7.1) implies that

$$\log \ell_B' - \log \ell_A' > \log \ell_B - \log \ell_A, \qquad (7.1a)$$

and hence that $a'b' > ab$, and similarly for the other inequalities.[10] Summing the inequalities (7.2) we obtain $a'e' > ae$, which implies that the range of costs of production of commodities in country II exceeds the corresponding range in country I. It is precisely this 'stretching' of the range of costs in country II as compared to country I which ensures that the commodities at the A end of the range are produced at a lower cost in country II, while those at the E end are cheaper in country I. It is possible to draw Figure 7.2 in such a way that o and o' coincide, so that $w = w'$; or that the costs of production of a particular commodity coincide. For example, if b and b' were to coincide in Figure 7.2, commodity B would be produced in both countries and may be exported by either of them. Both Mangoldt and Graham believed that this case where a commodity is produced in common was likely to occur in practice, but there is no theoretical justification for this belief in a model characterized by constant costs.

Edgeworth's five-commodity example is a special case of a more general Ricardian n-commodity model which can be used to illustrate the law of comparative advantage presented in Chapter 2. According to the Deardorff–Dixit–Norman (DDN) theorem proved there, the inner product of country I's net import vector and the difference between the autarky price vectors of countries I and II is non-negative. Because of the special structure of the present model, it can be shown that if a 'borderline' commodity (as defined below) is chosen as numeraire, this inner product is the sum of $(n - 1)$ positive numbers. This demonstrates the truth of the DDN theorem for a special case where none of the components of the inner product is negative. If any other type of commodity were chosen as numeraire, the inner product remains of course positive, but its sign cannot be verified as easily since it is the difference between a set of positive and a set of negative numbers. In order not to make this section overly long, these results are elaborated in the Appendix to this chapter.

7.2 Vilfredo Pareto's general equilibrium approach to trade theory[11]

Pareto's name is associated with the general equilibrium approach which he learnt from Léon Walras, made his own and developed further.[12] He first applied this approach to the international trade context in two papers in the *Giornale degli Economisti* (1894, 1895), then in Volume II of the *Cours d'économie politique* (1897) and finally in the *Manual of Political Economy* (1906, 1971).[13] Gottfried Haberler (1936, p. 3) bestowed high praise on the *Giornale degli Economisti* papers, stating that 'the only important theoretical advance [since the classical theory] has been the application, notably by Pareto, of general equilibrium analysis to the problems of international trade'.

In a similar vein, the other pioneer of the modern theory of international trade, Bertil Ohlin, argued that

> it is astonishing that the Anglo-Saxon literature on international trade has overlooked that Pareto did not bring some minor modifications of the classical doctrine, but attacked the problem in an entirely different way.... He has drawn the obvious consequence that the mutual interdependence theory must be valid for several markets as well as for one, and thus has provided at least a stepping stone for the construction of an alternative theory of international trade. (Ohlin, 1933, p. 564)

In the first edition of his book, Ohlin concluded a four-page discussion of Pareto and his school by noting the similarities and differences between Pareto's trade model and his own (to be discussed in Chapter 8). He found it 'not surprising that the equations worked out by Pareto and kept with comparatively small alterations by his pupils resemble those presented in Appendix I of this book.... A study of their writings a few years earlier would have saved me some trouble and work'. However, he concluded that Pareto and his followers only provided 'a starting point for an alternative theory' and 'have not, so far as I know, attempted to build up a concrete theory of international trade, alternative to the classical one' (1933, pp. 564, 567).

In the first part of the article entitled 'Mathematical theory of the foreign exchanges',[14] Pareto (1894) set out a general equilibrium model for an economy X, first in autarky, then linked by trade to economy Y. The equations of which it consists, based on 'the formulas of Prof. Walras', relate to different individuals, firms, commodities and factors of production. Pareto assumed that the prices of imports in one community exceed those of the other community's exports by their commercialization, transportation and insurance expenses. As in J. S. Mill's case, he assumed balance of trade equilibrium since 'every country must pay for what it receives'. These equations are sufficient in number to determine the prices and quantities of commodities produced and of factor services, as well as the net exports of each commodity from X to Y.

Pareto wrote a follow-up article entitled 'Mathematical theory of international trade' (Pareto, 1895), partly as a rejoinder to Edgeworth (1894), most of which dealt with trade in only two commodities using Marshallian offer curves. In concluding it, Edgeworth had discussed possible generalizations of his results:

> In entering upon the more complicated part of the subject, it is well to recall Professor Marshall's warning words: 'When a great many symbols have to be used, they become very laborious to any one but the writer himself,' and 'it seems doubtful whether any one spends his time well in reading lengthy translations of economic doctrines into mathematics, that have not been made by himself'. (Edgeworth, 1894, p. 440)

Marshall's words came from the first edition of his *Principles of Economics*. Edgeworth went on to refer to Pareto's 'able article' of 1894, but coupled this praise with some reservations on the scope of application of the Walrasian formulas. His reference to Walras and Pareto was preceded by the astonishing statement: 'I do not know that any fresh conclusions are presented by the case of many variables. Accordingly it may be left to the reader to elaborate that case' (1894, p. 442). This is reminiscent of Mill's statement, quoted in Chapter 6, that 'trade among any number of countries, and in any number of commodities, must take place on the same essential principles as trade between two countries and in two commodities' (Mill, 1920, p. 588).[15]

Pareto's reaction to Edgeworth's remarks is worth quoting, since it epitomizes the methodological difference in approach between an economist of the Lausanne school and a well-trained mathematician like Marshall who, surprisingly enough, sought to minimize the use of mathematics in his economic writings:[16]

> The conditions mentioned are expressed mathematically by equations. Prof. Marshall – according to what Prof. Edgeworth reports – apparently complains that many symbols are needed for this. We are sorry, and if it had pleased the good Lord to create the world so as to make the economic phenomenon simpler we would be very glad, but unfortunately we must accept things as they stand, and describe them as we are able to. Whoever studies science must only try to discover the truth, of the rest we care little or nothing. (Pareto, 1895, pp. 479–80)

If there are only two traded goods, Pareto's solution corresponds to the intersection of Marshallian offer curves. Pareto pointed out the more limited scope of Edgeworth's analysis compared to his own, while recognizing the pedagogical value of his diagrams:

> The method of Prof. Edgeworth and ours do not exclude each other, but investigate different parts of the phenomenon. Prof. Edgeworth considers particular cases; he lists no less than $2^8 = 256$ of them; we look for general properties, common to those various cases.... It is moreover not very clear to us how the method of Prof. Edgeworth could be extended to real cases, in which one must consider not just two, but a rather large number of commodities.... For teaching we certainly prefer the geometric method used by Prof. Edgeworth to the long analytical considerations we have had to make here in order to treat the problem in the most general case. (Pareto, 1895, pp. 486, 497)

Pareto reproduced his simultaneous equation model of trade involving many commodities, factors of production and consumers in Volume II of his *Cours d'économie politique* (Pareto, 1897). In the *Manual of Political Economy*, he adopted a more streamlined procedure by dispensing altogether with an explicit mathematical model. As compared to equilibrium under autarky, if community X trades, say, 100 commodities with community Y, the amounts traded represent 100 additional variables whose determination requires 100 extra equations. After allowing for transportation and similar costs, Pareto equated the prices of commodities in both communities. If they share an international commodity money as numeraire, this yields 99 equations. The remaining equation required for a solution is the balance of trade condition. If X and Y instead have their own monies, the exchange rate of one in terms of the other represents an extra unknown. The 101 equations needed to solve the system are the balance of trade condition and the equality of the 100 commodity prices (including the two commodity monies, via the exchange rate). The trade equilibrium can thus be determined by adding, to the closed-economy equations, 100 additional equations if an international money exists, or 101 if each community has its own money.

After noting that 'the earliest ... attempt [to set forth the neo-classical trade model in very general terms] appears to be that of Pareto', John Chipman (1965b, p. 688) expressed the reservation that 'it is rather significant that he was not able to develop the theory much beyond the counting of equations and unknowns, providing at best a loose (neither necessary nor sufficient) criterion for existence of equilibrium'. While Pareto's model is indeed defective if one applies contemporary standards of mathematical rigor, one must recognize that at the time it was unrivaled in scope and set the stage for advances in the theory of international trade in the twentieth century. It was a harbinger of developments such as Ohlin's work elaborated in Chapter 8, which was based on similar insights into the nature of general equilibrium.

Pareto and the theory of comparative advantage

Unlike Ohlin, Pareto recognized the usefulness of Ricardo's principle of comparative costs. Not content with the versions inherited from Ricardo, J. S. Mill and J. E. Cairnes, he generalized this principle in line with his own work on utility (which he later renamed 'ophelimity') and general equilibrium. He noted that an advantage of his formulas for a trade equilibrium was that

> they serve in our course in pure Political Economy to demonstrate Ricardo's theory of comparative costs, which thus acquires much greater rigor, and can be formulated as follows: in order for the barter of a commodity B to occur between two closed markets, it is necessary that the costs, **expressed in utility**, should be different in the two markets. (Pareto, 1894, p. 154; bold lettering in the original)

Using Cairnes's formulation of 'Ricardo's theorem', with costs expressed in utility rather than money terms, Pareto argued that 'Cairnes does not show, and could not show only with his theory, the equality of those costs for different individuals' (Pareto, 1895, p. 484).

In the *Cours*, Pareto expanded in considerable detail on the significance of the theorem of comparative costs and he used a different nomenclature. He replaced the Jevonian terms 'total utility' and 'final degree of utility' (the latter corresponding to marginal utility) with 'ophelimity' and 'elementary ophelimity'. In Volume I he showed that the price ratio between two commodities B and C, p_b/p_c, is equal either to the ratio of the elementary ophelimities of each individual consuming them, or to the ratios of their 'ophelimity costs' to each individual, defined as the sum of the elementary ophelimities which an individual sacrifices in order to obtain those commodities. Let b_s, b_t be the input coefficients for good B, and c_s, c_t the corresponding coefficients for good C, where S and T are two representative inputs of services which an individual can either consume directly or offer for sale. Defining ϕ_{ib} and ϕ_{is} as the elementary ophelimities (that is, the marginal utilities) of individual i relating to good B and service S, Pareto (1896, p. 49n) obtained

$$\frac{p_b}{p_c} = \frac{\phi_{ib}}{\phi_{ic}} = \frac{b_s\phi_{is} + b_t\phi_{it} + \ldots}{c_s\phi_{is} + c_t\phi_{it} + \ldots}, \tag{7.3}$$

so that prices are proportional both to elementary ophelimities and to ophelimity costs. Since (7.3) applies to any two individuals 1 and 2, we have

$$\frac{b_s\phi_{1s} + b_t\phi_{1t} + \ldots}{c_s\phi_{1s} + c_t\phi_{1t} + \ldots} = \frac{b_s\phi_{2s} + b_t\phi_{2t} + \ldots}{c_s\phi_{2s} + c_t\phi_{2t} + \ldots}. \tag{7.4}$$

Pareto pointed out that if, instead of (7.4), the first fraction 'was larger or smaller than the second, trade would continue. That is Ricardo's principle of the theory of *comparative costs*' (ibid.). In Volume II of the *Cours*, he commented that 'the theory of comparative costs is therefore not specific to international trade, and can also apply to individuals who compose an economic aggregation' (Pareto, 1897, p. 213). He generalized his formulas to allow for the fact that the ophelimity that an individual receives from certain services is not direct, since he may derive no personal satisfaction from them, but indirect, since he can sell them in order to buy other commodities.

Pareto criticized Mill for using the labor theory of value, where commodities are produced by labor alone, in the trade chapters of his *Principles of Political Economy*, and complained of Cairnes's 'very imprecise manner' of expression, given the ambiguity surrounding the latter's use of the term 'sacrifices' in connection with the production of commodities. He argued that the theorem of comparative costs 'can hardly be enunciated with precision by economists who do not utilize the mathematical method' (Pareto, 1897, p. 210).[17] The above equations allow one to appreciate better his objections to Cairnes's formulation:

> One could really say that there exists a certain person named 'society', and that it is the sacrifices made by that person that one considers. In reality, society is composed of different people, and the 'sacrifices' they make, while cooperating in production, are heterogeneous quantities, which one cannot sum together. A thing does not have an objective cost in terms of ophelimity, it has subjective costs, different according to the different individuals.... Cairnes seems to think that the *cost* (in ophelimity terms) of commodities is composed of *labor* and *abstinence*. In that form, the theory of comparative costs is not only inexact, it is false.... To speak of the 'sacrifices' of England makes no sense. In reality, there are Englishmen who make 'sacrifices'.... When one must decide if it is better to use a piece of land to develop a coal mine or to cultivate wheat, one considers neither 'sacrifices' nor 'abstinence', which in this case can only have an absolutely insignificant influence. One considers only the different quantities of economic goods that one can obtain from this land, according to how it is used. (Pareto, 1897, pp. 211, 222)

After citing part of the same passage, Ohlin noted that 'evidently Pareto has in mind a sort of *marginal* individual opportunity costs which, when measured in terms of his "ophélimité," are proportional to prices' (1933, p. 566). The passage shows that Pareto thought in terms of opportunity costs when he conceptualized the optimum use of economic resources. As Ohlin himself observed, he can therefore be viewed as an anticipator of Haberler (1930). The real cost theory of Cairnes and Viner will be contrasted with the opportunity cost theory in section 8.1.

A few pages after setting out his comparative cost theory in terms of individual ophelimities, Pareto decided that he could not use it for operational purposes. Thus, 'in order to have an idea, without recourse to mathematics, of equilibrium in international trade, let us for the moment resolutely sacrifice rigor for clarity'. He then presented an illustration involving a village X composed of two inhabitants, a farmhand and a shoemaker, who trade with region Y. 'We only consider labor in production, and neglect all types of capital service' (Pareto, 1897, p. 216) – the very assumption for which he had just criticized Mill! Pareto used this simplified model to analyze barter trade flows, and how monetary flows can assist the adjustment process if one economy's price level is too high compared to the other's. This allowed him to distinguish between real and nominal wages, and to show that a country can export some commodities even if its wage exceeds the other country's.

Pareto added an illustration with a surprisingly modern flavor, followed by some statistics of Japan's trade with Britain and France:

> If Y is Europe and X Asia, one understands how European industries can, in spite of paying high wages, stand up to the competition of Asian industries, which only pay their workers minimal wages. A very remarkable confirmation of this theory is provided by the evolution of import and export flows in Japan. (Pareto, 1897, pp. 220–21)

He contrasted the growth of British exports to Japan in the last quarter of the nineteenth century, which was vigorous in spite of high British wages, with the slower growth of French exports, 'wisely "protected" by protective tariffs'. It is interesting that Pareto, in arriving at these policy implications, not only avoided using his own model, but did not hesitate to use, while acknowledging its limitations, the simpler Ricardian one that he had earlier excoriated for assuming that all costs are labor costs. His trade model presents itself as an ingenious mathematical *tour de force*, but of such complexity that even its creator had to resort to the simpler, more operational Ricardo–Millian one for policy purposes.[18]

Pareto's paradox

Ricardo's model of comparative advantage fascinated Pareto, just as it did some of its other critics. In Chapter 9 of the *Manual* Pareto resorted to it in order to contest one of Ricardo's assertions. He showed that if two agents fully specialize in their commodities of comparative advantage, the world output of one of the commodities may decline below its autarky level, making one of the agents worse off than before. Chipman (1965a) dubbed this phenomenon 'Pareto's paradox'. Pareto referred to a footnote where Ricardo illustrated comparative advantage with the example of two men, one of whom exceeds his competitor by one-fifth in making hats and one-third in making shoes. Ricardo (1951a, p. 136n) had asked: 'will it not be for the interest of both, that the superior man should employ himself exclusively in making shoes, and the inferior man in making hats?'[19] In response, Pareto argued that this was a possible but not a necessary outcome. He showed by a numerical example that the output of one of the commodities can decline if specialization occurs, and that the larger output of the other commodity may not offer a sufficient compensation for this.

Chipman (1965a) subsequently demonstrated, in the case where each individual devotes half of his expenditure to each good, that Pareto's criterion that the world vector of commodity outputs with full specialization exceeds the world vector of pre-trade outputs is equivalent to 'Mill's inequality'. The latter, described in Chapter 6 and applied here to two individuals rather than two countries, states that the maximum output of the good in which each person has a comparative advantage exceeds the other person's maximum output of the same good. In light of the critique which Chipman's assumption of the putative form of Mill's utility function attracted and his subsequent retraction of it, it should be noted that even if individuals spend different fractions of their incomes on each good according to Cobb–Douglas utility functions, complete specialization by both of them, implied by inequality (6.3), is optimal if and only if the resulting output of each good exceeds the amount they jointly produced before trading with each other.

Let the maximal amounts of goods A and B producible by individuals I and II be (a', b') and (a'', b''), and let the fractions of time they spend producing these goods before trade be $(1 - \theta', \theta')$ and $(1 - \theta'', \theta'')$.[20] Let $a''/b'' > a'/b'$, so that individual I has a comparative advantage in good B, and assume both individuals to specialize after trade. Following Pareto (1971, p. 370n), the total output of each good exceeds that produced before trade if

$$a'' > (1 - \theta')a' + (1 - \theta'')a'' \tag{7.5}$$

and

$$b' > \theta' b' + \theta'' b''. \tag{7.6}$$

These inequalities can be combined to yield

$$b'/b'' > \theta''/(1 - \theta') > a'/a''. \tag{7.7}$$

Although Pareto did not derive from specific utility functions the fractions of time that the individuals spend producing the two goods in autarky, these fractions can be interpreted as the exponents (α', β') and (α'', β'') of the consumption of these goods in Cobb–Douglas utility functions. (7.7) then becomes

$$a''/b'' > \beta''a''/\alpha' b' > a'/b', \tag{7.8}$$

which is equivalent to (6.3) if the latter is interpreted as a pair of strong rather than weak inequalities. Pareto's criterion (or the absence of Pareto's paradox), stipulating that the world output of each good under full specialization exceeds its value under autarky, thus implies that individuals who spend constant (though different) fractions of their incomes on the two commodities find it optimal to become fully specialized. The assumption of unitary elasticity of substitution in consumption that underlies the above utility functions is of course very restrictive. Extending Pareto's reasoning in terms of individuals to countries, Chipman noted that

> Pareto stated his conditions as necessary ones, but they are neither necessary nor sufficient in general. That is, even if Pareto's criterion is satisfied, if the elasticity of substitution is small enough it will still be necessary for one country to produce both commodities; and conversely, even if Pareto's criterion is not satisfied, provided the elasticity of substitution is large enough, it may still happen that equilibrium is characterized by complete specialization. (Chipman, 1965a, p. 489)

Free trade or protection?

In his 1895 article and again in the *Cours* (Pareto, 1897, pp. 222–7), Pareto derived the welfare implications of his trade model. He used his equations of welfare change to argue that protectionism amounts to a 'destruction of wealth' owing to the 'sacrifices of ophelimity' occasioned by the increase in the factor services needed to produce the same consumption bundle as before. His position on the advantages of free trade was unequivocal. Though he agreed with Edgeworth (1894), whose offer curve diagram he reproduced, that if the foreign country's offer curve is inelastic a tariff can be beneficial to the home country, he added that 'if such cases are possible in theory, they are not equally so in practice' (Pareto, 1895, p. 498). In the *Cours* (pp. 228–9) Pareto warned that even monopolies are subject to competition from substitute products.

A few pages later, Pareto italicized the following proposition: '*it follows that if you want to protect an industry it is preferable, from the strictly economic viewpoint, to provide it with a direct subsidy rather than a protective duty*' (p. 232). This exemplifies what has been called the 'specificity rule' for economic policymaking, that 'it is more efficient to use policy tools that are closest to the sources of the distortions separating private and social benefits and costs. Intervene at the source' (Lindert, 1986, p. 149). It echoes the analogous prescriptions of Alexander Hamilton and John Rae.[21]

Given the uncompromising support for free trade that Pareto expressed in his early writings, it is interesting to trace the evolution of his thought to the much more modulated attitude that he displayed in the *Manual* and in his later sociological writings. This derives from his changed attitude towards *laissez-faire*, a methodological metamorphosis described by Tarascio as follows:

Pareto himself was dissatisfied with the *Cours*, as evidenced by his refusal to sanction a reprint and also by his self-criticism in the Preface of the *Manuale di economia politica*, wherein he referred to himself as the 'author of the *Cours.*' His main criticism of his earlier work, and perhaps the most devastating he could make from his own point of view, was that he had allowed sentiment to interfere with scientific objectivity. (Tarascio, 1968, p. 44)

In the *Manual*, Pareto noted that the growth of industry can be promoted by either protectionism (as in Russia) or free trade (as in England). Indeed, he put the choice of a trade regime as an open question to be decided on the merits of the case:

From all the preceding it can be seen how complex is the practical and synthetic problem of knowing whether protection is preferable to free trade or *vice versa*. In this general form, the problem is insoluble anyway because it has no precise meaning. It is [instead] necessary to [consider a particular] problem, which can be expressed thus: given all the economic and social conditions of a country at a given time, to find, for that country at that time, which system is preferable, protection or free trade. The following reasoning is incorrect because it neglects some essential conditions of the problem: protection entails a destruction of wealth, accordingly in every era and for every country protection is detrimental and free trade advantageous. (Pareto, 1971, p. 377)

Pareto emphasized that a country's choice of a trade regime does not determine its prosperity or stagnation: 'It is not possible to judge the effect[s] of protection, or of free trade, by comparing the countries where they exist, because these countries differ on many other points' (p. 381). He then singled out the following statement he had made in the *Cours* (1897, p. 240) as incorrect:

'England, thanks to its faithfulness to the principles of liberal political economy, continues to see its prosperity increase....' The author was wrong to accept, without submitting it to a sufficiently strict examination, a proposition current among the liberal economists and which seemed to them to [be axiomatic]. Moreover ... the author should not have been so positive about the fidelity of England to the principles of liberal economics. (Pareto, 1971, p. 382)

Pareto's agnostic stance in the *Manual* towards the relative benefits of free trade and protectionism was in line with the ethical neutrality he had started to advocate. He now envisaged the choice of a trade regime as the pragmatic solution of a choice problem involving non-economic as well as economic variables. Even though he had begun to modify his views towards free trade, Pareto noted in the *Manual* that it has been said that protection could be useful to protect infant industries, which, later, having become adult, would no longer need it. It cannot be denied *a priori* that such could sometimes be the case, but there is no known example of it. All the industries born under a system of protection have always sought more and more protection, and the day has never come when they declared they could do without it. (Pareto, 1971, p. 375)

In his last major mature work, the *Trattato di sociologia generale*, he modified even that position, noting that

the increase in economic production may be great enough to exceed the destruction of wealth caused by protection; so that, sum total, protection may yield a profit and not a loss in wealth; it may therefore prove (though not necessarily so) that the economic prosperity of a country has been enhanced by industrial protection. (Pareto, 1935, pp. 1549–50)

Hamilton, Rae and List would have agreed wholeheartedly with Pareto's revised position.

Concluding observations

Whether we stress his contributions as a general equilibrium theorist, welfare economist or perceptive sociologist, Pareto's performance in the area of international trade theory and policy commands respectful attention. The breadth of his interests goes a long way to compensate for certain flaws which have been pointed out, such as his presuming that matching the numbers of equations and unknowns is sufficient to determine a general equilibrium solution which makes economic sense for two trading economies. Pareto's general equilibrium model of trade between two countries, comprising many consumers, commodities and factors of production, remains his most impressive achievement. His critique of classical trade theory has helped to elucidate the conditions under which complete specialization in Ricardo's trade model leads to an increase in welfare. Pareto's utilization of the Ricardian model (despite its limitations) has a decidedly modern flavor, since he used it to show that more advanced economies (such as the Europe of his day), freely trading with the less developed Asian ones, can compete with them despite their higher wages.

Among the welfare implications that Pareto drew from his trade theory was his latter-day realization that the choice between free trade and protection should be made on pragmatic grounds, by maximizing welfare broadly defined so as to include non-economic as well as economic variables. His changed outlook towards protection aptly illustrates his methodological metamorphosis from a *laissez-faire* economist to one wishing to free himself from ethical preconceptions. As pointed out in Maneschi (1993b), Pareto anticipated the basic ideas underlying the political economy of protection that were rediscovered 50 years later by public choice theorists such as Downs, Buchanan, Tullock and Olson. The notion that protection is endogenously determined, in terms of the economic rewards which its expected beneficiaries hope to reap from it, came naturally to a keen observer of sociological phenomena such as Pareto. A final bonus associated with Pareto's discussion of protectionism was his articulation of a proposition rediscovered (also 50 years later) by Lipsey and Lancaster (1956), and named the theory of second best.

7.3 Enrico Barone's pioneering diagram of neoclassical trade equilibrium

Vilfredo Pareto's friend and follower Enrico Barone is best known to the economics profession for his 1908 paper in the *Giornale degli Economisti* on 'The Ministry of Production in the Collectivist State', which appeared in an English translation in Hayek (1935). Through a system of equations, Barone 'established the formal equivalence of the basic economic categories between a society based on private ownership in perfectly competitive conditions and a socialist society' (Caffè, 1987, p. 195). 1908 was a banner year for Barone, for that was also the year of publication of his *Principi di Economia Politica*, a textbook written in a simple style for beginners. Trade theorists are acquainted with this textbook mainly because of its back-to-back supply and demand curves for a particular commodity in two trading markets, in which one country's exports equal the other's imports, and transport costs are equated to the vertical distance between the origins of the two quadrants of the diagram. Although such diagrams had been developed earlier by Cunynghame and have a partial equilibrium character, Barone used them effectively for the pedagogical purpose of illustrating the gains from trade.[22] An even more notable contribution found in the same chapter on foreign trade of the *Principi* was the first general equilibrium diagram of a neoclassical economy in autarky and in trade, outlining both the changes in resource allocation and the gains brought by trade. Before Barone's diagram was brought to the profession's attention,[23] the first such diagram was reputed to have been presented in a lecture given by Viner in 1931 (as outlined in Viner, 1937), soon followed by Lerner (1932, 1934) and Leontief (1933). Barone's diagram illustrated the trade equilibrium of a small country facing given terms of trade rather than that of two trading economies as in the diagrams of Lerner and Leontief. This was also the first occasion when the graph of a community's production possibility frontier appeared in print, although there had been anticipations of

Figure 7.3   Barone's 1908 neoclassical trade diagram

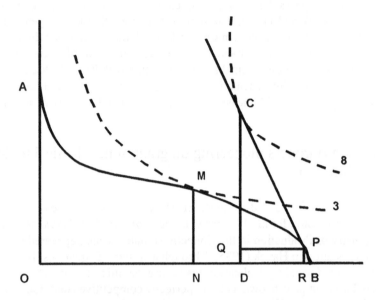

it in Pareto's *Manual*. It was previously believed that this curve was invented much later by Young (1928) or Haberler (1930, 1933).

Barone's diagram was embedded in a long footnote which followed his discussion of the Ricardian theory of comparative costs. It was preceded in this footnote by two of its building blocks. The first was the production possibility frontier AB (which Barone called the 'curve of indifference of production'), indicating all possible transformations of good A, plotted on the vertical axis, into good B, plotted on the horizontal axis.[24] Although labor was the only factor of production he considered, Barone assumed that the rate of transformation was not constant. His production possibility frontier is peculiar in that it shows a convex region of increasing returns followed by a concave region of decreasing returns. Barone did not explain the reason for this particular nonlinear shape, but was not dogmatic about it since it 'could be that shown or another' (Barone, 1908, p. 89).[25] If the economy produces MN of good A and ON of good B, the slope of the tangent at point M indicates the economy's 'comparative cost'. Barone then drew a diagram with two indifference curves ('curves of indifference of tastes') and explained how the transition from the lower to the higher one is associated with an increase of welfare. His third and final diagram, shown in Figure 7.3, combined the previous two diagrams, and showed the transition from autarky equilibrium at point M to trade equilibrium at points P ('production point') and C ('consumption point'). He also indicated the trade triangle CQP, where exports QP of good B pay for imports CQ of good A. The increase in welfare made possible by trade is shown by the passage from the indifference curve tangent to AB at point M, indexed 3, to that tangent to CP at C, indexed 8. In order for trade to be possible, Barone assumed the existence of a 'gap' between the slopes of PC and of the tangent at M. He called his diagram 'a more complete exposition of the theorem of comparative costs'.[26]

In the Preface to his *Principi*, Barone (1908, p. 6) explained that 'one of the purposes I have constantly had in mind in this elementary course has been to give a relatively extensive treatment to what we can call *dynamic* phenomena, because they essentially represent reality'. He went on (pp. 6–7) to compare the market to a large and very complicated machine subject to a large amount of 'friction'. A dislocation of any of its component parts does not lead to an instantaneous shift to a new point of equilibrium but by a slow and gradual displacement towards it, and it may never be reached because of a new disturbance to the system. It is essential to study both the general equilibrium configuration of the mechanism in question and the dynamic phenomenon of adjustment to disturbances, since a failure to do so can lead to conclusions that are very far from reality.

In his foreign trade chapter, Barone provided an illustration of the need to take dynamic factors into account when he evaluated the relative advantages of free trade and protection in the presence of terms of trade fluctuations. The latter are not a cause for concern if, as shown in Figure 7.3, there is a sizable gap between the terms of trade PC and the comparative cost ratio given by the slope of AB at point M. While fluctuations in the terms of trade, given by the slope of PC, change the location of point P, they do not alter the direction of trade. But if the difference between PC and the tangent at M is small, slight shifts in PC can move P alternately to the left and right of M, causing the desired direction of trade to change. But the capital invested in A or in B is not easily disinvested when such reversals of comparative advantage occur. The negative rents accruing alternately to A-capital and to B-capital can lead to a destruction of wealth considerably greater than that caused by protection (Barone, 1908, p. 97).

As an example of the dilemma that a country may face, Barone cited one whose economic structure is halfway between that of an advanced industrial country and that of a country with a developed agricultural sector. A slight rise in the price of agricultural goods would lead it to close factories and bring previously abandoned land into cultivation; and a slight fall in this price to abandon the land and establish new factories. Such fluctuations in the terms of trade cause not only a wastage of capital but a reluctance to invest new savings; hence 'a societal damage compared to which the one resulting from protection can sometimes be the lesser evil. This is one of those many cases, in which not taking into account the *dynamic* facts and limiting oneself only to the consideration of *equilibrium*, can lead to conclusions which diverge very much from reality (see *Preface*)' (Barone, 1908, p. 95).

Barone had previously used his back-to-back trade diagrams to measure the deadweight losses caused by prohibitive duties as well as more moderate ones, and noted that such duties always cause a 'destruction of wealth'. But such destruction must be set against any benefits, or prevention of losses, which protection may entail. One of these may be the government revenue brought by a duty; another, the possible lowering of the import price (though Barone did not take this terms of trade improvement to its logical conclusion, the concept of the optimal tariff); a third, the prevention of devastating terms of trade fluctuations. Barone heartily endorsed Pareto's rejection (cited in the previous section) of the blanket statement that free trade is advantageous and protection harmful to *any* country at *any* time. Dynamic factors 'temper greatly the free trade thesis and explain how, even through simple considerations of an economic nature, one cannot erect free trade to an absolute dogma, without taking into account the special conditions in which a *given* country finds itself at a *given* time' (Barone, 1908, p. 96).

In spite of his quintessentially neoclassical trade diagram, we are thus led to a much more qualified view of Barone's neoclassicism. He did not share the neoclassical faith in a purely mechanistic view of the economic phenomenon, which implies that any economic transformation caused by a change in economic conditions can be simply reversed by an equal and opposite change.[27] He attached instead much importance to the frictions rampant throughout the economic system, and his outlook was self-consciously dynamic rather than static. His support for protection under certain circumstances had nothing in common with the protectionist positions advocated by Alexander Hamilton, John Rae or Friedrich List. But like them and like Pareto, Enrico Barone evinced an open mind towards a policy like free trade, and an appreciation of the gap which can easily intrude between an economic model and the reality it is designed to portray.

Appendix: Comparative advantage in the multicommodity Ricardian model

Adopting a different and more general notation than that used in section 7.1, assume that the home (H) and foreign (F) countries, denoted by lower- and upper-case letters respectively, can potentially produce n commodities with fixed labor coefficients per unit of output given by $a = (a_1, ..., a_n)$ and $A = (A_1, ..., A_n)$. Number commodities in decreasing order of the home country's comparative advantage, so that

$$\frac{a_1}{A_1} < \frac{a_2}{A_2} < \cdots < \frac{a_k}{A_k} < \frac{a_{k+1}}{A_{k+1}} < \cdots < \frac{a_n}{A_n}. \qquad (A7.1)$$

Let w and W be the wage rates in H and F, and let superscripts a and t refer to the autarky and trade equilibria. Assume that when free trade is established

$$\frac{a_k}{A_k} < \frac{W^t}{w^t} < \frac{a_{k+1}}{A_{k+1}}, \qquad (A7.2)$$

so that commodity k $(k+1)$ is the Home (Foreign) country's *borderline* export commodity, a term which designates the commodity in which each country's comparative advantage is least. Choose k as the numeraire good. Since k is produced in H both before and after trade, and in F before (but not after) trade, we have

$$w^a a_k = w^t a_k = W^a A_k = 1, \qquad (A7.3)$$

so that

$$w^a = w^t = 1/a_k \qquad (A7.4)$$

and

$$W^a = 1/A_k. \qquad (A7.5)$$

The n-commodity autarky price vectors of H and F, p^a and P^a, are given by

$$p^a = w^a a \qquad (A7.6)$$

and

$$P^a = W^a A. \qquad (A7.7)$$

If $m = (m_i)$ is H's net import vector, and we substitute (A7.4) into (A7.6) and (A7.5) into (A7.7), we obtain

$$(p^a - P^a)m = \left(\frac{a}{a_k} - \frac{A}{A_k} \right) m = \sum_{i=1}^{n} \frac{A_i}{a_k} \left(\frac{a_i}{A_i} - \frac{a_k}{A_k} \right) m_i. \qquad \text{(A7.8)}$$

If $i < k$, the ith term in parentheses after the summation sign in (A7.8) can be seen from (A7.1) to be negative while, from (A7.1) and (A7.2), $m_i < 0$ since $w^t a_i < W^t A_i$. Hence all terms in (A7.8) relating to $i < k$ are positive. If $i = k$, the corresponding term in parentheses in (A7.8) is zero, so that its product with $m_k < 0$ is zero. For commodities indexed $i > k$, the ith term in parentheses is seen from (A7.1) to be positive while, from (A7.1) and (A7.2), $m_i > 0$ since $w^t a_i > W^t A_i$. Hence terms corresponding to commodities for which $i > k$ are positive. Since $(n - 1)$ of the terms of the summation on the RHS of (A7.8) are positive and the kth term is zero, the inner product $(p^a - P^a)m$ is strictly positive. This confirms the validity of the DDN theorem for the Ricardian multicommodity model.[28] This result is much stronger than that generally found in a multicommodity neoclassical trade model, where (as discussed and illustrated in Chapter 2) the inner product of these vectors is positive even though some of its elements may be negative.

Define $\pi_i = p_i^a / p_i^t$ to be the ratio between the autarky and the world price of commodity i in the home country, $\Pi_i = P_i^a / p_i^t$ the corresponding ratio in the foreign country, and $\pi = (\pi_i)$ and $\Pi = (\Pi_i)$ the vectors containing them. We obtain

$$(p^a - P^a)m = \sum_{i=1}^{i=n} (p_i^a - P_i^a)m_i = \sum_{i=n}^{i=1} (\pi_i - \Pi_i)p_i^t m_i = \sum_{i=n}^{i=1} (\pi_i - \Pi_i)V_{mi},$$

$$\text{(A7.9)}$$

where $V_{mi} = p_i^t m_i$ and $V_m = (V_{mi})$ is the vector of H's net imports valued at world prices. As pointed out in Chapter 2, the positive correlation between $(p^a - P^a)$ and m implies, by a simple extension of corollary 1 of Deardorff (1980, pp. 950–52), a positive correlation between $(\pi - \Pi)$ and V_m. This is illustrated in Figure A7.1, where the vertical axis measures $(\pi_i - \Pi_i)$ and the horizontal axis V_{mi}. The NE quadrant contains points relating to commodities $(k + 1)$ through n for which F has lower autarky prices, leading it to export them. The SW quadrant contains points relating to commodities 1 through $(k - 1)$ for which H has the lower autarky price, and which it exports. Since the numeraire commodity k entails $p^a_k = P^a_k$, the point corresponding to it lies on the horizontal axis, to the left of the origin since $m_k < 0$.

Consider now, as choice of numeraire, not a borderline commodity, but commodity 1 in which the home country's comparative advantage is greatest. Following the same procedure as above, it can be shown that H has no commodities whose autarky price is lower than F's, and that $(k - 1)$ of its k export goods have higher autarky prices. To comply with the DDN theorem, the sum of the $(n - k)$ positive elements in (A7.9) relating to commodities $(k + 1)$ through n must be larger in absolute size than the sum of its $(k - 1)$ negative ones relating to commodities 2 through k. This is illustrated in Figure (A7.2), where the point corresponding to the numeraire commodity 1 lies on the horizontal axis to the left the origin. While the points corresponding to F's export commodities continue to be in the NE quadrant, those corresponding to H's export commodities 2 through k are now found in the NW quadrant. Inequality (A7.9) implies that the sum of the areas of the rectangles (not drawn) subtended by the points in the NE quadrant must exceed that of the rectangles subtended by the points in the NW quadrant. Since the trade balance condition implies that the sum of the bases of these imaginary rectangles in the NE quadrant equals the sum of their bases in the NW quadrant, the import-weighted average height of these rectangles in the NE quadrant must exceed the export-weighted average height of the corresponding rectangles in the NW quadrant. In other words, on average the autarky prices of the home country's imports exceed the foreign country's autarky prices by a larger margin than in the case of its exports.

Similar results to those in the Ricardian model with a finite number of commodities follow in the Ricardian model of Dornbusch, Fischer and Samuelson (1977) for a continuum of commodities indexed over the closed interval $[0, 1]$. If commodity k is the common borderline commodity of the two countries, and is used as the numeraire, the prices of all H's or F's export commodities are lower in autarky than the other country's, leading to identical signs for corresponding components of the vectors $(p^a - P^a)$ and m, and hence to a positive value of $(p^a - P^a)m$.

Figure A7.1 Correlation between autarky prices and net import values when borderline commodity k *is numeraire*

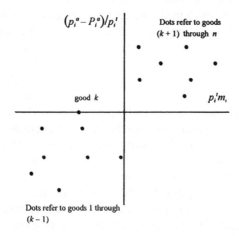

Figure A7.2 Correlation between autarky prices and net import values when commodity 1 *is numeraire*

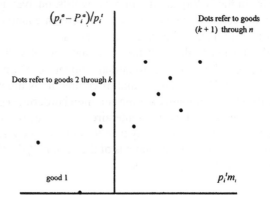

Notes

1. As mentioned in Chapter 6, Whewell as well as Marshall attempted to translate Mill's theory of international values into mathematics, but Marshall ignored Whewell in his writings.
2. When he consolidated his three-part article, Edgeworth (1925) omitted the lengthy footnote in which he interpreted Mill's numerical examples with diagrams.
3. Not everyone became converted to the use of offer curves in analyzing international trade problems. While acknowledging the appeal of the symmetry of offer curves, where each axis measures the quantity of a commodity, Viner (1937, p. 542) 'found it much more convenient as a rule to follow the procedure which Marshall rejects, i.e., to make the vertical axis represent terms of trade rather than the total quantity of one of the commodities', yielding what Viner referred to as 'terms-of-trade diagrams'.
4. Marshall's offer curve was later extended to show two branches in the first and third (or second and fourth) quadrants as shown in Figure 2.1, where the second branch illustrates a reversal of comparative advantage. Since Marshall did not associate comparative advantage with his offer curves, it is not surprising that he did not discover this second branch.
5. Marshall did not take his own advice that 'some writers have however laid so much stress on the word "demand" in [the phrase "reciprocal demand"], as to imply that the problem of international trade is one of demand rather than supply: and this is a reason for emphasizing the interdependence of supply and demand' (Marshall, 1923, p. 161).
6. A scholar who studied Marshall in depth observed that 'the main purpose of this theoretical apparatus [of offer curves] was to examine the effects of tariffs' (Whitaker, 1987, p. 361).
7. After referring to Marshall (1879), Hicks (1946, p. 61) stated laconically that 'Marshall's theory is repeated, but without gain in clarity, in *Money Credit and Commerce*, Appendix'.
8. Graham's critique gave rise to several rejoinders. His views and those of his opponents are summarized in Viner (1937, pp. 448–51, 548–55), Chipman (1965a, 493–5), Caves (1960, 44–57) and Gomes (1990, chapter 6).
9. Marshall was subsequently criticized for resurrecting in this appendix the Ricardian theory that he had endeavored to modify in his other writings. Thus Mason, as cited by Haberler (1930, pp. 356–7), commented that 'it seems strange, upon the appearance of his last book, to find [Marshall] clinging to a branch of the tree which he had himself already cut off some years before' (Mason, 1926, p. 86).
10. This was not noted by Edgeworth and Viner, who did not assume inequality (7.1), nor by Haberler, who assumed the existence of a chain of comparative advantage but did not use Edgeworth's diagram. While in Figure 7.2 the distances between a, b, c, ... compared to those between a', b', c', ... measure *comparative* advantage, the distances of these points from their respective origins measure *absolute* advantage. Thus $o'a'$ exceeds or falls short of oa according as country I has an absolute advantage or an *absolute* disadvantage over country II in commodity A, the commodity in which its *comparative* disadvantage is greatest.
11. Maneschi (1993b) contains a fuller discussion of Pareto's approach to trade theory and policy.
12. Pareto's name figures in trade-theoretic articles usually combined with the word 'optimum', as if the concept of a 'Pareto optimum' constituted the be-all and end-all of Pareto's contribution. This parallels Pareto's fame as a general economic theorist, of which it has been said that 'it is disappointing that this reputation should be constructed on the basis of such a small part of his work' (Kirman, 1987, p. 808).
13. One reason for Pareto's neglect as a trade theorist may be that the *Giornale degli Economisti* papers in which he first elaborated his theory have never been translated into English.
14. Translations from Pareto (1894, 1895, 1897) are by the author. With regard to the *Manual*, it is unfortunate, as Jaffé has noted, that its English version (Pareto, 1971) was translated from the French *Manuel* rather than the Italian *Manuale*, since the *Manuel* is itself a poor translation of the Italian original, except for the completely rewritten Appendix and for certain other revised passages. 'A consequence of this dereliction has been to turn several of Pareto's often

exasperatingly difficult, but still coherent, analytical passages into gibberish' (Jaffé, 1972, pp. 1194–5). In quoting from Pareto (1971), I have therefore taken the liberty of substituting in square brackets my own translations of certain passages in the *Manuale*.

15. Five years earlier Edgeworth had shown respect for the general equilibrium approach when he stated that 'the great lesson to be learnt is this. The equations are *simultaneous*, and their solutions *determinate*. That the factors of economic equilibrium are simultaneously determined is a conception which few of the literary school have received' (cited in Chipman, 1965b, p. 715).

16. As the successor (and former student) of Marshall in Cambridge stated, 'in [Marshall's] own practice, even where he had worked something out with the help of mathematical machinery, he was at immense pains to wrap up the mathematical skeleton of his argument, so that the timid should not know it was there' (Pigou, 1953, p. 6).

17. Ohlin (1933, pp. 565–6) commented that even though Pareto 'does not formally reject the Ricardian doctrine of comparative costs ... Pareto's doctrine is fundamentally different from Ricardo's and that of the later classical writers. Pareto rejected all attempts to measure costs in objective terms, i.e., he discarded the basis of the whole classical theory of value'. However, he was skeptical about Pareto's concept of ophelimity and did not use it in his book.

18. Recall that Pareto had similarly agreed that Edgeworth's offer curve diagram was preferable to his own equations for the pedagogical aim of illustrating a trade equilibrium.

19. Ricardo's footnote was discussed in endnote 12 of Chapter 4 in connection with the generalization to two countries of Ricardo's example of specialization by two individuals.

20. I have changed Pareto's notation for the maximal amounts of the two commodities which the individuals can produce. Pareto used the values $a' = x$, $b' = y$, $a'' = 1$, $b'' = 1$.

21. This proposition was stated by Meade (1955) and illustrated graphically by Corden (1957). It was then generalized by Johnson, who showed that '[domestic] distortions do not logically lead to the recommendation of protection, in the sense of taxes on international trade; instead, they lead to the recommendation of other forms of government intervention which do not discriminate between domestic and international trade and which differ according to the nature of the distortion they are intended to correct...[This proposition] follows directly from the well-known first-order conditions of Pareto optimality' (Johnson, 1965, pp. 5, 9). None of these authors seemed aware that particular examples of this proposition, such as that relating to infant industries, had been anticipated by other writers.

22. Barone's diagram and some theoretical objections to it are set out in Viner (1937, pp. 589–91).

23. Maneschi and Thweatt (1987).

24. Translations from Barone (1908) are the author's.

25. Since the equilibrium occurs on the concave part of the production possibility frontier, its convex section can be neglected. Curves with a similar nonlinear shape were subsequently presented by Young (1928) and Tinbergen (1945) to depict a commodity produced under decreasing costs and another produced under increasing costs. Tinbergen's diagram was designed to illustrate Graham's contention that the protection of a decreasing cost industry may be beneficial. On this, see Caves (1960, pp. 169–74), who reproduces Tinbergen's diagram.

26. Barone's entire footnote is translated in Maneschi and Thweatt (1987), who also comment on priorities in formulating the neoclassical international trade diagram.

27. In discussing neoclassical methodology, Georgescu–Roegen (1966, p. 18) has noted that 'no other science illustrates better than economics the impact of the enthusiasm for mechanistic epistemology upon its evolution'.

28. Note that the above result also holds if the $(k + 1)$th commodity, the borderline export commodity of F, is chosen as numeraire. The proof follows as before, *mutatis mutandis*. If both countries produce commodity k in the trade equilibrium, m_k is unsigned but the term in parentheses corresponding to kth commodity in (A7.8) is zero, so that the kth term of the summation is again zero.

8. Neoclassical Trade Theory: Gottfried Haberler, Eli Heckscher and Bertil Ohlin

The first half of the 1930s signaled an important turning point in the history of international trade theory. The twin peaks of what Gomes (1990, p. 102) has referred to as 'the 1930s watershed' are two books published in the same year, Haberler (1933) and Ohlin (1933). The first was written in German and appeared in an English translation in 1936 with the title *The Theory of International Trade with its Application to Commercial Policy*. Bertil Ohlin's *Interregional and International Trade* had a more immediate international impact since it was published in English. The twin peaks in question were preceded by several smaller pinnacles. Haberler anticipated the key trade-theoretical chapter 12 of his book with a paper (Haberler, 1930) which generalized the constant-cost assumption of the Ricardian comparative advantage model to the case of increasing costs, attracting the attention of economists such as Lerner. Ohlin's book was inspired by the other founding document of the Heckscher–Ohlin theory, a paper published in Swedish by Eli Heckscher 14 years earlier in 1919. Another anticipation of Ohlin's 1933 book was his 1924 doctoral dissertation entitled *Handelns Teori*, which has only recently been translated into English as *The Theory of Trade* (Ohlin, 1991).

While the books of Haberler and Ohlin molded subsequent developments in trade theory, most of the profession regards Ohlin's (elaborating Heckscher's insights) as the more significant of the two. It inspired the Heckscher–Ohlin–Samuelson (H–O–S) theory which emerged as the mainstream theory of trade after World War Two thanks to a series of papers by Paul Samuelson and others (Samuelson, 1948, 1949; Stolper and Samuelson, [1941] 1949; Rybczynski, 1955). These greatly simplified Ohlin's factor endowment theory, and made it both more rigorous and capable of being illustrated graphically. Chipman (1965a, p. 479) has referred to the H–O–S paradigm as 'probably the most complex and impressive theoretical structure that has yet been developed in economic thought'. But he is also a strong supporter of Haberler, whose 1930 'reformulation of the theory of comparative costs ... revolutionized the theory of international trade' (Chipman, 1987, p. 581). Haberler is well known to trade theorists not only for his book on trade theory, but for several influential papers including 'Some Problems in the Pure Theory of International Trade' (Haberler, [1950] 1968) and *A Survey of International Trade Theory* (Haberler, 1961). Chapter 12 of his book went beyond his 1930 paper in several respects, such as the construction of a model based on specific factors of production, that is, on factors which can be used in some sectors of the economy but not in others. The distributional implications which Haberler derived from his model are reflected in what has appropriately been called the 'Haberler theorem' (Kenen, 1994). Although Haberler did not specify his model mathematically, this was accomplished many years later by Samuelson (1971) and Jones (1971). The specific-factors model has been an important addition to the trade literature, and has spawned an empirically fruitful literature centering on its 'Dutch disease' variant.

Because of the differences in outlook and approach between Haberler on the one hand, and Heckscher and Ohlin on the other, some may question juxtaposing their names in a chapter devoted to the second generation of pioneers of neoclassical trade theory. In his magisterial three-part survey of trade theory, Chipman referred to Haberler's theory as a strand of 'The Neo-classical Theory' (Chipman, 1965b) and to Heckscher–Ohlin's as 'The Modern Theory' (Chipman, 1966). But both theories can be called 'neoclassical' since, as discussed below, they are applications of the general equilibrium theory promulgated by one of the founders of neoclassical economics, Léon Walras.[1]

Section 8.1 begins with the generalization of the theory of comparative costs that Haberler introduced in 1930 and elaborated in his 1933 book. It compares the concave transformation curve he derived for this purpose with Barone's discussed in Chapter 7. The imperfect substitutability between commodities is conditioned by the presence of specific factors, and Haberler's role in pioneering the specific-factors model is stressed. Although Haberler's insights into the causes of comparative advantage did not go much further than Ricardo's, he deftly modeled how the passage of time affects an economy's trade equilibrium. This is manifested by a change in the curvature of the transformation curve, and hence in the opportunity cost of commodities, between the short run and the long run. Another example of the dynamics of Haberler's trade theory is his graphical depiction of the infant industry argument for protection.

The precursors of Heckscher and Ohlin are discussed in section 8.2, which argues that none of them went much beyond the rather obvious association of plentiful factors of production with the export of commodities in which these factors are embodied. Section 8.3 discusses Eli Heckscher's memorable paper of 1919 in which the outlines of what became the Heckscher–Ohlin theory of trade are set out in crisp and crystal-clear fashion. His paper contains ramifications of the theory that sometimes go beyond those found in Ohlin's magnum opus of 1933, which is examined in section 8.4 and compared to Heckscher's paper. That section goes on to discuss Ohlin's characterization of the theory of comparative costs as a *deus ex machina* and his disdain for the term 'comparative advantage', probably because of its association with that theory; the important subsidiary role played by economies of scale as a cause of trade; and the appendix of his book in which he formulated a general equilibrium model of two trading regions. The concluding section 8.5 evaluates the legacies of Haberler, Heckscher and Ohlin. The H–O–S model which was subsequently constructed on the basis of the insights of Heckscher and Ohlin is analyzed in Chapter 9.

8.1 Gottfried Haberler's defense and elaboration of comparative cost theory

Haberler's writings on the theory of international trade began with a spirited defense of the theory of comparative costs, combined with an extension of its basic underlying assumptions so as to make it compatible with contemporary developments in the neoclassical theory of value. His intention was not to overthrow the Ricardian theory, but to liberate it from the shackles of a discredited theory of value in order to reaffirm its validity. His attitude was thus diametrically opposed to that of Ohlin, who saw himself as a revolutionary anxious to introduce an alternative theory of trade in which comparative costs had no role to play.

In two of his earliest writings, Haberler (1929, 1930) defended the theory of comparative costs from some attacks launched against it. In his 1929 paper, he responded to a critique voiced by Angell (1926) regarding the stability of equilibrium in a two-commodity Ricardian model, and showed that a stable equilibrium results if the model is expanded to more than two commodities. He deflected another attack by Burns (1928) who, after rediscovering 'Pareto's paradox' discussed in Chapter 7, had mistakenly argued that it militated against free trade. In both these papers, and in greater detail in his 1933 book, Haberler advanced further than Edgeworth in extending the Ricardian model to many commodities, as was outlined in Chapter 7. He concluded his 1929 paper with the tantalizing remark that 'a much more serious objection' could be raised against the comparative cost theory, which he would voice on another occasion.

That occasion was a paper he wrote in German (Haberler, 1930), first translated into English as Haberler (1985a). His main purpose was to reformulate the theory of comparative costs so that it does not have to rely on an 'antiquated' labor theory of value. He argued that 'for the authors who reject the labor theory of value, the theory of comparative costs founders on the same cliffs as the former, that is, on the fact that there simply exists no units [sic] of real cost, neither in the shape of days of labor nor in any other shape' (1985a, pp. 7–8). The 'real cost' theory was briefly discussed in Chapter 7 in connection with Pareto's attack on its premises. It attributes the value of commodities to the disutility incurred in producing them, including labor effort and the alleged 'waiting' or 'abstinence' associated with the use of capital. Haberler rejected it in favor of the rival 'alternative cost' or 'opportunity cost' theory of the Austrian school, which postulates that a commodity is worth the value of the commodities which must be sacrificed in order to produce it.

Theorists such as Viner (1937, pp. 483–93, 508–26) who were sympathetic to the real cost approach criticized opportunity cost theorists for their lack of awareness of the special assumptions on which the validity of their theory depends. Haberler subsequently granted that his construction of a transformation curve depends crucially on assumptions such as perfect competition in product and factor markets, inelastic supplies of factors of production, and the indifference of factors to the industry which employs them. Samuelson (1948, p. 182) described the last two assumptions as 'empirically gratuitous'. In response, Haberler ([1950] 1968, p. 214n) aptly noted that Stolper and Samuelson ([1941] 1949) had also assumed inelastic factor supplies in their construction of a transformation curve via an Edgeworth–Bowley box diagram.[2] Viner, in turn, has agreed that certain elements of cost, such as land-use costs, have no 'real' counterpart and can only be measured in terms of opportunity cost. There has therefore been a convergence of views between these two schools of thought.[3]

Haberler's opportunity cost approach was embodied in what he termed the 'substitution curve', nowadays known as transformation curve or production possibility curve (or frontier), whose slope (as Barone had already noted in 1908) represents the opportunity cost of one commodity in terms of the other. In his 1930 paper, Haberler illustrated it for the cases of constant and increasing costs, as shown in panels (a) and (b) of Figure 8.1. His 'classical' (linear) production possibility frontier, now familiar from all textbooks in international trade, is shown in panel (a). Haberler drew two such frontiers, one for each trading country, and related their slopes to the labor theory of

Figure 8.1   Haberler's transformation curves: (a) classical, (b) neoclassical,
(c) specific-factors

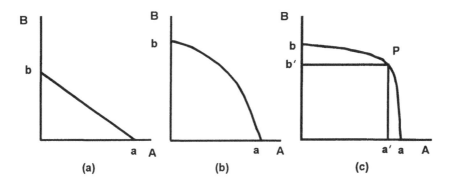

value since they equal the ratios of the unit labor coefficients of the two goods in the two countries. The curve shown in panel (b) generalizes the classical model by assuming that 'there are many means of production which cooperate in the production of goods A and B in different mixes, different according to type and volume of output'. The concave shape of this transformation curve illustrates 'the law of diminishing returns for A in terms of B and for B in terms of A' (1985a, p. 9). Haberler went on to note that the actual combination selected on the curve *ab* depends on demand, and that the relative price which prevails equals the slope of the transformation curve (or marginal rate of substitution) at that point.

It is instructive to compare Haberler's concave transformation curve with that which Barone had drawn twenty-two years earlier, shown in Figure 7.3. One difference is that Barone's curve, having an inflection point, was both convex and concave, though (as noted in section 7.3) this feature played no role in the equilibrium reached. Barone used his diagram to illustrate the economy's equilibrium both in autarky and in trade. He identified the post-trade consumption and production points, the associated trade triangle and the gains from trade, none of which appear in Haberler's diagrams. In a paper he wrote two decades later to survey the elaborations of the theory of international trade that had meanwhile occurred, Haberler did include consumption points, justifying their location by a vague appeal to 'demand conditions'. Unlike Barone and a host of economists who followed the lead of Lerner and Leontief, he scrupulously avoided the use of community indifference curves, noting that 'a shift in production will usually be accompanied by a redistribution of income. This precludes the uncritical application of community indifference curves' (Haberler, [1950] 1968, p. 215).

In the final section of his 1930 paper, Haberler argued that the existence of gains from trade does not depend on the mobility or specificity of the factors of production. He recognized that some factors are highly specific to their sectors and will be hurt by a shift in demand away from their products. In such cases the adverse distributional effects of free trade may make protectionism politically difficult to avoid. The degree of mobility of factors affects the shape of the transformation curve, but as long as at least one factor (likely to be labor) is mobile between sectors, 'there will always be a rate of substitution, albeit not necessarily a constant one' between commodities (1985a, p. 9). In sum, the theory of comparative costs remains valid in the presence of a multiplicity of factors of production, and its validity is not impugned either by the factors' degree of mobility or specificity, or (though Haberler here returned to the classical one-factor case) by the existence of more than two commodities.

Haberler's specific-factors model

In his 1933 book, Haberler presented his pure theory of trade in chapters 9–12. He discussed four theories that can account for trade flows: the Ricardian theory of comparative costs; that based on reciprocal demand, due to Marshall and J. S. Mill; Pareto's general equilibrium theory; and partial equilibrium models such as those used by Schüller and Barone.[4] His eclectic approach is shown by his assertion that 'these four theories are not mutually exclusive; on the contrary, they supplement one another' (Haberler, 1936, p. 123).

Haberler reiterated the intention expressed in his 1930 article that he wished to generalize, rather than reject, Ricardo's comparative cost theory. He accepted the latter as a 'provisional hypothesis', then proceeded to modify it by (1) introducing money, (2) extending it to more than two goods and more than two countries, (3) introducing transport costs, (4) allowing for increasing or decreasing (instead of constant) costs, (5) using offer curves to determine the terms of trade, and (6) postulating heterogeneous factors of production such as different qualities of labor and sector-specific factors. Chapter 12 of Haberler's book went much further than his 1930 paper in elaborating the nature of his basic model, and its implications for income distribution and trade policy. In connection with points (4) and (6), Haberler stressed that the specificity of factors causes the transformation curve to assume a concave shape.[5] As more of the mobile or non-specific factors are transferred from one sector to another, diminishing marginal returns appear in the latter matched by increasing marginal returns in the former. Because of increasing costs in the expanding sector, 'the division of labour will ... be carried less far than under constant costs' (1936, p. 143).

When the specific-factors model was formalized many years later, it is unfortunate that Jones (1971) and Samuelson (1971) neglected to mention Haberler's pioneering anticipation of their models.[6] One reason for Haberler's neglect as the inventor of the specific-factors model may be that his formulation lacked the mathematical underpinnings that are nowadays the *sine qua non* of models. But remarkably he was able to convey the essence of the model both verbally and diagrammatically (with the exception noted below), and to obtain short-run and long-run policy implications.[7] Jones (1971) called it originally a three-factor model, but it is now mostly referred to as the specific-factors model. Samuelson (1971, p. 367) named it, rather infelicitously, the 'Ricardo–Viner case'.[8] Some authors have even blurred the distinction between this model and the Heckscher–Ohlin model since they both give rise to a concave transformation curve.[9] The reasons for this concave shape are however quite different in the two models. In the specific-factors case, it is a question of variable marginal returns to the mobile factor when it is combined with the specific factors. In the H–O–S case, if two sectors use two factors in different proportions at a common factor-price ratio and one sector expands, its marginal cost rises since it needs to attract the factor it uses intensively from the other sector, bidding up its price.

In his 1933 book, in addition to the two types of transformation curve which he had presented in 1930, reproduced in panels (a) and (b) of Figure 8.1, Haberler added a third one designed to portray his specific-factors model, shown in panel (c). The bulge or kink at point P indicates the difficulty of substituting good A for good B in the short run, so that 'there will be a marked change in relative prices if an alteration in demand causes a shift in production'.[10] In general, the transformation curve is flatter 'the greater the proportion of the available factors which can be employed in producing either the one or the other commodity' and 'the longer the time allowed for production to adapt itself' in response to a disturbance. Although most means of production, even labor, are specific in the short run, 'in the long run ... [labor] is the least specific and most adaptable factor of all' (1936, pp. 178–9, 194).[11]

Unlike in models based on the labor theory of value, Haberler noted that in the specific-factors model the opening of trade leads to large changes in income distribution.[12] These are '(1) a rise in the prices of those factors which are specific to the export industries of a country... (2) a fall in the prices of whatever factors are specific to those industries in which the country has a comparative disadvantage... (3) a rise in the prices of non-specific factors ... since [trade] will increase the total output, but this rise will be less than the rise under (1)' (1936, pp. 193–4). These assertions should be compared with the more accurate ones contained in what Kenen appropriately denoted as the 'Haberler theorem':[13]

> A change in relative prices raises the real earnings of the factor used specifically in the industry whose output price has risen and reduces the real earnings of the factor used specifically in the industry whose output price has fallen. The real earnings of the mobile factor (labor) fall in terms of the good whose price has risen and rise in terms of the good whose price has fallen. (Kenen, 1994, p. 94)

In the simplest case where each of two factors is specific to a sector while another factor (say labor) is mobile between them, a rise in the price of one of the goods causes labor's wage to fall in terms of that good and to rise in terms of the other, so that the impact on the real wage is ambiguous. Haberler's conclusion that 'in the long run the working-class as a whole has nothing to fear from international trade' is comparable to a similar statement made by Ohlin (referred to in Chapter 9) and is equally unwarranted.[14] Haberler granted that trade may harm some non-competing groups of workers. Since these groups are examples of specific factors, in the short run they 'may suffer heavy reductions in income when for one reason or another they are faced with more intense foreign competition' (1936, p. 195). If wages are downwardly rigid, some factors can become chronically unemployed. Since the resulting fall in national income can be obviated by protection, Haberler allowed this as an exception to the general case in favor of free trade.

There are few hints in chapter 12 of a rationale for the comparative advantage which countries enjoy in certain goods. The only time Haberler ventured into this area was when he commented on Taussig's (1927) views regarding the influence of different types of labor supply on the pattern of trade:

> it is clear that [the nature of international trade] will be strongly influenced by the presence in one country of social strata and of closed groups of workers not present in other countries, if this results in an abundant and cheap supply of certain kinds of labour. Taussig gives as an example Germany's export of chemicals and especially of coal-tar products, which is largely due to the presence of an abundant supply of qualified chemists and trained assistants. (Haberler, 1936, p. 193)

The fact that certain non-competing groups of workers are 'not present in other countries' makes Taussig's explanation of trade consistent with that derived from a specific-factors model, but Haberler did not follow up on this hint with any general theory of comparative advantage. He merely added that while 'Taussig's exposition is most ingenious and persuasive ... the treatment of non-competing groups in the classical theory, even as he presents it, cannot be termed theoretically complete and systematic' (ibid.).

Haberler illustrated the Ricardian roots of his trade theory by starting with the classical comparative cost theory and generalizing it step by step until it merged with general equilibrium theory. Before expounding the classical theory, he warned that 'we shall end by discarding [the labor theory of value], with all its assumptions, without having to discard the results obtained from it: these will remain, just as a building remains after the scaffolding, having served its purpose, is removed' (1936, p. 126). His construction of a transformation curve based on increasing opportunity costs, far from invalidating, strengthened Ricardo's insights into the gains from specialization according to comparative advantage. The link between Haberler and Ricardo may be even closer than Haberler suspected. Following Findlay (1974), Chapter 4 formulated the Ricardian system as a simplified form of a specific-factors model consisting of an agricultural sector and a manufacturing sector. Labor is the mobile factor common to both sectors, land is specific to agriculture and no factor is specific to manufacturing, so that the returns to labor in it are constant. As Findlay showed, these assumptions yield a concave transformation curve, analogous to that derived by Haberler in 1930. Factor specificity seems a natural assumption to make in a Ricardian system formulated along these lines, since Haberler (1936, p. 194) noted that 'in the long run, material means of production which are highly specific are found mainly in agriculture and consist of land of various qualities and of natural resources of all kinds.... In other spheres, such as manufacturing and commerce and transport, highly specific material factors play only a minor part in the long run'. Findlay's model, as well as the dynamic model of Ricardian trade presented in section 4.4, thus combine Haberler's as well as Ricardo's insights.

Dynamics of Haberler's trade theory

Haberler offered some original insights into the short-run as well as long-run implications of protection and free trade for resource allocation, income distribution and national welfare. Already in 1930, he had pointed out that the transformation curve was likely to be flatter in the long run than in the short run. The reason, elaborated in his book, is that factor mobility is much smaller in the short run when factors tend to be more sector-specific. Since different time horizons must be taken into account, 'our doctrine is by no means a purely static one. It does not relate only to a hypothetical final equilibrium, in which there is no incentive for further movements of factors between industries. It applies also to short periods' (1936, p. 179).

Figure 8.2   (a) Haberler's short-run and long-run transformation curves,
*   (b) the infant-industry argument*

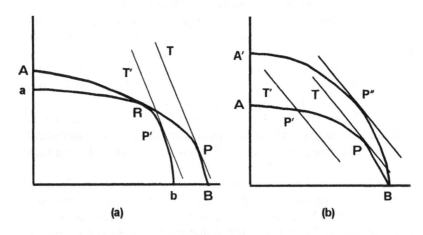

Haberler ([1950] 1968) represented this graphically as shown in panel (a) of Figure 8.2, where R is the economy's equilibrium point under autarky. If the opportunity to trade becomes available at the terms of trade shown by PT or P'T', and some factors of production are immobile in the short run, production moves to point P' on the inner transformation curve *ab*, while consumption goes to T'. In the long run, most factors become mobile and it becomes easier to transform good A into good B. The transformation curve becomes the outer curve AB, production moves to P and consumption to T.

The difference in curvature between the inner and the outer transformation curves depends on the degree of specificity or immobility of the factors of production. Haberler (1936, p. 179n) granted that 'the twofold division into short and long run is an oversimplification. As Marshall has suggested, we should assume a whole series of "runs" of different lengths'. Since Haberler had stressed this distinction between the short-run and long-run implications of his trade model already in the 1930s, it is surprising, as Mayer (1974, p. 955) noted, that standard trade models failed to make a similar distinction and remained static in nature. In this respect, Haberler's specific-factors model displays greater versatility than the H–O–S model.

Another example of dynamics in Haberler's trade theory is his analysis of the infant-industry argument for protection, for which he provided the diagram shown in panel (b) of Figure 8.2. The free trade equilibrium is shown by production at P on the transformation curve AB and consumption at T. If sector A is now protected with a duty and the terms of trade are constant, production in the short run shifts from P to P' and consumption from T to T'.

In the long run the protected industry become more productive and the transformation curve shifts out to A'B. If free trade is restored, the production point becomes P" while consumption may be on either side of P", allowing either good to be exported. The consumption point may even coincide with P", in which case all trade is eliminated. In any of these cases, the economy is clearly better off than in the initial free trade equilibrium. Haberler ([1950] 1968, p. 228) expressed the dynamics of this change by noting that 'the essence of the infant-industry argument is that a movement on the transformation curve will bring about an irreversible shift of the curve itself'.

After making his diagrammatic case for infant-industry protection, Haberler (p. 229) observed that while the argument has been supported in principle by 'most leading economists', to make the case does not mean that it is easy to implement in practice: 'to generalise about the overall importance of the infant-industry effect, and to evaluate it in concrete cases is an extremely difficult task which requires not only theoretical acumen, but intimate empirical knowledge of industrial development and above all, historical perspective'.

8.2 Precursors of Heckscher and Ohlin

In chapter 1 of his magnum opus, in a section entitled 'Notes on similar viewpoints in works by earlier writers', Bertil Ohlin observed that

> the fact that the productive factors enter into the production of different commodities in very different proportions, and that *therefore* (relative prices of the factors being different in different countries) an international specialization of production is profitable, is so obvious that it can hardly have escaped notice. Yet this fact was long ignored in international trade theory. (Ohlin, 1967, p. 20)

Ohlin was correct on both counts. The factor endowments theory is indeed 'obvious' and did not escape notice. But it was basically ignored even by those writers who cited various examples of the effects of factor endowments on trade and income distribution. Ohlin listed as precursors only two nineteenth-century economists, Sismondi and Longfield. As Power (1987, p. 298n) argues, 'a possible explanation for Ohlin's somewhat misleading discussion is that he was not overly interested in tracing antecedents and that he simply threw together a section in haste, based ... on the footnote in Viner's review of Angell's *The theory of international prices*'. The fact that this footnote of Viner (1926, pp. 621–2) mentions the same two economists cited by Ohlin (1967, pp. 20–1) makes this a plausible hypothesis. Ohlin preceded these references with the statement that 'it is not surprising, then, to find [the study of varying factor proportions] touched upon not by the English classical school but in French works'. But the sole reference to the latter was Sismondi's 1803 book *De la richesse commerciale*. Viner (1937, p. 503) dismissed this work with the remark that 'Sismondi ... was at this time still a rather slavish disciple of Adam Smith and may conceivably have found his inspiration even on this question in the *Wealth of Nations*'. Viner was surprised that Ohlin did not regard Longfield as a member of the British classical school, possibly because he was Irish rather than English. He went on to add:

> The classical economists, it is true, revealed no great interest in the detailed explanation of the forces which determined the nature of the international specialization existing in their time. But they did not wholly ignore the question, and when they did touch on it their adherence to the doctrine of comparative costs did not prevent them from dealing with it on lines similar in essentials to those followed by Ohlin. (Viner, 1937, p. 504)

To support this last statement, Viner (1937, pp. 504–7) quoted passages by Smith, Ricardo, Malthus, McCulloch and Cairnes, and mentioned several minor writers of the classical school including some American and Continental ones. Power (1987) added several other passages, including significant ones by Adam Smith. The latter had been noted earlier by Hollander (1973) and Bloomfield ([1975] 1994), and were quoted in Chapter 3. They increase the plausibility that Sismondi was indeed inspired by Smith. Power also presented a passage containing an anticipation of Heckscher–Ohlin by Turgot, but argued that Turgot's thoughts on trade derived from his translations of two of Josiah Tucker's works and from his correspondence with Tucker.[15] No one has questioned the originality of Longfield's anticipation of Heckscher–Ohlin, though it is strange (as Power points out) that Ohlin quoted from his *Lectures on Political Economy* (1834) rather than his *Three Lectures on Commerce* (1835), which provides some clearer examples.

Gomes (1990, p. 115) added the American economist Stuart Wood to the list of nineteenth-century anticipators of the Heckscher–Ohlin theory. Although another list can be made for the twentieth century, there seems little point in doing so, since none of the writers cited by Ohlin, Viner, Power or Gomes actually assembled all the basic building blocks of the theory, including identical technology across countries and differential factor intensities across commodities, and none of them announced the birth of a new theory of trade. A possible reason for this is that the Heckscher–Ohlin theory depends on the concept of a production function, which only entered the literature in the late nineteenth century. As Gomes (1990, p. 115) commented regarding these anticipators' insights, 'the accounts are often superficial, generally falling short of any deeper analyses as to why the factor-endowment explanation should provide the basis of trade in general'.

Eli Heckscher cited a couple of economists, Henry Sidgwick and Knut Wicksell, not so much as anticipators but as important catalysts for his own thoughts on the factor endowments theory. Wicksell's role is discussed in the next section.

8.3 Eli Heckscher and the causes of comparative advantage

Eli Heckscher's 1919 paper, translated into English as 'The Effect of Foreign Trade on the Distribution of Income', is one of the major milestones in the history of the theory of international trade. It has been rightly referred to as a *'tour de force'* (Samuelson, 1981a, p. 151), and was one of the sources of inspiration for Bertil Ohlin's 1924 doctoral dissertation *Handelns Teori*. The latter was expanded into Ohlin (1933), which in turn led to the Heckscher–Ohlin theory. Heckscher's paper appeared in its first English translation, in a slightly abridged form, in the American Economic Association's *Readings in the Theory of International Trade* (Ellis and Metzler, 1949), with a Prefatory Note by Heckscher. A new translation of its unabridged version (with 'substantive corrections') recently appeared in Heckscher and Ohlin (1991). The English-speaking public can now read for the first time a section of great historical interest (section 7) containing Heckscher's comments on Sidgwick and Wicksell, where he observed that his article 'owes its origin to Knut Wicksell's criticism of an earlier book of mine' (Heckscher, 1991, p. 43). In his review Wicksell had alleged that a worldwide scarcity of raw materials abroad would stimulate their production in Sweden, leading to a rise in rents, a fall in wages and hence the emigration of labor.[16]

The new theory of trade that Heckscher proposed in his paper was designed to supplement the Ricardian theory in an important respect: 'Our main concern is not with the influence of foreign trade on national income, but with its influence on the distribution of that income and more specifically on *the prices of the various factors*'. In analyzing this effect, Heckscher was led to examine the foundations of the received theory of foreign trade, in particular *'the reasons for differences in comparative costs among countries*. It is a puzzle that until now so little attention has been paid to this basic issue in Ricardo's theory of foreign trade – a theory that has yet to be successfully challenged' (1991, pp. 46–7). In any attempt to trace the evolution of the rationale for comparative advantage, Heckscher's comment is of great interest. His surprise that the issue of the sources of comparative advantage had not been addressed in a formal way before is understandable, even though the Heckscher–Ohlin theory did not lack anticipators as noted in the previous section. In Heckscher's view, as implied by the title of his paper, comparative advantage and functional income distribution are closely related. Differences in the abundance of factor endowments combined with differences in the factor intensities of commodities give rise under autarky to differences in commodity prices across countries:

> A difference in the relative scarcity of the factors of production between one country and another is thus a necessary condition for differences in comparative costs and consequently for international trade. A further condition is that the proportions in which the factors of production are combined not be the same for one commodity as for another. In the absence of this second condition, the price of one commodity relative to that of another would be the same in all countries regardless of differences in relative factor prices. (Heckscher, 1991, p. 48)

Heckscher added as a third condition of trade the 'tacit assumption' that '*the same technique is used to produce a given commodity* in different countries' (p. 49). The same three assumptions were later made by Ohlin and by economists working within the H–O–S paradigm.

Just as noteworthy as the preconditions for trade to take place were the stunning implications of trade for income distribution that Heckscher deduced:

> Foreign trade in the overwhelming majority of cases *will* alter the distribution of income.... Trade must continue to expand until an *equalization of the relative scarcity of the factors of production among countries* has occurred.... A difference in comparative costs between countries will *create* trade but such a difference is not necessary for the *continuance* of established trade. On the contrary, the differences in comparative costs between countries inevitably disappear as trade expands. Differences in the relative prices of factors of production are thus eliminated even in the absence of movements of these factors, provided that techniques are the same in the trading countries....
>
> We must next inquire whether the equalization will be *absolute* as well as *relative*, that is, whether rent, wages, and interest for the same qualities of the factors of production will *constitute* the same real return in all trading countries. This proposition has not been demonstrated thus far, but it is an inescapable consequence of trade. (Heckscher, 1991, pp. 51–5)

In both trading countries the prices of scarce factors are thus lowered by trade while those of abundant factors are raised. Because one country's abundant factors correspond to its trading partner's scarce ones, trade leads to the international convergence of factor prices. Underlying this effect of trade on income distribution are variations in marginal rates of transformation and hence in comparative costs. While in a classical model these are exogenously given and not affected by trade, Heckscher noted that they obey a different law in a neoclassical world . The difference between countries' comparative costs causes trade to arise in the first place, but is then erased by the very trade it engenders. Moreover, once trade is established, a difference in comparative costs is no longer needed to ensure its continuation.

According to the second part of the above passage, trade has an even stronger (in fact, 'inescapable') implication for factor prices than their convergence, namely their equalization in real terms across countries. The factor price equalization theorem, to be discussed in Chapter 9, is one of the basic propositions of the Heckscher–Ohlin model, and depends for its validity *inter alia* on the important proviso that countries should not become fully specialized. Heckscher was aware of this qualification, for he went on to point out that factor prices are equalized only if 'harmonic equilibrium' prevails, which he defined as a state in which the trading countries use the same techniques of production. To achieve this state, factor proportions in the trading countries must not be too different. But 'such a state is generally inconceivable', since it 'demands ... that each country must have enough of its *most scarce* factor so that the proportions of factors in each branch of production can be the same as the corresponding proportions in other countries'. If harmonic equilibrium is not achieved, 'then it is not only possible, but necessary, that *the relative and absolute prices of the factors of production must differ in the two trading countries*' (1991, pp. 57–9).

According to Heckscher, 'harmonic equilibrium' did not prevail in the US before the mass immigration from Europe. The scarcity of labor was such as to drive wages higher than in Europe, just as land rents were lower. It was the discrepancy in wages – in spite of ongoing trade – which spurred immigration into the US. Factor migration or population growth thus become indispensable if world efficiency in production is to be attained. By allowing the possibility of factor migration, Heckscher differentiated his model from the classical one in yet another respect, rejecting the key classical assumption that factors are mobile within countries but immobile between them.[17] As another source of change in factor endowments, he mentioned the response of factor supplies to changes in their prices. This has 'the rather paradoxical result that when supply reactions are taken into account, foreign trade tends to *increase the relative differences in the supply of factor* [sic] *of production in different countries*' (1991, p. 60). Thus the increased (decreased) demand for a country's abundant (scarce) factor due to trade tends to raise (lower) its supply, leading to even more trade.

In spite of his reformist intentions, Heckscher turned out to be a revolutionary thinker. Though he resembled Haberler in wishing to provide a firmer basis for the theory of comparative costs, his rationale for the existence of comparative advantage in terms of factor endowments and differential factor intensities of commodity production resulted in the birth of a theory which eventually replaced the classical theory and became the mainstream theory of trade. It achieved this status mainly because of Heckscher's influence on his student Ohlin, whom we consider next.

8.4 Bertil Ohlin's *Interregional and International Trade*

Bertil Ohlin was fortunate to have had three great teachers, Knut Wicksell, Eli Heckscher and Gustav Cassel.[18] Ohlin's 1924 doctoral dissertation *The Theory of Trade*, translated into English in Ohlin (1991), is an admirably succinct version of his later book (Ohlin, 1933). Despite his reluctance to cite Heckscher, *The Theory of Trade* evinced the combined influences on Ohlin of Heckscher's 1919 paper and of the general equilibrium theory he learned from Cassel, as well as the impact of his visit to Harvard in 1922–23.[19] There he was Frank Taussig's student and benefitted from his contacts with two other students of Taussig, Jacob Viner and John H. Williams. He and Williams ended up sharing a critical attitude towards the classical school.

Ohlin's 1933 book *Interregional and International Trade* was an expanded English-language version of *The Theory of Trade*, and established his international reputation. It is permeated with Heckscher's brilliant insights into the causes of trade as well as with Cassel's view of the mutual interdependence of economic variables. An appendix contained an extension of Cassel's general equilibrium model of a closed economy to two trading regions. Ohlin's magnum opus will be compared both to Heckscher's 1919 paper and to the Heckscher–Ohlin theory which grew out of them. We first examine Ohlin's attitude towards the classical theory of comparative costs whose influence his book was attempting to supplant.

The theory of comparative costs as a *deus ex machina*

In contrast to the continuous line of development which Haberler traced from Ricardo to his own writings, and to Heckscher's expressed intention of providing firm economic support for Ricardo's concept of comparative advantage, Ohlin had a highly critical attitude towards the classical school and what he perceived as Heckscher's soft treatment of it. In his first reference to it in his 1933 book, he noted that a 'simple statement [of his own theory], which is nothing but a starting point for a real analysis, is evidently quite different from the classical doctrine of comparative cost'. After referring to Haberler (1930), he commented that 'such reasoning [in terms of opportunity costs] explains very little unless connected with a mutual interdependence price system and is as different from the doctrine of comparative cost as anything can be' (Ohlin, 1967, p. 8n).[20] After discussing the 'modifications' to the classical theory made by some writers, Ohlin commented:

> Both Heckscher and Taussig regard their discussion as a modification and addendum to the classical theory. Heckscher, for instance, looks upon his paper as an analysis of 'the antecedents of the law of comparative costs.' I cannot share this view. As a matter of fact, I do not think that it can be fitted into the classical labor cost theory at all. The assumption that the productive factors, except land, enter in the *same* proportion into *all* goods is vital to the classical theory. It cannot be ignored in any attempt at modification. (Ohlin, 1967, p. 22)

Since the theory of comparative costs was intimately connected with the classical labor theory of value, it was flawed by this association. Ohlin elaborated on this in Appendix III of his 1933 book, entitled 'Criticism of the classical theory of international trade', which was a revised and expanded version of Ohlin (1927). The only instance where classical economists allowed for changes in factor proportions and the associated diminishing returns was in the context of adding labor and capital in a fixed ratio to a stock of land. But in fact capital is normally not combined with labor in fixed proportions in every line of activity. The awkward 'modifications' of the labor theory of value which its adherents had to make, to allow for the existence of other factors of production such as capital, exposed that theory's inadequacy.

The association of the term 'comparative advantage' with the theory of comparative costs which Ohlin wished to discredit probably explains why this term hardly appears in his book. The two references to it in Appendix III placed it in an unflattering light by linking it to a multicommodity Ricardian model based on the labor theory of value.[21] Ohlin used this term in its common-sense meaning only on the last page of that appendix, while stressing that this was a 'loose way' of using it:

> When studying concrete cases, economists sometimes use such expressions as 'comparative advantage in the production of these goods' in a loose way, including all sorts of natural advantages, cheap capital, etc., and not in the least thinking in terms of the 'effectiveness of labour.' This seems to show the need of a theory in terms of money costs. Certainly both to business men and to economic geographers such an approach is more natural than that of the labour value theory. (Ohlin, 1933, p. 590)

When Ohlin sketched the outlines of his theory in Chapter 1 of his book, he italicized the proposition that '*each region has an advantage in the production of commodities into which enter considerable amounts of factors abundant and cheap in that region*' (1967, p. 12). The word 'advantage', which has

Smithian overtones, could equally well be replaced by 'comparative advantage'. Indeed the Heckscher–Ohlin theory, as pointed out in Chapter 9, has been interpreted as implying that a country abundant in a certain factor has a comparative advantage, or a lower comparative cost, in those commodities in whose production that factor is intensively used.[22] This usage is also consistent with the general law of comparative advantage discussed in Chapter 2, since autarky prices tend to be low for goods in whose production abundant factors are intensively used.[23]

Another reason for Ohlin's animosity towards the concept of comparative costs appears in the section of chapter 2 of his book entitled 'Generalization of one idea underlying [the] classical law of comparative costs', where he pointed out what he regarded as a basic weakness in the concept of Ricardian comparative advantage:

> According to the classical theory of value the possibility that a country may import certain goods, although they could have been produced with less labor at home than in the exporting country, has naturally been considered as an extremely important, even as *the* fundamental problem of international trade. Viewed from a consistent equilibrium theory of prices it is not so. (Ohlin, 1967, pp. 31–2)

His reason is that what counts for competitiveness are the money costs of production, not the amounts of a single factor of production embodied in commodities. A country may indeed produce a commodity using a smaller amount of a factor than the country from which it imports it, but that factor may be more valuable in another line of activity. Thus 'one will always prefer to use a greater quantity of a cheaper factor than a smaller quantity of a dearer one if the total costs are lower that way' (1967, p. 32). He illustrated his contention by means of the following example:

> The land that is best for rye, in the sense that a given amount of capital and labor will yield more rye there than on other sorts of land, may be used for wheat, while rye is imported from regions that only have land of second-rate quality.... In this analysis there is nothing peculiar. A mutual interdependence theory of interregional trade – based on money costs (prices) and not on real costs – has no use for a special law of comparative cost, which gives a flavor of paradox to a fairly simple relationship while being from other points of view a result of unnecessarily extreme simplifications. Indeed, this so-called law is only a special instance of the tendency to find the cheapest possible combination of productive factors. (Ohlin, 1967, pp. 32–3)

He added (p. 33n) that 'when the classical labor value theory is applied to the phenomenon of international trade, the law of comparative cost – of which one has, curiously enough, heard nothing in the analysis of domestic trade – is introduced as a *deus ex machina*'. Ohlin's hostility towards the classical school thus led him to dismiss Ricardo's principle of comparative advantage (and implicitly the four 'magic numbers' which defined it and gave birth to the field of international economics) as a mere *deus ex machina*. It is somewhat paradoxical that, following Heckscher's lead, Ohlin's book ultimately provided the first book-length explanation of the causes of comparative advantage based on international factor endowment differences.

Another nail which Ohlin wished to drive into the coffin of the theory of comparative costs was his denial that a region (region A) may not gain from trade, as occurs in the Mill–Whewell model when the terms of trade coincide with its autarky price ratio. His reasoning was eminently neoclassical:

> The change in production caused by trade implies a change in the relative scarcity of A's factors, with those contained mostly in A's exports rising relative to the others.... Only if trade did not change the relative scarcity of factors in A at all would it be conceivable for the terms of trade to be unaffected and for A to reap no gain at all. But such a case is impossible. (Ohlin, 1967, p. 30)

In other words, the country's transformation locus is not, and cannot be, the linear one of classical economics, but is inevitably concave. This implies that the price ratio must change between autarky and trade, leading to gains from trade and changes in factor scarcity.

Ohlin's other reason for trade

Heckscher and Ohlin did not attribute all trade to factor endowment differences. When he alluded to a possible absence of 'harmonic equilibrium', Heckscher had made a passing reference to another reason why techniques of production may differ between countries: 'the only possible exception would be differences in the absolute size of markets, which might lead to differences in the size of units of production and thus to differences in technique' (Heckscher, 1991, p. 47). To Ohlin's credit, he took this hint and expanded it into another major explanation of trade. Chapter 3 of his book, entitled 'Another Condition of Interregional Trade', argues that a powerful secondary reason for trade is economies of scale, due to the indivisibility of certain factors of production and the consequent need to concentrate activities geographically: 'this conclusion that interregional trade reduces the disadvantages of indivisibility corresponds to the previous conclusion that trade mitigates the disadvantages of an unequal geographical distribution of productive agents' (1967, p. 40). However, though he frequently referred to economies of scale in his book, Ohlin played down their relative importance as a cause of trade when compared to factor endowments:

> On the whole, it is certainly the differences in factor supplies that determine the course of interregional trade – unless regions are small – whereas the advantages of large-scale production are more in the nature of a subsidiary cause, carrying the division of labor and trade a little further than it would otherwise go, but not changing their main characteristics. (Ohlin, 1967, p. 39)

He omitted this important rationale for trade in his formal model in Appendix I of his book, discussed in the next subsection. Because of their inconsistency with the conditions of perfect competition, economies of scale were also ignored in the H–O–S model, and had to await the 'new trade theory' of the past two decades to be resurrected.

Ohlin's general equilibrium model and the Heckscher–Ohlin theory

Ohlin formalized his trade model in Chapter 3 of *The Theory of Trade* and in Appendix I of both editions of his book, entitled 'Simple Mathematical Illustration of Pricing in Trading Regions'. He relaxed Cassel's assumption that coefficents of production are fixed, allowing them instead to depend on factor prices, and went on to extend Cassel's general equilibrium model of an isolated region (which Cassel had borrowed without acknowledgment from Walras) to two trading regions. As mentioned in Chapter 7, it was only when Ohlin's 1933 book was almost ready for publication that he became aware of Pareto's work, which had likewise extended the Walrasian model to two trading regions. The models of Ohlin and Pareto both include many individuals, commodities and factors of production. Both authors assumed incorrectly that, to obtain an economically sensible solution, it is sufficient to ensure that variables and equations are equal in number. But their models differ in several important respects. First, Pareto introduced ophelimity functions relating to the individuals in his model, whereas Ohlin bypassed utilities and jumped straight to the demands for commodities as functions of commodity prices and individuals' incomes. Second, Ohlin (like Heckscher) assumed that the technical coefficients of production are identical functions of factor prices in both countries, that is, that production functions are the same everywhere. Third, unlike Pareto who assumed endogenous factor endowments, Ohlin took them to be exogenously given.[24]

In his two-region model, Ohlin assumed that all commodities are traded and produced under conditions of full specialization, with region A being the sole producer of commodities 1, 2, ... , m and region B of $m + 1$, ... , n. The equilibrium exchange rate x must be such that a region's imports match its exports in value. To determine the sets of imported and exported commodities, Ohlin compared their autarky prices in the two regions converted at the exchange rate x to determine where they are cheaper, implying they will be exported. As we know from Chapter 2, this procedure is in general incorrect, since a region may well end up exporting goods which in autarky are dearer there than in its trading partner. Aside from the absence of non-traded goods, the most peculiar of Ohlin's assumptions is that full specialization occurs so that no commodity is produced in both regions. This feature is inconsistent with Heckscher's 'harmonic equilibrium', where commodities are produced with the same techniques in all trading countries.

Ohlin departed from his own model in the text of his book, for example by considering (among others) incomplete specialization, endogenous factor supplies, interregional factor mobility and economies of scale. What, then, was the function of his general equilibrium model? Just as in the case of Pareto, Ohlin's model was far too general to be useful in deriving specific results, particularly those he sketched verbally in the text, such as the attribution of a region's comparative advantage to its factor endowment. Ohlin's aim seems to have been the more modest one of showing how to obtain in theory a determinate solution for a trading equilibrium, taking full account of the mutual interdependence between economic variables. His main goal was to differentiate his trade model from the classical one based on real costs. Another reason for formulating a very general model lay in the fact that 'orthodox economists have usually confined their analysis to two countries and two or three commodities. They have, however, not hesitated to apply to concrete problems the conclusions arising from such an analysis – a thoroughly dangerous procedure' (1933, p. 586). Through no fault of Ohlin, and as examined in Chapter 9, the dangers of 'two-ness' have also plagued the H–O–S model.

8.5 The legacies of Haberler, Heckscher and Ohlin

The seminal contributions of the three major pioneers of neoclassical trade theory were cast in the general equilibrium mold of neoclassical economics. As Caves (1960, p. 29) observed, 'joint credit for developing the modern simplified general equilibrium theory of trade has frequently been split between Heckscher–Ohlin, on the one hand, and Haberler, on the other.... Haberler's "opportunity costs" exposition essentially breaks into the general economic equilibrium at an intermediate point. His starting point is the set of output combinations of the various commodities which a country will produce in the face of various price ratios'. In spite of the title of chapter 12 of Haberler's book, 'International Trade and General Equilibrium', and of the formal model that Ohlin presented in Appendix I of his book, none of these pioneers produced a fully specified model capturing their basic insights. The 1933 books of Haberler and Ohlin nevertheless provided excellent starting points for a theory of international trade which could account for multiple factors of production and the possibilities of substitution between them in the production of commodities, and reflect the distributional changes induced by trade. Both books illuminated the ways in which an economy can respond to and gain from trade. The disparity between their approaches stems from their authors' different goals, training, methodological predispositions and the aspects of the real world they wished to capture. Their contributions are thus truly complementary. They inspired the next generation of economists, first and foremost Paul Samuelson, to develop mathematically the specific-factors and H–O–S models. In addition to the Ricardian model, these have become the trade models most beloved by textbook writers, and they provide plausible alternative explanations of trade and its welfare impact.

All three pioneers realized the gap separating the burgeoning neoclassical theory of value from a trade theory which had not yet broken free from the real cost perspective of the classical school. Both Heckscher and Haberler believed that useful insights were still available from the classical theory of comparative costs. Haberler presented it as a prelude to his own theory and pointed out the analogies between them. In contrast to this gradualist approach to paradigm change, Ohlin's attitude towards the classical school was dismissive and reminiscent of that of the originators and early adherents of the 'marginal revolution', who self-consciously pointed to the revolutionary character of their break with the past.[25] Despite the fact that Ohlin ignored the concept of comparative advantage in his book, a new rationale for this concept was subsequently advanced in terms of the Heckscher–Ohlin model itself. Ohlin was fortunate that his model could be easily recast in the general equilibrium framework pioneered a few years later by Hicks (1939) and Samuelson (1947). As outlined in Chapter 9, he found in Samuelson someone eager to simplify his model to the $2 \times 2 \times 2$ case, turning it into the mainstream H–O–S model of trade which acquired ascendancy over the field, casting some shade on Haberler's contemporaneous contributions.

Notes

1. Ohlin's approach was reminiscent of Jevons's in vigorously rejecting the classical theory as a prelude to setting out his own theory. The theory of mutual interdependence which he propounded, and the close integration of his trade theory with income distribution, justify his

being characterized as 'quintessentially neoclassical in his approach' (Flam and Flanders, 1991, p. 13). The transformation of classical into neoclassical trade theory occurred with certain leads and lags compared to the analogous transformation in the theory of value, constituting an interesting case study of the lurching process of paradigm change in two closely related fields. I am indebted to Claudio Sardoni for pointing out to me that Ohlin's general equilibrium model of trade (inspired by Walras, Pareto and Cassel) anticipated by several years the introduction of general equilibrium modeling into the theory of value in such works as Hicks (1939) and Samuelson (1947).

2. In Haberler's defense, Baldwin (1982, pp. 143–4) argued, with the H–O–S theory in mind, that 'it seems no more "empirically gratuitous" ... to assume that factors are fixed in supply and indifferent among various uses than to assume that production functions for any good are identical among all countries or that tastes are not only identical among nations but homothetic. Indeed, the usual simplified form of the Heckscher–Ohlin proposition requires (among others) the same assumptions that Haberler made'.

3. See also Caves (1960, pp. 12–4, 218–25). According to Maloney (1987, p. 103), 'much of the discussion which took place between English and Austrian economists concerned whether, and to what extent, the two doctrines logically came to the same thing'. Some English economists such as Wicksteed and Robbins espoused the Austrian viewpoint.

4. Haberler was clearly not acquainted with Barone's general equilibrium model of trade discussed in section 7.3.

5. Haberler attributed the distinction between specific and non-specific factors of production to his teacher Wieser, without providing any textual reference. He noted that Bastable (1903) made a similar distinction.

6. In a later paper, Jones and Neary (1984, p. 21) acknowledged that '[the specific-factors] model has its antecedents in the work of Cairnes and Bastable, and was used explicitly or otherwise in inter-war writings by Haberler and others who attempted to break out of the Ricardian straitjacket of constant costs'.

7. Haberler later noted that 'not being sufficiently skilful mathematicians, most of us resort to simplifications and allow for factors from which we abstract in our simplified models by means of somewhat vague verbal qualifications' ([1950] 1968, p. 214). After reviewing Haberler's collected writings, Findlay (1987b, p. 1346) remarked that 'among some of the things that [students today] would learn are that logic and rigor in economics can be sustained at the highest level without recourse to extensive mathematics'. A similar comment could be made regarding David Ricardo and J. S. Mill.

8. Referring to a famous paper by Viner (1931), Samuelson's justification was that 'the supply conditions of that model are of interest for their own sake since they portray what might be called the Ricardo–Viner case of pure rent'. Viner, to my knowledge, never formulated or discussed anything resembling the specific-factors model. According to Findlay (1987b, p. 1347), in attributing paternity to that model 'it would not be inappropriate for Haberler's name to be added to this distinguished lineage [of Samuelson (1971) and Jones (1971)]'. Indeed, a case could be made that his "opportunity cost" approach is more in conformity with the spirit of this model than the "real cost" approach of Viner'. Other economists, such as Kenen (1994) and Mayer (1974), have also recognized Haberler's early verbal and diagrammatic formulation of this model. Yet another name proposed by Magee (1980) for the specific-factors model is the Cairnes model, because of the association of the non-competing groups discussed by Cairnes (1874) with industry-specific factors.

9. Caves (1960, pp. 30–31) asserted that 'the conclusion remains, then, that Haberler's analysis, embodied in the "transformation function," is basically a condensed presentation of the Heckscher–Ohlin model.... Haberler ... deduces a transformation curve concave to the origin that is equivalent in most ways to the one arising from Ohlin's model'. More correctly (pp. 33–4), he added that 'the Haberler and Samuelson explanations of the derivation of the

transformation curve are basically complementary'. According to Gomes (1990, p. 108), Haberler's explanation for the curvature of the transformation curve in terms of specific factors is 'similar to that commonly used today to account for the shape of the curve in terms of factor-intensity differences: i.e. products can be classified in terms of their relative K-intensity or L-intensity in production'.

10. Haberler noted that if no factors can be transferred between sectors, the transformation locus degenerates to the right angle b'Pa', where P is the only efficient point of production.

11. This was denied by Viner (1937, p. 533), who claimed that 'in the long run it would seem to be free capital and not labor which is the least specific [of the factors]'.

12. Income distribution also changes in response to price changes in the H–O–S model. Interpreting the specific-factors model as a short-run version of the H–O–S model, Mayer (1974) showed that the short-run impact of a price change on a factor's return can take the opposite sign from its long-run impact. Tariff protection given to a sector can raise the returns of all its factors in the short run, contrary to the result postulated by the long-run Stolper–Samuelson theorem. Mussa (1974) and Neary (1978) also distinguished the short-run from the long-run distributional implications of the specific-factors model. Magee (1980) confirmed empirically that factors lobby in accordance with their short-run, not their long-run, interests.

13. Kenen (1994, p. 94) added that 'Haberler did not prove this theorem completely but was among the first economists to examine the behavior of real earnings in a specific-factor model'.

14. In critiquing Haberler's reasoning, Viner (1937, p. 533) correctly argued that '[labor's] real income might still rise with a removal of tariff protection even though its money income and its relative share in the national money income and the national real income all fell, if it was an important consumer of the hitherto protected commodities, and if the prices of these commodities fell sufficiently as a result of free trade to offset the reduction in money wages in the new situation'.

15. Power (1987, p. 292) mentioned the providentialist theory discussed in Chapter 3 as another anticipation of Heckscher and Ohlin. If Providence has scattered natural resources randomly around the world, this would furnish one of the building blocks of the Heckscher–Ohlin theory, which is differential factor endowments across regions.

16. On the strength of this insight, Wicksell has been named one of the precursors of the Stolper–Samuelson theorem discussed in Chapter 9 (Flam and Flanders, 1991, p. 32n). In order to rebut Wicksell's allegation, Heckscher used the theoretical considerations he had outlined in the previous sections of his paper. He agreed that wages would be lowered by the demand shock considered by Wicksell, but denied that emigration from Sweden would ensue. The greater demand for raw materials would have raised rents and lowered wage rates overseas before the shock affected Sweden. As soon as Sweden started to export more raw materials, its wages would decline to the level of the rest of the world because of the tendency towards factor-price equalization but never sink below this level, so there would be no economic incentive to emigrate.

17. After introducing international factor mobility into his trade model, Heckscher even managed to anticipate a result reached 40 years later by Robert Mundell (1957), that perfect factor mobility would cause all trade to cease since 'the factors of production would always move to the places where they were needed' (Heckscher, 1991, p. 61).

18. The excellent Introduction of Flam and Flanders to *Heckscher–Ohlin Trade Theory* (Heckscher and Ohlin, 1991), which they edited, includes interesting biographical information on both Heckscher and Ohlin, and traces the intellectual influences on them.

19. In the Preface to *The Theory of Trade*, Ohlin thanked Heckscher for his 'guidance, advice, and criticism' and acknowledged 'the influence of his pathbreaking paper, both conscious and unconscious', as well as the 'important similarities to Heckscher's treatment' of one of the chapters. But in the text itself, Heckscher's name appears only in three one-line footnotes.

20. 'Very little' in this passage from Ohlin (1967) was an emendation of 'nothing' in Ohlin (1933, p. 14n). The 1967 revised edition of Ohlin's book, from which I mostly quote in this chapter, is an abbreviated version of the first edition. In addition to omitting and abridging several chapters, Ohlin (1967, p. vii) made changes in Parts One and Two 'modernizing the terminology and removing minor ambiguities'. While he omitted two appendices of the first edition (which have been referred to in this chapter), he retained the mathematical appendix and added a valuable new one entitled 'Reflections on Contemporary International Trade Theories'.

21. Ohlin pointed out in this connection that the supply-side data provided by the theory of comparative costs does not suffice to establish the borderline between the sets of exported and imported commodities. For this the balance of trade condition and reciprocal demands are needed, as was shown in Chapter 7. Since Appendix III was omitted in Ohlin (1967), the latter's index does not even contain the term 'comparative advantage'.

22. Samuelson attached the title 'The neo-classical presentation of comparative advantage' to the section of his 1948 paper on factor price equalization containing his graphical illustration of the Heckscher–Ohlin theorem in terms of food exported by America and clothing exported by Europe. In the concluding paragraph of that section, he noted that 'so far this differs in only one important respect from John Stuart Mill's completion of the Ricardian comparative cost theory. We have dropped the assumption of *constant returns* (or of a single labor theory of value)' (Samuelson, 1948, pp. 170–72).

23. Gomes (1990, p. 114) concurs that '[Ohlin's] theory was not a rejection of comparative advantage, but merely a restatement of it along neoclassical lines as part of a more general theory of the causes of trade'.

24. Ohlin relaxed this assumption of his formal model in the text itself, allowing for both endogenous factor supplies and international factor mobility. Several chapters of Ohlin's book are in fact devoted to international labor and capital movements.

25. See Mirowski's (1984) characterization of the iconoclastic attitudes of Jevons and Walras *vis-à-vis* their predecessors.

9. The Heckscher–Ohlin Theory Encounters the New Trade Theory

This chapter examines the developments in trade theory and the new insights gained into the nature of comparative advantage which took hold in 1941 and gathered momentum after World War Two. Thanks to some strategic simplifications of the theories of Heckscher and Ohlin examined in Chapter 8, Paul Samuelson and his followers rigorously elaborated the Heckscher–Ohlin theory, causing it to replace the Ricardian or real cost theory as the mainstream theory of trade in the post-war period.[1] Samuelson's contributions to this development were so fundamental that his name has appropriately been added to those of the two Swedish economists as the co-founder of the so-called Heckscher–Ohlin–Samuelson (H–O–S) theory of trade. As Ethier (1982a, p. 389) noted, 'this model is often identified as "the" modern theory of trade'. When in 1968 the American Economic Association published its second anthology of articles in international economics (Caves and Johnson, 1968), all six articles contained in Part I, entitled 'Theory of Comparative Advantage', were founding documents or applications of the H–O–S theory.[2]

The main features of the H–O–S theory, which is described in all textbooks of international economics, are presented in sections 9.1 and 9.2 in the context of two countries, two commodities and two factors of production (the so-called $2 \times 2 \times 2$ model). Extensions of this theory to many factors and commodities are examined in section 9.3. The relationship of the H–O–S theory to the writings of Heckscher and Ohlin is discussed in section 9.4 as a prelude to a consideration in section 9.5 of the 'new trade theory' that emerged in the last two decades to explain trade in the context of differentiated products, imperfect competition and economies of scale. While some of its models dispense altogether with the notion of comparative advantage, others take a very dynamic view of its creation.

Concluding thoughts on comparative advantage, and an overall assessment of the impact of the new trade theory on its relevance as a key concept of the theory of international trade, are presented in Chapter 10.

9.1 Paul Samuelson and the Heckscher–Ohlin–Samuelson model

As we saw in Chapter 8, Ohlin (1933) offered in Appendix I a formalization of his theory couched as a Walras–Cassel general equilibrium model of two trading regions with n commodities, r factors of production and s individuals. The model was so general that it offered no insights into the factor endowments theory itself, which was the main subject of the book, or the nature of comparative advantage, a term which Ohlin in any case assiduously avoided. The very general nature of Ohlin's formal trade model was eagerly seized on by the next generation of economists, spearheaded by Paul Samuelson, as a golden opportunity to create a scaled-down version capable of throwing greater light on the factor endowments theory. Many years later, in his Foreword to Heckscher and Ohlin (1991), Samuelson stated (p. ix) that 'neither [in 1924], nor in 1933 and 1967, did Ohlin descend from full generality to strong and manageable cases – such as two factors of production and two-or-more goods. What a pity. Not only did Ohlin leave to my generation these easy pickings, but in addition he would for the first time have really understood his own system had he played with graphable versions'. In a later volume commemorating the fiftieth anniversary of the Stolper–Samuelson theorem, Samuelson clarified his remark that Ohlin had not understood his own system:

> What put general equilibrium, so to speak, on the undergraduate classroom map after 1941, was bringing it out of the realm of n+m equations and n+m unknowns to the beautifully simple diagrams of land and labor, cloth and corn. Finally a *manageable* general equilibrium system – one with texture and content – was at hand. Never again could an Ohlin not understand his own system, as when he denied the logical possibility of perfect factor-price equalization! (Samuelson, 1994, p. 345)

What Samuelson clearly understood, to the benefit of future generations of students of trade theory, was the fact that a model does not lose its general equilibrium character by being reduced to a very small number of dimensions, such as $2 \times 2 \times 2$. His trade model gave birth to hundreds of papers based on it as well as to two-sector growth models which, though mostly applied to a closed economy, also feature two goods, a consumption good and a capital good, and two factors of production, capital and labor.

The H–O–S theory is based on the following assumptions, some of which (leaving dimensionality aside) coincide with those made by Heckscher or Ohlin, while others are quite foreign to their conceptual frameworks:[3]

(a)   There are two countries, two commodities and two factors of production.
(b)   Production functions display constant returns to scale.
(c)   The law of diminishing marginal product applies to increases in one input, the other remaining constant.
(d)   Production functions are identical in both countries.
(e)   Commodities differ in their factor intensities, and one commodity intensively uses the same factor at all factor price ratios.
(f)   Commodities and factors of production are qualitatively identical in the two countries.
(g)   The movement of commodities between countries is not subject to transport costs or trade impediments.
(h)   There is perfect competition in commodity and factor markets.
(i)   Factors of production are inelastically supplied and immobile between countries.
(j)   Relative factor endowments differ between countries.
(k)   Demands are identical and homothetic in both countries.

Assumption (e), the 'strong' Samuelsonian factor intensity assumption, implies that there are no factor intensity reversals. In other words, a commodity cannot be labor-intensive at one set of factor prices and land-intensive at another set.
  A further assumption is needed for the factor price equalization theorem:

(ℓ)   Neither country specializes in its export commodity.

Given these assumptions, the H–O–S theory consists of the following four 'core propositions':

(1)   The Heckscher–Ohlin theorem, which states that the country abundant in a certain factor exports the commodity which intensively uses that factor in exchange for the other commodity.
(2)   The Stolper–Samuelson theorem, which in its 'essential version' states that 'an increase in the relative price of a good increases the real wage of the factor used intensively in producing that good, and lowers the real wage of the other factor'.[4]
(3)   The factor price equalization theorem, which states, given the additional assumption (ℓ), that trade equalizes real factor prices in the two countries.
(4)   The Rybczynski theorem, which states that if commodity prices are constant and one factor expands, the output of the commodity that intensively uses that factor grows in a greater proportion, while the output of the other commodity declines.

These four legs of the Heckscher–Ohlin stool can be subdivided into two sets of pairs. Theorems 1 and 4 are concerned with quantities of factors of production and of commodity outputs, while 2 and 3 have to do with factor prices and commodity prices. Alternatively, theorems 1 and 3 relate to two economies in a trading equilibrium, while 2 and 4 apply as much to a closed as to an open economy. Samuelson almost single-handedly proved the first three theorems, starting with theorem 2 (Stolper and Samuelson, [1941] 1949) and moving on to theorems 1 and 3 (Samuelson, 1948, 1949). Theorem 4 was proved by Rybczynski (1955).

While the way in which Samuelson went about proving these theorems is of historical interest, other authors subsequently (as is often the case) found more expeditious ways of doing so. Especially noteworthy was the article of Ronald Jones (1965), who used 'hat algebra' to derive his main results, a technique that has been widely imitated. Jones discovered and named the 'magnification effect' which will be used in the next section to derive the four theorems which constitute the Heckscher–Ohlin theory.[5]

9.2 Ronald Jones's magnification effect

Let p and q be the prices of goods X and Y, and X and Y their outputs. These outputs are produced with constant returns to scale using as inputs L (labor) and T (land), whose prices are w (wage) and r (rental). The unit factor requirements are a_{ij} ($i = L, T; j = X, Y$), measuring the quantity of factor i needed to produce one unit of good j. They are chosen so as to minimize the unit production cost of good j. Let good X be labor-intensive, so that

$$\frac{a_{LX}}{a_{TX}} > \frac{a_{LY}}{a_{TY}} \tag{9.1}$$

at all factor price ratios. Because of the assumption of perfect competition in product markets, price equals unit cost in each sector, so that

$$a_{LX} w + a_{TX} r = p \tag{9.2}$$

and

$$a_{LY} w + a_{TY} r = q. \tag{9.3}$$

Let $\theta_{TX} = a_{TX} r/p$ be the share of land and $\theta_{LX} = 1 - \theta_{TX} = a_{LX} w/p$ the share of labor in producing good X. Similarly $\theta_{TY} = a_{TY} r/q$ is the share of land and $\theta_{LY} = 1 - \theta_{TY} = a_{LY} w/q$ the share of labor in producing good Y. Replacing

Jones's 'hat algebra' with 'star algebra', let $z^* = d \ln z = dz/z$ denote the relative change in any variable z. Total differentiation of (9.2) and (9.3) yields

$$(1 - \theta_{TX})w^* + \theta_{TX} r^* = p^* - (\theta_{LX} a_{LX}^* + \theta_{TX} a_{TX}^*) = p^* \qquad (9.4)$$

and

$$(1 - \theta_{TY})w^* + \theta_{TY} r^* = q^* - (\theta_{LY} a_{LY}^* + \theta_{TY} a_{TY}^*) = q^*. \qquad (9.5)$$

The expressions in parentheses in the middle terms of (9.4) and (9.5) sum to zero because the assumption of cost minimization implies that the slope of each isoquant equals the ratio of factor prices.

Assumption (9.1) implies that the share of land in producing Y exceeds its share in producing X, or

$$\theta_{TY} > \theta_{TX}. \qquad (9.6)$$

Subtracting (9.5) from (9.4), we obtain

$$p^* - q^* = (\theta_{TY} - \theta_{TX})(w^* - r^*). \qquad (9.7)$$

If $p^* > q^*$, (9.7) and inequality (9.6) imply that $w^* > r^*$, so that changes in the wage-rental ratio w/r are positively associated with changes in the price ratio p/q. Since (9.4) and (9.5) show that p^* and q^* are weighted averages of w^* and r^*, it follows that

$$w^* > p^* > q^* > r^*. \qquad (9.8)$$

Similarly, if $p^* < q^*$, then $w^* < p^* < q^* < r^*$; and if $p^* = q^*$, then $w^* = p^* = q^* = r^*$. This is Jones's 'magnification effect' for prices, so-called because any commodity price changes are magnified in the factor price changes they entail. It is illustrated for $w^* < p^* < q^* < r^*$ in Figure 9.1, where $p^* > 0$ in panel (a) and $p^* = 0$ in panel (b). In both panels the horizontal axis plots the closed interval from 0 to 1, while the vertical axis measures relative growth rates. On the horizontal axis, mark off distances equal to the shares of land in the production of X and Y, θ_{TX} and θ_{TY}, and measure ordinates at those points equal to p^* and q^*. If the points (θ_{TX}, p^*) and (θ_{TY}, q^*) are joined by a straight line, its ordinates corresponding to the abscissas 0 and 1 measure w^* and r^* respectively. This can be proved from the similarity of the triangles w^*p^*E and w^*r^*F in panel (a), which implies that $w^*E/w^*F = p^*E/r^*F$, or

Figure 9.1   (a) Price magnification effect, (b) Stolper–Samuelson theorem

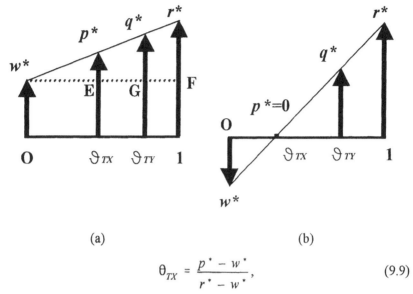

(a)   (b)

$$\theta_{TX} = \frac{p^* - w^*}{r^* - w^*}, \tag{9.9}$$

which is equivalent to (9.4). Applying the same procedure to the triangles w^*q^*G and w^*r^*F, we obtain

$$\theta_{TY} = \frac{q^* - w^*}{r^* - w^*}, \tag{9.10}$$

which is equivalent to (9.5). This establishes the correctness of the graphical procedure used to derive w^* and r^*. Using the same procedure in panel (b), we note that $p^* = 0$ together with $q^* > 0$ imply that $w^* < 0$.

Both panels of Figure 9.1 illustrate the magnification effect, since it is clear that in either case the difference between r^* and w^* exceeds that between q^* and p^*. Panel (b) establishes the *Stolper–Samuelson theorem* by showing that, if the price of the land-intensive good rises while that of the other good remains constant, the rental of land rises in an even greater proportion than q, while the wage of labor falls in terms of either good. A modification of panel (b) also serves to prove the *factor price equalization theorem*. It is clear that if $q^* = p^* = 0$, then $w^* = r^* = 0$. Hence, if the starred symbols are interpreted as differences between two countries rather than changes over time in the same country, the equality of commodity prices brought about by free trade leads to the international equality of factor prices.

Moving on to the other two theorems which relate to changes (or differences) in factor endowments and the corresponding commodity output changes (or differences), consider an economy where the production of commodities yields full employment to the given endowments of labor, L, and land, T, so that

$$a_{LX} X + a_{LY} Y = L \qquad (9.11)$$

and

$$a_{TX} X + a_{TY} Y = T. \qquad (9.12)$$

Let $\lambda_{LY} = a_{LY} Y/L$ and $\lambda_{LX} = 1 - \lambda_{LY} = a_{LX} X/L$ be the fractions of labor employed in producing goods Y and X; and $\lambda_{TY} = a_{TY} Y/T$ and $\lambda_{TX} = 1 - \lambda_{TY} = a_{TX} X/T$ the corresponding fractions of land. Assumption (9.1) implies that the fraction of land used to produce Y exceeds that of labor, or

$$\lambda_{TY} > \lambda_{LY}. \qquad (9.13)$$

Total differentiation of (9.11) and (9.12) yields

$$(1 - \lambda_{LY})X^* + \lambda_{LY} Y^* = L^* - (\lambda_{LX} a_{LX}^* + \lambda_{LY} a_{LY}^*) \qquad (9.14)$$

and

$$(1 - \lambda_{TY})X^* + \lambda_{TY} Y^* = T^* - (\lambda_{TX} a_{TX}^* + \lambda_{TY} a_{TY}^*). \qquad (9.15)$$

If all commodity and hence factor prices remain constant ($p^* = q^* = w^* = r^* = 0$), the unit factor requirements a_{ij} are likewise constant, so that (9.14) and (9.15) simplify to

$$(1 - \lambda_{LY})X^* + \lambda_{LY} Y^* = L^* \qquad (9.14a)$$

and

$$(1 - \lambda_{TY})X^* + \lambda_{TY} Y^* = T^*. \qquad (9.15a)$$

Subtracting (9.15a) from (9.14a), we obtain

$$(\lambda_{TY} - \lambda_{LY})(X^* - Y^*) = L^* - T^*. \qquad (9.16)$$

From (9.13), $1 > (\lambda_{TY} - \lambda_{LY}) > 0$. Hence if $L^* > T^*$, $X^* > Y^*$, and a change in the endowment ratio L/T leads to a magnified change in the same direction in the output ratio X/Y. But (9.14a) and (9.15a) imply that L^* and T^* are weighted averages of X^* and Y^*. Hence

$$X^* > L^* > T^* > Y^*, \qquad (9.17)$$

which expresses Jones's magnification effect on the quantity side. Similarly,

Figure 9.2   (a) Quantity magnification effect, (b) Rybczynski theorem

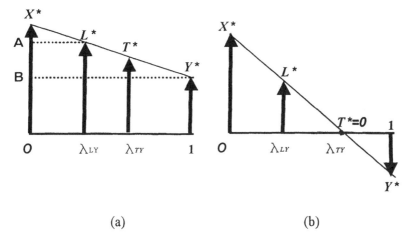

(a)   (b)

if $L* < T*$, then $X* < L* < T* < Y*$. If balanced factor growth occurs (or $L* = T*$), then $X* = L* = T* = Y*$.

The magnification effect expressed by inequalities (9.17) is illustrated in Figure 9.2, which is constructed on similar principles to Figure 9.1. In panel (a) both factors grow, while in panel (b) only labor does. Along the unit interval on the abscissa axis, mark off the fractions of labor and land in sector Y, λ_{LY} and λ_{TY}, and plot the points $(\lambda_{LY}, L*)$ and $(\lambda_{TY}, T*)$. If these points are joined with a straight line, its ordinates corresponding to the two extremes of the unit interval, 0 and 1, are $X*$ and $Y*$. To show this, note that in panel (a) $X*AL*$ and $X*BY*$ are similar triangles, so that $AL*/BY* = X*A/X*B$. This can be rewritten as

$$\lambda_{LY} = \frac{X* - L*}{X* - Y*},\qquad (9.18)$$

which is the same as (9.14a). Similarly, one can obtain an expression for λ_{TY} equivalent to (9.15a).

Panel (b) plots the special case where $L* > 0$ and $T* = 0$. Since this implies that $Y* < 0$, it illustrates the *Rybczynski theorem* which states that, given constant prices, if a factor grows and the other remains constant, the output of the good which intensively uses the growing factor rises in a greater proportion, while the output of the other good declines.

Two versions of the *Heckscher–Ohlin theorem* were identified by Jones ([1956] 1979), one based on relative physical factor abundance, the other on relative factor prices under autarky. According to the latter 'price' version, a country exports labor-intensive goods if its wage-rental ratio is lower before

Figure 9.3   The Heckscher–Ohlin theorem

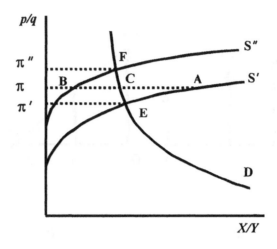

trade. This follows immediately from the Stolper–Samuelson theorem. If the starred symbols in Figure 9.1 are interpreted as differences between countries, a lower wage-rental ratio under autarky implies a lower price of the labor-intensive good, which is exported with the opening of trade. According to the former 'quantity' version, the Heckscher–Ohlin theorem implies that the country with the greater ratio of labor to land, L/T, exports the labor-intensive good. This version of the theorem follows as long as demand conditions do not neutralize the supply-side determinants of relative outputs. To ensure this requires assumption (k), that demands are identical and homothetic in both countries, so that they demand goods in the same proportion at a given price ratio regardless of their income levels. If the starred symbols in Figure 9.2 are interpreted as differences between two countries' factor endowments, it is clear that if they face identical commodity prices after trade, the labor-abundant country produces a higher ratio of X to Y. Since, at the post-trade price ratio, both countries consume the two goods in the same proportion, the labor-abundant country must export the labor-intensive good in exchange for the land-intensive one.

    If demand forces are neutralized by making assumption (k), factor endowments determine autarky prices as shown in Figure 9.3, which plots the relative price of X, p/q (or π), against the ratio of commodity outputs, X/Y. The curve D traces for both countries the relative demand for X in relation to Y as an inverse function of their price ratio. The curves S' and S" plot the ratios of commodities produced in the labor-abundant country I and the land-abundant country II as functions of p/q. Their positive slope conforms to the concavity of the two countries' transformation curves. S′ lies to the right of S″ since, by the Rybczynski theorem, at any commodity price ratio the relative output of the labor-intensive good X is higher in the labor-abundant country. The intersections E and F of S′ and S″ with the relative demand curve D indicate the relative prices under autarky of I and II, π' and π'', and their relative commodity outputs. The labor-abundant country I thus has the lower relative price of the labor-intensive good. At the terms of trade π, intermediate between π' and π'', country I increases, and country II decreases, its relative output of the labor-intensive good as shown by points A and B. The worldwide demand ratio at point C is an average of the countries' relative commodity outputs, as predicted by the Heckscher–Ohlin theorem.

Figures 9.1, 9.2 and 9.3 are related as follows. The Rybczynski theorem shown in Figure 9.2 explains why S′ lies to the right of S″ in Figure 9.3. The latter shows that country I has a comparative advantage in good X since it has a lower autarky value of p relative to q as compared to country II. Interpreting the relative changes in Figure 9.1 as indicating the differences between the two countries, this implies that country I has a lower wage rate and a higher rental rate than country II before trade, which is consistent with the 'price' version of the Heckscher–Ohlin theorem. With the equalization of commodity prices after trade, a modified version of Figure 9.1 shows that factor prices are also equalized as long as neither country becomes specialized.

9.3 Extensions to many commodities and factors of production

The $2 \times 2 \times 2$ model presented in the previous two sections has been the *pièce de résistance* of the theory of international trade in the post-war period. Part of its appeal is that it is the smallest general equilibrium system that can be used to explore the basic insights of Heckscher and Ohlin. Their theory can be easily illustrated graphically in commodity space or factor space, in terms of either prices or quantities.[6] Even when extended to many commodities, it is not surprising that it fell short of expectations as a description of reality. A memorable application of the model that limited it to two factors of production, capital and labor, but extended it to hundreds of export- and import-competing commodities, raised more questions than it answered. Using a 1947 input–output table of the American economy, Leontief (1953) discovered a disconcerting fact which became known as the Leontief Paradox. Despite the general impression of economists and policymakers that the US, right after World War Two, was the world's most capital-abundant economy, Leontief found that it exported labor-intensive and imported capital-intensive commodities. His finding unleashed a torrent of papers which attempted to explain this apparent contradiction of the Heckscher–Ohlin model. Some advanced explanations such as factor intensity reversals, demand reversals or the effects of tariffs. Further empirical tests extended the factor endowments model to include other factors such as natural resources and different classes of skilled and unskilled labor.[7] When Leontief himself and other researchers retested his model using later data, the paradox sometimes disappeared (often by a small margin), but in other cases was even strengthened. Although it disappeared in tests carried out in the past two decades, this does not explain why the paradox arose in the first place. Leamer (1980) claimed that there was no paradox since Leontief's test was invalid. The US in the immediate post-war period ran a trade surplus and was a net exporter of both capital and labor services. Since its ratio of net capital exports to net labor exports exceeded the capital-labor ratio relating to home consumption, Leamer concluded that the US was in fact capital-abundant. A rich literature has by now accumulated on empirical tests of the pattern of trade of the US and other countries, so rich that it is impossible to do it justice here. Much of it enhanced our understanding of the sources of comparative advantage by moving away from factor endowments in terms of undifferentiated labor and capital to their disaggregation into various forms of human capital and categories of labor by skill level.

The Leontief paradox also gave an impetus to theoretical extensions of the $2 \times 2 \times 2$ Heckscher–Ohlin model to more than two commodities and two factors.[8] As Jones pointed out in his insightful '"Two-ness" in Trade Theory: Costs and Benefits' ([1977] 1979), models which move beyond two dimensions in goods or factors can reflect phenomena that are qualitatively impossible to portray in two dimensions, such as complementarity in production or consumption, extreme specialization in production, or distributional effects among more than two factors. He argued that $2 \times 2 \times 2$ models, where the two commodities and factors are subject to the drastic changes implied by the magnification effect, are misleading since they neglect what he terms the 'excluded middle'. In a multifactor world, some factors may remain relatively unaffected by some price changes, in contrast to the prediction of the Stolper–Samuelson theorem. In a multicommodity world, a small economy is likely to specialize in production much more than in consumption. Again, this contrasts with the $2 \times 2 \times 2$ Heckscher–Ohlin model, where both commodities are typically produced as well as consumed.

In another landmark paper, Samuelson (1953) explored the generalization of the factor endowments model to many goods and factors. Jones ([1977] 1979, pp. 311–2) observed that subsequent generalizations followed two paths. One attempted to replicate the details of two-sector model results in an *n*-dimensional world, and required the imposition of conditions on the underlying matrices that are economically hard to interpret. Another path, followed by Ethier and Jones himself, was to explore possible generalizations without imposing such restrictive conditions, even if the insights of the $2 \times 2 \times 2$ case are thereby lost. For example Ethier (1974, 1982b, 1984) formulated the multidimensional analogues of the four main theorems of the Heckscher–Ohlin theory in terms of correlations similar to those used in Chapter 3 to define the general validity of comparative advantage. The generalization of greatest interest here relates to the pattern of comparative advantage resulting from factor endowments, and hence to the Heckscher–Ohlin theorem in its quantity version. Given identical and homothetic tastes, factor price equalization, and at least as many goods as factors, Ethier (1982b, p. 342) showed that 'on average a country tends to import those goods which make most intensive use of the country's relatively scarce factors', where factor scarcity is defined as in Vanek's model considered below.[9]

The Leontief Paradox and the models discussed in the next two subsections imply that the factor 'capital' can be treated in the Heckscher–Ohlin model on the same footing as labor or land. Since capital in fact is not a homogeneous putty-like substance but is composed of many heterogeneous commodities, neo-Ricardian writers have rightly questioned this procedure (Harcourt, 1972; Steedman, 1987). Their qualms are examined in section 10.4.

Chains of comparative advantage and the Heckscher–Ohlin model

If the Heckscher–Ohlin model is limited to two factors but extended to many commodities, an important question is whether commodity production in two trading countries is subject to a chain of comparative advantage, similar to that discovered by Haberler for the classical model and examined in Chapter 7. In an early exploration of this issue, Jones claimed that the Heckscher–Ohlin model was characterized by such a chain without specifying the underlying conditions:

> Ordering the commodities with respect to the capital/labor ratios employed in production is to rank them in order of comparative advantage. Demand conditions merely determine the dividing line between exports and imports; it is not possible to break the chain of comparative advantage by exporting, say, the third and fifth commodities and importing the fourth when they are ranked by factor intensity. (Jones, [1956] 1979, pp. 12–13)

Bhagwati (1972) showed that Jones's contention is incorrect if factor prices are equalized. He assumed two countries, I and II, that produce many commodities using capital (K) and labor (L). Their endowment ratios are such that $(K/L)' > (K/L)''$, so that country I is capital-abundant. Each country's capital-labor ratio can be shown to be a weighted average of the capital-labor ratios of the goods it produces, the weights being the fractions of the labor force in each sector. For example, if country I produces two goods X and Y, we have the identity

$$(\frac{K}{L})' \equiv \frac{L_X}{L}\frac{K_X}{L_X} + \frac{L_Y}{L}\frac{K_Y}{L_Y} \equiv (1- \lambda_{LY})\frac{K_X}{L_X} + \lambda_{LY}\frac{K_Y}{L_Y}, \qquad (9.19)$$

where λ_{LY} is the fraction of the labor force in sector Y. Identity (9.19) can be generalized to any number of commodities, and shows that the *average* capital-intensity of commodities produced by country I must be higher than that of those produced in country II. This is consistent with country I producing some very labor-intensive commodities in sufficiently small amounts and with correspondingly low weights λ_{Li}. Let factor price equalization prevail so that the two countries face isocost lines with the same slope equal to their wage-rental ratio. Given identical and homothetic tastes, and all commodities consumed in both countries, Bhagwati showed graphically that it is possible for country I to export commodities that are more labor-intensive than some of country II's exports. Hence, 'the "comparative advantage" chain can be crisscrossed by the actual trade pattern in the Heckscher–Ohlin model' (Bhagwati, 1972, p. 1053).

While a chain of comparative advantage fails in that model if factor price equalization prevails, Deardorff (1979) showed that it exists under free trade as long as factor prices in the trading countries are unequal. This result, which Bhagwati (1972) asserted but did not demonstrate, follows because the two countries now have unit isocost lines of different slopes. Being a high-wage country, country I then specializes in the more capital-intensive goods since it can produce them more cheaply than country II, and vice versa. The unit-value isoquant of a good of intermediate capital-intensity may by chance be tangent to both countries' unit isocost lines, in which case it can be produced in both countries and exported by either of them. Deardorff went on to show that the chain of comparative advantage whose existence is assured under free trade with unequal factor prices also holds if there are (a) impediments to trade, or (b) intermediate goods and free trade, but not (c) intermediate goods and impeded trade. He also showed that these results generalize to many countries instead of only two, with or without intermediate goods, as long as free trade prevails. An implication of his findings is that if there is free trade among three countries with unequal factor prices, the country with the intermediate wage-rental ratio imports commodities which are both more capital-intensive and more labor-intensive than those it exports.

Jones's multicommodity generalization of the Heckscher–Ohlin model

Jones (1974) generalized the Heckscher–Ohlin theorem to many commodities for small economies with different capital-labor ratios that share the same technology and the same homothetic tastes. He drew tangents to adjoining unit-value isoquants, and derived the unit-value locus for the world economy as the inner envelope of these tangent line segments and isoquants. Countries either specialize in a single good or produce a combination of two goods. A country produces one commodity if its factor endowment ray through the origin intersects this locus where it coincides with an arc of a unit-value isoquant, and two commodities if it intersects it on one of the line segments tangent to two isoquants. The slope of the unit-value locus at its intersection with the endowment ray yields the economy's wage-rental ratio. Consequently there is no possibility of factor price equalization between two economies, unless their endowment rays are very close and intersect the locus along the same linear segment. Since all countries consume all commodities, a country with an intermediate factor endowment ratio imports some commodities that are more capital-intensive, and others more labor-intensive, than its own exports.

Jones argued that his multicommodity model reconciles the Ricardian and Heckscher–Ohlin models: while in the Ricardian model the differences in labor productivity between the trading countries are taken as given and unexplained, in his model the difference between their relative factor endowments determines the techniques they choose and the associated labor productivities. If production functions are internationally identical, two countries produce commodities with different capital-labor ratios as long as they have different factor prices. Whereas 'the Ricardian and Heckscher–Ohlin models are distinguished from each other by the assumption concerning a commonly shared technology ... moving to a multicommodity setting allows this strict distinction to be blunted' (Jones, [1977] 1979, p. 321). However, there is no reason to believe that Ricardo would have agreed that production functions are the same everywhere, or that capital is a homogeneous substance like labor.

In a neoclassical framework, Jones's model is a useful antidote to the 2 × 2 × 2 version of the Heckscher–Ohlin model which suggests that factor price equalization and incomplete specialization are a 'normal' outcome, so that both trading countries end up satisfying part of their consumption of importable goods with domestic production. It implies instead that as a rule factor prices are not equalized by trade, and that countries concentrate on the production of a very small range of commodities (or even a single one), importing all the others. Since unequal factor prices across countries are a fact of everyday experience, and many small countries do concentrate their exports on a handful of commodities, it has realism on its side. It also highlights a danger of 'two-ness', the propensity to generalize the insights gleaned from a two-dimensional model to a multidimensional world. Jones used his model to show how a developing country's comparative advantage is modified over time as capital accumulates. As its capital-labor ratio rises, its exports are gradually transformed from labor-intensive to capital-intensive commodities.

The Jones model can be interpreted as a degenerate case of a multicountry Deardorff model where each country produces one or at most two commodities. It also yields a chain of comparative advantage since each country produces only one or two commodities with factor intensities close to its endowment ratio. The key to obtaining a chain of comparative advantage under free trade in both the Deardorff and Jones models is the failure of what Bhagwati referred to, rather curiously, as the 'not unimportant' case of factor price equalization.

Vanek's chain of factor endowment ratios

Given factor price equalization and identical homothetic tastes, Vanek (1968) generalized the Heckscher–Ohlin model to many factors of production, obtaining what became known as the *Heckscher–Ohlin–Vanek (HOV) theorem*. Let c be a country's consumption share in world output, which coincides with its output share if trade is balanced. Let V_i be its endowment of factor i and V_{wi} the corresponding world endowment ($i = 1, \ldots, m$). In a multifactor world, a country is said to be abundant in factor i if its share of the world supply of that factor exceeds its consumption share, or $V_i > cV_{wi}$. Given factor price equalization, the HOV theorem states that a country exports the services of abundant factors and imports those of scarce factors (Leamer, 1980, p. 496; 1984, p. 15). Renumber factors so that

$$\frac{V_1}{V_{w1}} > \frac{V_2}{V_{w2}} > \ldots > \frac{V_j}{V_{wj}} > c > \frac{V_{j+1}}{V_{w(j+1)}} > \ldots > \frac{V_m}{V_{wm}}. \tag{9.20}$$

Given Vanek's definition of factor abundance, the HOV theorem implies that the country exports the services of the first j factors and imports those of the last $m - j$ factors. If trade is balanced, the value of c can be shown to be a weighted average of the V_i/V_{wi} ratios, weighted by the world earnings shares of each factor, $w_i V_{wi}/\Sigma w_i V_{wi}$, where w_i is the wage of the ith factor. Vanek's chain of factor endowments is illustrated in Figure 9.4 for $j = 7$ and $m = 15$. The horizontal axis plots the 15 factors of production ranked in descending

Figure 9.4   Vanek's chain of factor endowment ratios

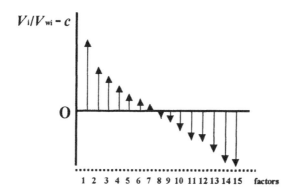

order of abundance, and the vertical axis the difference between V_i/V_{wi} and c, where positive values (indicated by upward pointing arrows) signify factors whose services are exported, while negative values (indicated by downward pointing arrows) signify factors whose services are imported.

Leamer (1984, p. 15) commented that 'this way of reexpressing the Heckscher–Ohlin theorem properly emphasizes the point that it is factor services that are being exchanged through trade. Commodities serve only as a bundle within which factor services are wrapped'. Ohlin had also stated that trade ultimately implies the exchange of factors:

> Australia trades wool and wheat against manufactures because the former products require much land of grades found in large quantities in that region, whereas manufactures require large quantities of labor and certain gifts of nature, such as coal and iron mines, which are scantily supplied in Australia. *Thus, certain grades of land are exchanged for labor and for other grades of land.... One can say that trade implies an exchange of abundant factors for scantily supplied factors.* (Ohlin, 1967, pp. 19–20; emphasis added)

When the number of commodities exceeds that of factors, prediction of factor service trade is determinate under the HOV assumptions, but no prediction can be made about the exports or imports of particular commodities. This indeterminacy is clear from Bhagwati's (1972) analysis, since many different subsets of commodities can in theory be produced and exported by each country. A commodity which is one country's export in one of these subsets may well be the other country's export in another subset.[10] This is consistent with a labor-abundant country exporting a specific amount of labor services in exchange for those of other factors.

While Vanek's theorem is logically correct given the underlying assumptions, there is something almost tautological about the statement that a labor-abundant country has a comparative advantage in goods which on average embody more labor than other factors.[11] It is reminiscent of Samuelson's (1948, p. 182) reference to 'such fatuities as: the tropics grow tropical fruits because of the relative abundance there of tropical conditions'. More importantly, the HOV prediction that trade reflects factor abundance has not been confirmed empirically, and this points to the unrealistic nature of its underlying assumptions. Not only does the HOV theory assume factor price equalization, but by focusing only on factor endowment differentials it ignores other influences on trade such as demand differences, technological differences and economies of scale. This failing, and suggestions for an alternative model, are discussed in section 10.2.

9.4   Gains and losses in the transition from Heckscher and Ohlin to Heckscher–Ohlin

The Heckscher–Ohlin–Samuelson and Heckscher–Ohlin–Vanek models differ in significant ways from the writings of both Heckscher and Ohlin. It is instructive to examine these differences to assess what has been lost and gained in the transition from the first statements of the theory to its subsequent metamorphosis. Some of the Ohlin's ideas were never incorporated in the Heckscher–Ohlin model and recently found their way into the new generation of trade models examined in the next section. The main differences between Heckscher and Ohlin, on the one hand, and the H–O–S and HOV models on the other, can be summarized as follows.[12]

Verbal economics versus formal economics. The strength and, at the same time, a limitation of the $2 \times 2 \times 2$ model is that, by neutralizing all other effects on trade except factor endowments, the relationship between the two is obvious. The geometric and mathematical trappings of the H–O–S and HOV models contrast with the economics of Eli Heckscher and Bertil Ohlin, which is largely verbal except for a few simple algebraic examples used by Heckscher, and some diagrams, economic statistics and the mathematical Appendix I of Ohlin. As argued in Chapter 8, the latter's elaborate Walras–Cassel model was in the nature of an 'optional extra', since it played no functional role in the derivation of any of his results. While the Heckscher–Ohlin model captures some of the central insights shared by Heckscher and Ohlin, it omits from consideration a number of features that it could not easily incorporate but were considered, especially by Ohlin, to be of prime importance for a full explanation of the sources of trade. Some of these, noted below, derive from the great sense of realism that permeates Ohlin's magnum opus.[13]

Economies of scale. One of these features is economies of scale, whose important role in Ohlin's work was discussed in Chapter 8. They are not compatible with the H–O–S model which, given its assumption of perfect competition in product and factor markets, assumes that the internationally identical production functions display constant returns to scale. Ohlin frequently referred to economies of scale in his book, and devoted the whole of chapter 3 to an examination of how their existence modifies trade flows. When he later summarized their impact, he remarked that

> the economies of large-scale production also cause an interregional division of production; they must be considered along with trade due to different factor supplies. The proportions in which the factors are used in the production of a commodity depends [sic] not only upon their prices but also upon the quantity to be produced. Consequently, different technical combinations may be used at the same time in different countries to produce the same commodity. (Ohlin, 1967, pp. 63–4)

The very existence of economies of scale negates one of the basic assumptions of the H–O–S theory, that production functions are identical everywhere, an assumption that Ohlin himself had made in an earlier chapter! Only with the 'new trade theory' did economies of scale regain their rightful place in a full explanation of trade flows.

Qualitative differences in commodities and factors of production. One of the key assumptions of the H–O–S theory is that commodities and factors of production are qualitatively identical in all countries. Land is land, no matter where located, as are labor and capital. Wheat and automobiles are also identical, no matter where produced. These assumptions are of course in flagrant contradiction to the facts. Ohlin was aware of this, and discussed qualitative differences of commodities and factors in chapter 6 of his book, coining the terms subfactors and subcommodities to describe subsets of these within which qualitative differences can be neglected. He noted that the existence of subfactors is one reason why factor prices are not equalized by trade. Qualitative differences among commodities lead to the phenomenon that 'in many countries the same sort of commodity is both imported and exported. This is partly due to the costs of transport, partly to the fact that the imported and exported commodities are of different quality' (1967, pp. 65–6). In other words, though Ohlin did not use these terms, product differentiation leads to intraindustry trade. This insight cannot be accommodated by the H–O–S theory, whose assumption that goods are homogeneous rules out intraindustry trade.[14] The large and increasing amount of such trade between the industrialized countries, despite the fact that factor endowments are fairly similar among them, led economists to seek an explanation of trade not based on endowments and eventually gave birth to the new trade theory. In the last appendix containing his 'Reflections on Contemporary International Trade Theories', Ohlin raised the question if his theory can explain the trade of developing countries. He responded that 'the considerable international quality differences with regard to labor have to be considered. Therefore account has to be taken of a substantial number of factors of production' (Ohlin, 1967, pp. 315–6). It was clear to him that an industrialization process requires changes in the supply and quality of factors. He also noted that internal factor mobility can be very restricted in developing countries, and that international trade can lead to unemployment rather than factor reallocation to other lines of activity.

Exogenous versus endogenous factor supplies. Though there have been some attempts to allow for labor-leisure choices and international factor migration, the H–O–S and HOV theories have generally assumed that factor endowments are purely domestic, inelastically supplied and fully employed.[15] This is again contrary to the intentions of both Heckscher and Ohlin. One of the criticisms which Ohlin directed at the classical economists was precisely the Ricardian assumption that factors are domestically mobile but internationally immobile, which he wished to replace with that of partial factor mobility both nationally and internationally. Heckscher and Ohlin also allowed for feedback effects from trade to factor endowments, which are again ruled out of court by the H–O–S model. As pointed out in Chapter 8, both economists observed that the impact of trade on factor rewards increases the abundance of the abundant factors as well as the scarcity of the scarce factors, thus raising both the difference between countries' endowments and the volume of trade beyond those associated with inelastic factor supplies. Thanks to his stay at Harvard and acquaintance with John Williams, Ohlin went further than Heckscher. He adopted Williams's view (noted in Chapter 6) that trade changes a country's endowments not just in quantitative terms but qualitatively, since many become specific to the export sector and cannot be shifted to other uses. This contrasts with the methodology, usually adopted by trade theorists, of postulating given factor endowments, finding a country's equilibrium under autarky, and comparing the resulting prices to its partner's autarky prices to determine comparative advantage and the direction of trade. If the endowments are themselves partly caused by trade, this procedure should obviously be modified, and replaced by a process of mutual causation between trade and factor endowments. This process is reminiscent of Adam Smith's productivity theory of trade and has been incorporated in some recent trade-and-development models.

The four core propositions of the Heckscher–Ohlin theory. Of the four theorems discussed in section 9.1, the only one that can be associated with the two Swedish pioneers is the Heckscher–Ohlin theorem itself (Flam and Flanders, 1991, p. 25). As noted in Chapter 8, Heckscher asserted that factor price equalization is theoretically possible but empirically unlikely if the factor endowments of the trading regions are not sufficiently close. Ohlin (1967, p. 26) had a different perspective: while trade does reduce the relative scarcity of each trading region's scarce factors, 'complete equality of factor prices is ... almost unthinkable and certainly highly improbable'.[16] The failure of factor price equalization can of course be attributed to his assumption of complete specialization. Ohlin, however, justified this result by an appeal to real world conditions which were always paramount in his mind, such as the existence of transport costs or trade impediments, imperfect domestic or interregional factor mobility, and other types of 'friction'.

It is difficult to find traces of the Rybczynski theorem in the writings of either author. The implications of the Stolper–Samuelson theorem were denied by Ohlin. Just as Haberler (1936) had done, though with less justification in view of the different natures of their models, Ohlin denied that a factor like labor can ever lose from free trade: 'the relative decline in the price of [a factor], say labor, compared to another, say land, does not necessarily mean that the wage level is lowered in terms of goods. Should Australian labor be worse off because of international trade? Of course not' (Ohlin, 1967, pp. 30–31).[17]

If all four theorems are viewed as hanging together or falling together, one can say that neither author provided a rigorous proof, verbal or otherwise, of the theory with which their joint names are associated. The Heckscher–Ohlin theorem itself crucially depends on assumption (k) of section 9.1, that demands in the trading countries are identical and homothetic. While Ohlin (1967, p. 10) did note that 'if differences in supply between the regions are balanced by differences in demand, the relative price of all factors and relative commodity prices will be the same', he added that 'differences in supply [are] probably as a rule more important than differences in demand. In a loose sense, therefore, differences in equipment of factors of production will be the cause of trade', which hardly expresses the implications of assumption (k). The contention of Heckscher and Ohlin that factor abundance leads to factor cheapness, and to the relative cheapness of commodities in which these factors are embodied, was derived from eminent common sense based on real world observation, but had to await a Paul Samuelson to turn it into a rigorous proposition.[18]

Complete or incomplete specialization. As noted in section 8.4, the model in Ohlin's Appendix I ruled out economies of scale but postulated complete specialization in both regions. In the text itself, however, full specialization was discussed only in chapter 3 in connection with factor indivisibility and economies of scale. Thanks to the work of Samuelson and others, economists now link the degree of specialization attained to the relation between the numbers of goods and factors. Complete specialization causes factor price equalization to fail, invalidating one of the Heckscher–Ohlin theory's core propositions. Ohlin's assumption of complete specialization helps to explain his view that factor prices are not equalized by trade, although he also attributed this phenomenon to transport costs and real world imperfections such as factor immobility.

Dimensionality. Samuelson introduced rigor by reducing the two-region, n-commodity, r-factor, s-inhabitant general equilibrium model of Ohlin to the $2 \times 2 \times 2$ dimensions in which it is nowadays usually presented. While this has the pedagogic advantage of allowing the four Heckscher–Ohlin theorems to be rigorously derived, the lack of empirical support for such a stripped-down version of the model led to attempts to extend it once again to more than two factors and two commodities, as detailed in section 9.3. More importantly, the factor endowments model was regarded as a fertile field of application for general equilibrium theorizing, and Samuelson himself (1953) took a major hand in investigating the extension of this model to many goods and factors, with the ramifications outlined above. There is some irony in the fact that, after jettisoning the very general version of the model of two trading regions originally proposed by Ohlin in favor of a much reduced version, economists have now returned to models of a similar degree of generality, though armed with a set of mathematical tools which Ohlin did not possess. This seems a good illustration of the French dictum *reculer pour mieux sauter*.

Statics versus dynamics. With its assumptions of given tastes, technology and factor endowments, the H–O–S theory is designed to analyze comparative static equilibrium changes rather than dynamic processes. Ohlin was more interested in the process by which equilibrium is reached, witness the numerous chapters of his book which deal with elements of change such as factor movements, their relation to commodity movements, and the adjustment process to various types of international disturbance with its accompanying monetary implications.[19]

Some attempts have been made to dynamize the H–O–S theory. The $2 \times 2 \times 2$ model has been blended with the literature on two-sector growth models applied to closed economies by assuming that the two traded commodities are a capital good and a consumption good. The consequences of capital accumulation and population growth for long-run comparative advantage could then be traced (Oniki and Uzawa, 1965). Jones's (1974) model relating to small countries in a multicommodity world, discussed in the previous section, implies that comparative advantage shifts in the direction of capital-intensive commodities if capital accumulates faster than population grows. Dynamic determinants of comparative advantage were also introduced by Findlay (1970b) into a model with two consumer goods and a non-traded capital good.

He showed that, in the long run, factor proportions and hence comparative advantage depend on the relationship between the propensity to save and the rate of population growth. As one might expect, the higher the former and the lower the latter of these parameters, the greater the probability that the country in the long run will specialize in the capital-intensive consumer good. Factor endowments are thus endogenous rather than exogenously given.

9.5 The brave new world of the 'new trade theory'

Partly because of the Leontief Paradox and the unsatisfactory results of the empirical tests of the HOV model, the Heckscher–Ohlin theory has been challenged in the past two decades by a 'new trade theory' some of whose models dispense altogether with the notion of comparative advantage. This challenge was made possible by advances made in the theory of industrial organization, which were extended to the international trade arena by Krugman, Helpman, Grossman, Ethier, Brander, Spencer, Lancaster and others. The mainstream H–O–S theory which assumed perfect competition in all commodity and factor markets, sustained by ubiquitous constant returns to scale, represents for a pioneer of the new trade theory the 'homeostatic' view 'that there is a natural pattern of specialization and trade, determined by underlying characteristics of countries, and that automatic forces tend to restore this natural pattern' (Krugman, 1987a, p. 41). The new theory allowed instead for phenomena such as increasing returns to scale, external economies and differentiated products, and the associated imperfectly competitive market structures such as monopolistic competition, oligopoly and the existence of multinational corporations. The theory of monopolistic competition, which coincidentally emerged in the same year as the books of Haberler and Ohlin, offered the prospect of generalizing trade theory to market structures other than perfect competition. Trade could be shown to arise even between economies which are identical with respect to factor endowments and technical knowledge.

Although there had been earlier attempts to formulate models based on increasing returns to scale, 'the literature did not seem to offer the possibility of a fruitful marriage of increasing returns and comparative advantage as explanations of trade. Ironically, this failure may have been in part because of an excessive loyalty to the *techniques* of conventional models – production possibility curves, offer curves, and so forth' (Krugman, 1987b, p. 65). As pointed out in section 8.4, Ohlin himself was a strong advocate of such as 'fruitful marriage'. The other pioneer of neoclassical trade theory, Haberler, also realized the importance of broadening its scope in that direction.

When Haberler analyzed increasing returns in his book, he pointed to the benefits of trade in reducing the monopoly power they engender, and remarked in Smithian fashion that their existence 'is not only no argument against the unrestricted international exchange of goods, but is, on the contrary, one of the most important arguments in favour of it. For one of the main advantages of international trade is that it widens the extent of the market....' (1936, p. 205). In the Preface of the English edition of his book, he made the prophetic remark that the theory it outlined 'requires further development, in two main directions. The theory of imperfect competition and the theory of short-run oscillation ... must be applied to the problems of international trade. It will soon be possible to do this in a systematic way, since much progress has been made in both fields in recent years' (1936, p. v). He cited the 'two outstanding books' on imperfect competition of Edward Chamberlin and Joan Robinson. But almost half a century passed before progress in this direction was realized with the new trade theory, some of which is indeed based on Chamberlinian models of monopolistic competition.

Section 8.4 described the importance that Ohlin gave in his 1933 book to increasing returns to scale, with their accompanying specialization, as a cause of trade and as a source of gains from trade in addition to factor endowments. His anticipation of the new trade theory is rather remarkable for its details as well as its general thrust. Ohlin stated some of its basic contentions, that thanks to economies of scale even regions with identical factor endowments can gain from trade, and that the particular industries in which each region specializes are a matter of chance:

> Assume that a number of regions are isolated from each other, and that their factor endowments and their demand are so balanced that the relative prices of factors and commodities are everywhere the same. Under the assumptions of Chapter I, no trade is then possible. As a matter of fact, insofar as the market for some articles within each region is not large enough to permit the most efficient scale of production, division of labor and trade will be profitable. Each region will specialize on some of these articles and exchange them for the rest. *The character of this trade will be entirely a matter of chance if factor equipment is everywhere the same, for it doesn't matter whether a certain region specializes in one commodity or another*, just as uniformly endowed individuals can with equal advantage specialize in any kind of work. (Ohlin, 1967, p. 38; emphasis added)

Ohlin went on to make the point that some industries subject to economies of scale are in fact labor-intensive, while others are capital-intensive, so that 'the different growth of these industries in different regions causes a shift in the demand for factors of production and makes their relative scarcity unequal.... This makes further division of labor profitable' (ibid.). He also denied the realism of the premise in the above passage that endowments and demands can balance out so as to yield identical prices. Since this is unlikely, trade originates from both differences in endowments and economies of scale. This is also the implication of models such as Helpman (1981), who subtitled his paper 'A Chamberlin–Heckscher–Ohlin Approach'. Ohlin also remarked on the importance of history and accident in molding comparative advantage, a factor stressed in particular by Krugman.[20] Other authors referred to this as *hysteresis*, the title of one of the chapters of Grossman and Helpman (1991), who show that research activity can become concentrated in the country that acquires a technological lead in an industry. Ohlin's view was that

> the location of an industry in one region and not in another might simply be due to chance, the industry having gained strength in that particular region and having reached an efficient scale. Since it cannot profitably be carried on in every region because the total demand is too small, it tends to remain where it was first located.... *If the actual location of production is not that which the available factors would seem to indicate, the usual explanation is that this location was natural in earlier times, and when certain industries have once been established in a place, there is a tendency for them to remain there. Friction of various kinds here is responsible.* (Ohlin, 1967, p. 39; emphasis added)

Although Ohlin qualified his statement by observing that 'as time goes on ... the tendency toward a more economical location and trade will break through' (ibid.), he offered several examples of cases where 'friction' dominates the location of industry.

Unlike the Heckscher–Ohlin theory with its agreed list of underlying assumptions, the new trade theory is characterized by great heterogeneity in the models its practitioners have used. This very diversity makes it difficult to generalize about the brave new world it has opened for international trade theorists. An assessment of its implications for whether comparative advantage is still relevant, and what forms it takes, is necessarily based on a sample of its models. Some of them provide a theoretical scaffolding for 'noncomparative-advantage trade', to use Krugman's (1990, p. 4) term, a phenomenon that Ohlin fully anticipated. One of the great achievements of the new trade theory is to provide a satisfactory explanation of the intraindustry trade that characterizes most of the advanced economies and many of the developing ones. In diametrical opposition to the prediction of the H–O–S theory for the volume of interindustry trade, that of intraindustry trade has been shown to be greater, the more similar are the trading countries' factor endowments. Some of the new models are hybrid ones that combine the novel insights into the determinants of trade with traditional explanations based on factor endowments and hence on 'comparative advantage'. The ability of the new trade theory to be hospitable to this older tradition, and allow it to yield a complementary explanation of trade, is regarded by its advocates as one of its strengths.

Krugman (1987b) subdivided models based on increasing returns into three classes, based on Marshallian external economies, Chamberlinian monopolistic competition, and an oligopolistic market structure where firms compete in Cournot fashion. The first two of these have relevance for comparative advantage. As noted in Chapter 7, a Marshallian approach to trade with increasing returns at the industry level was proposed by Graham (1923) and revived by Ethier (1979, 1982a, 1982c), who proposed a new way of thinking about world trade equilibria in terms of an *integrated world economy*. The latter is characterized by factor price equalization and thus behaves as if all factors of production were located in a single economy. Ethier's technique allowed progress to be made in modeling hitherto intractable phenomena such as increasing returns to scale, of whose empirical importance economists had been aware since the days of Adam Smith. Economies of scale lead to gains from trade as long as the increasing returns industries increase their output over the pre-trade level. Additional gains may result from the exploitation of comparative advantage as countries export commodities which embody their relatively abundant factors. Trade can then be interpreted as the export of the services of relatively abundant factors in exchange for those of scarcer factors, accompanied by the exchange of goods made cheaper by the geographical concentration of increasing returns industries, though the specific industries which locate in a country are indeterminate.

The same type of trade characterizes the second class of models, based on Chamberlinian monopolistic competition between firms producing differentiated products in an integrated world economy. If countries differ in factor endowments but this difference does not prevent factor prices from being equalized, intraindustry trade in differentiated manufactures whose production is subject to economies of scale is combined with interindustry trade involving the net export of manufactures from the capital-abundant country for a homogeneous good produced under constant returns to scale by the labor-abundant country. The volume of intraindustry trade increases with the similarity between factor endowments, and if factor endowments are identical all trade is intraindustry in nature.[21] Gains from trade include a greater variety of products and lower prices due to a higher scale of output. Because of the similarity of factor endowments which characterizes it, intraindustry trade softens the impact of trade on the gains or losses of particular factors of production, in contrast to interindustry trade and its associated Stolper–Samuelson theorem.

Increases in productivity via a Smithian division of labor can be depicted by learning curves where cumulative past output determines current productivity. They are featured in the model of dynamic comparative advantage of Krugman (1987a), which harks back to Arrow's (1962) learning-by-doing model and falls in the Marshallian class of increasing returns models. The assumption that the industry learning curve is external to firms allows perfect competition to prevail. Krugman represents the international spillover of external economies by the parameter δ, with $\delta = 0$ denoting zero spillover or purely national learning effects, and $\delta = 1$ complete spillover or a world learning curve. For values of δ between 0 and 1, labor productivity rises faster in the country which first produces a traded good. Krugman (1987a, p. 47) observed that 'Like a river that digs its own bed deeper, a pattern of specialization, once established, will induce relative productivity changes that strengthen the forces preserving that pattern. Clearly, history matters here even for the long run.... Comparative advantage is "created" over time by the dynamics of learning, rather than arising from underlying national characteristics'. He proceeded to apply his model imaginatively to such diverse issues as Japanese infant industry protection designed to cause a permanent shift in comparative advantage ('the narrow moving band'), the longer-run implications of the 'Dutch disease' for a country's comparative advantage, and the 'competitive consequences of Mrs. Thatcher'.

Assumptions about the nature of international spillovers have played an important role in other models. Grossman and Helpman (1991, chapters 7 and 8) examined polar cases where spillovers are international and national in scope. In the case of international spillovers, analyzed in a chapter entitled 'Dynamic Comparative Advantage', economies are divided into a highly human-capital-intensive sector specializing in research and development (R & D), a manufacturing sector that produces innovative products and an unskilled-labor-intensive sector that produces traditional manufactures. Activity in the R & D sector leads to the output of innovative goods, and fixed costs in the latter 'take the form of upfront research outlays'. If factor price equalization prevails, international trade follows a Heckscher–Ohlin pattern accompanied by intraindustry trade, with the human-capital-rich country exporting a greater quantity of innovative goods than it imports and importing traditional manufactures. Both countries carry out R & D and introduce new products at identical rates in the steady state.

This scenario changes dramatically when spillovers are purely national and knowledge behaves like a local public good. Now history matters in the sense that initial conditions determine the ultimate outcome. R & D activity eventually takes place in only one of the two countries since 'a country that begins with a head start in the accumulation of knowledge often widens its productivity lead over time'. However, there is room here for policy intervention in the form of a subsidy to R & D to reverse this outcome. Once the lagging country has caught up with and surpassed the leading one, the subsidy can be removed without imperiling its new relative standing. This has been referred to as 'a clear case of policy *hysteresis*; a temporary policy can have permanent effects' (Grossman and Helpman, 1991, pp. 233, 207). Their model has implications resembling those of Krugman (1987a), even though technology improves via R & D expenditure rather than a learning curve.

Whether spillovers are national or international in scope has important implications for comparative advantage. International spillovers guarantee that technology is the same everywhere, no matter which country has undertaken the R & D expenditure which improves it. This then allows factor endowments to determine a pattern of trade which includes intraindustry trade, and where the Heckscher–Ohlin theorem has a residual role to play. In models where spillovers are national or partly national in scope, another type of comparative advantage appears with Ricardian features. It is created either by learning by doing, national cumulative output being the key to productivity increases, or by the tendency of R & D (and with it the production of high-technology goods) to concentrate in one country. History and accident are now responsible for the eventual trade outcome, though there is room for policy intervention to garner for a country the advantages of specialization in high-technology goods. Such models of created comparative advantage are sophisticated versions of the infant-industry argument reviewed in Chapter 5. They are similar in nature to another family of models, the so-called 'technology gap' models which postulate that more advanced countries are more productive in all industries, but most productive in the more technologically intensive ('upscale') ones (Krugman, 1986). Countries are characterized by the number of years (uniform across industries) that they lag behind best-practice requirements. The two-country version of this model is a dynamic version of Ricardo's wine–cloth example, where the more advanced country has an absolute advantage in all goods (and hence a higher wage rate), and a comparative advantage in those whose labor productivity rises at a faster rate. A narrowing of the technological gap by the less advanced country can make the more advanced one worse off, a result which has been duplicated in other models of the new trade theory.

Models which derive from the 'imitation lag' model of Posner (1961) and the product-cycle model of Vernon (1966) do not fit comfortably into either a Ricardian or a Heckscher–Ohlin mold. They postulate a world divided into an industrialized, innovating 'North' and a 'South' where production facilities are either transferred by Northern firms to the South to take advantage of its lower costs, or where Southern firms themselves imitate the new technologies. Vernon's theory intrigued orthodox trade theorists since its publication, but was at first too heterodox to be formally modeled. Krugman (1979b) attempted this first, assuming that new products are invented in the North and adopted with a lag in the South. Trade between North and South in a new product takes place until the North's monopoly position has been eroded. This temporary monopoly position allows Northern workers to earn a higher wage than Southern ones.

A weakness of Krugman's model was his assumption that the rate of innovation in the North and of technology transfer to the South were exogenously given. Other models endogenized the North's superiority by ascribing it to expenditure on R & D, assumed to be sufficient as well as necessary to lead to new products. Imitation in the South likewise requires prior expenditure on R & D (Grossman and Helpman, 1991, chapter 11). Other authors believed, more realistically, that investment in R & D need not be crowned with success in the development of new products, and constructed Schumpeterian models of the product life cycle where R & D races are viewed as 'invention lotteries'. The probability of winning each race is proportional to the resources devoted to R & D, and each race has losers as well as winners. Firms that win the R & D race monopolize the product for a period of time, after which their patent expires and the product can be produced at lower cost in the South.

In conclusion, some of the trade that characterizes the models of the new trade theory is intraindustry in nature and can indeed be described *à la* Krugman as noncomparative-advantage trade, since it takes place even between countries with identical factor endowments. However, many of its models accord an explicit role to the creation of comparative advantage via learning by doing, R & D expenditure, or government policy. Unlike the textbook presentations of the Ricardian and Heckscher–Ohlin models, the comparative advantage featured by them is typically dynamic in nature, and reminiscent of the way it was envisaged by Adam Smith and some of the 'creators' of comparative advantage discussed in Chapter 5. Section 10.3 examines the extent to which the new trade theory can be traced back to Adam Smith rather than Ricardo, and whether Ricardo's traditional position as the father of the theory of international trade is thereby jeopardized. Section 10.4 considers the family of neo-Ricardian trade models, and the rest of Chapter 10 attempts to derive conclusions on the relevance of comparative advantage in the perspective of the past two and a half centuries of economic thought.

Notes

1. The key contributions are Stolper and Samuelson ([1941] 1949), Samuelson (1948, 1949) and Rybczynski (1955).
2. Two of these articles are Samuelson (1949) and Rybczynski (1955). The 1941 article of Stolper and Samuelson had already been reprinted in the AEA's first book of readings (Ellis and Metzler, 1949). As the editors of the second book of readings stated in the Preface, 'the great bulk of research in the static "pure" or real theory of international trade has come to center upon simple general-equilibrium models, especially the so-called two-by-two-by-two version of the Heckscher–Ohlin model.... The contributions in the first section of the volume ... lie almost entirely within the framework of this highly popular model and, taken as a group, seem to "close" it by covering all functional relations needed to make it determinate' (Caves and Johnson, 1968, p. vi). In connection with Mundell (1957), also reprinted in that volume, they observed that the theory of international factor movements had also become closely integrated with the Heckscher–Ohlin model. References to the H–O–S model are in fact scattered throughout the other selections of that book.
3. This list of assumptions (with some modifications) is drawn from Samuelson (1949, pp. 181–2).
4. The 'essential version' is the term used by Deardorff (1994b, p. 13) to denote the most general version of this theorem. The original formulation of Stolper and Samuelson, relating to the introduction of trade in a closed economy, states that it benefits the abundant factor and hurts the scarce factor.
5. See Chipman (1966), Jones and Neary (1984), Jones (1987), and international economics textbooks such as Caves, Frankel and Jones (1993) or Krugman and Obstfeld (1994), for alternative presentations of the Heckscher–Ohlin theory.
6. The diagrams favored by writers of textbooks of international trade to present the Heckscher–Ohlin theorem usually illustrate the biases towards the horizontal or vertical axes of the two countries' transformation curves induced by their relative factor endowments.
7. Leontief's results point to the dangers of 'two-ness' on the factor side. As Jones ([1977] 1979, p. 313n) stated, 'if a two-factor (capital and labor) ranking is relied upon to provide comparisons when other factors are available in differing amounts (and prices), obvious errors can be made. For example, it proved inappropriate to examine American trade patterns solely on the basis of capital and labor endowments and requirements when other factors, such as natural resources, were present but unaccounted for'.
8. The Leontief Paradox has been analyzed by de Marchi (1976) as a fascinating case study of the varied reactions of the economics profession when confronted with a significant anomaly in their scientific research program. He identified four types of reaction, the most significant of which 'belongs to the third group, led by Samuelson though over a fifteen year period embracing a succession of prominent theorists, who chose to all but ignore the Leontief paradox. This behaviour was entirely consistent with the research programme pursued by Samuelson in three important papers of 1948, 1949 and 1953' (de Marchi, 1976, p. 115). The Samuelsonian research program acquired a life of its own as a field of application of general equilibrium theory to trade issues, and was not to be deterred by an anomaly which could be explained in terms of various kinds of real world imperfections. The reaction of de Marchi's fourth group was to seek an alternative to the factor endowments model. Their efforts eventually matured into the models of the new trade theory considered below, which can be interpreted methodologically as a 'progressive problem shift' (Bensel and Elmslie, 1992). See also Blaug (1992, chapter 11) and Gomes (1990, pp. 123–7).
9. Ethier generalized an earlier finding of Dixit and Norman (1980, p. 100) based on more restrictive technological assumptions.
10. The indeterminacy of the output pattern when the number of commodities exceeds that of factors was pointed out by Samuelson (1953). For examples and graphical illustrations, see Dixit and Norman (1980, chapter 4).

11. As Blaug (1992, p. 191) observed, 'the replacement of the HOT [Heckscher–Ohlin theorem] by the HOVT [Heckscher–Ohlin–Vanek theorem] has subtly altered the question being asked: instead of explaining the trade flows in actual commodities, we end up explaining the factor-content of trade patterns, a harmless procedure if the factor-proportions theory is true but not otherwise'.

12. This section has benefitted from the Introduction of Flam and Flanders (1991), particularly the section entitled 'Heckscher and Ohlin versus Heckscher–Ohlin Theory'.

13. Ohlin's own later reactions to the H–O–S literature are revealing. In 'Reflections on Contemporary International Trade Theories', Appendix II of Ohlin (1967), he stated that because of its abstraction from several conditions of the real world, 'I have found the intensive preoccupation with the factor proportions model after World War II – which started with Paul Samuelson's [1948] penetrating article ... – to have a gradually declining "marginal utility"'. Ohlin cited Leontief's test as a failure because 'he considers only two factors of production. Each of the simplifications made in the model constitutes a more or less important deviation from reality, and therefore no "close fit" can be expected'. He rejected the idea that 'only results presented in the form of explicit theoretical models of an extremely simplified nature are of scientific value' and concluded by asserting that 'economic theory models are a good thing – indeed, quite necessary – but a "model mania" that rejects other methods of analysis must be shunned' (1967, pp. 310–11, 319). It is interesting to note that Haberler shared similar views when he concluded that 'the Lerner–Samuelson theory [of factor price equalization], though formally correct, rests on such restrictive and unrealistic assumptions that it can hardly be regarded as a valuable contribution to economic theory', though he did grant 'its elegance and pedagogic value'. He contrasted it with 'Ohlin's more modest and somewhat unprecise contention ... to the effect that trade will tend to bring about a partial equalization of factor prices' (Haberler, 1961, p. 20).

14. Aside from product differentiation, another reason for intraindustry trade is the above-mentioned existence of economies of scale, which are also inconsistent with the H–O–S theory.

15. Jones (1980) constructed a model where some factors – which he labels footloose – are internationally mobile and move to the country that offers them the highest return. The patterns of production and trade in two countries depend then on *absolute advantage*, determined by the productivity of the footloose input in each country in a particular industry, as well as on *comparative advantage* determined by the relative productivity of an immobile input such as labor in each of two industries.

16. In his article entitled 'Ohlin Was Right' where he presented his Ricardo–Viner (or specific-factors) model, Samuelson (1971) confirmed that under its assumptions factor price equalization is incomplete.

17. In analyzing the Australian case for protection, Marion C. Samuelson (1939) argued that what can befall a particular non-competing group can also affect 'broad categories of land and labor'. Her contention was formally vindicated by Stolper and Samuelson, who concluded their paper ([1941] 1949, p. 356) by observing that 'in Australia, where land may perhaps be said to be abundant relative to labour, protection might possibly raise the real income of labour'. M. C. Samuelson, Edgeworth and Pigou were ranked by Paul Samuelson (1981b) as anticipators of the Stolper–Samuelson theorem.

18. If, in the absence of assumption (k), demand conditions offset supply conditions and cause the country with the higher L/T ratio to export the land-intensive good, how is comparative advantage to be defined? According to Jones ([1956] 1979, p. 10), 'the meaning of comparative advantage in production is reflected in the production bias arising from differences in factor endowments.... In this sense, it is meaningful to state that the capital-rich country has a comparative advantage in producing the capital-intensive commodity'. This usage of the term, however, would be inconsistent with that adopted in Chapter 2, which requires a country to export commodities whose autarky prices, *on average,* are lower than those of its trading partner whether because of supply-side or demand-side factors.

19. Ohlin (1967, p. 314n) resented the suggestion of Myrdal (1957, chapter 11) that the Heckscher–Ohlin theory centers around the notion of equilibrium and is therefore static in nature. He went on (p. 318n) to cite sections of nine chapters of his book that deal with dynamic aspects of trade theory.
20. Part II of Krugman's (1990) collection of his articles is entitled 'Cumulative Processes and the Role of History'. See also Krugman (1991).
21. Models of this type include Krugman (1979a), Dixit and Norman (1980), Lancaster (1980), Helpman (1981). For a synthesis, see Helpman and Krugman (1985) and Krugman (1987b).

10. The (Almost) General Validity of Comparative Advantage

10.1 A retrospective of comparative advantage

Ever since individuals and communities have exchanged goods and services, explanations have been sought for the comparative advantage they evince. The sources of comparative advantage are many and various (Chapter 2), and include different tastes, technologies, factor endowments and the ability to reap economies of scale. Factor endowments are available in different proportions in different countries (Heckscher–Ohlin theory) or are resources present in one community to the exclusion of others ('availability' theory of trade). The ancients appeared to have this last theory in mind when they identified different parts of the world with particular commodities with which they were endowed. The universalist theory of trade was first given a naturalistic interpretation, but this was followed by a theological one: Providence deliberately scattered resources in a random fashion among countries so as to force different peoples to trade and hence to realize that they depend on each other (Chapter 3).

Trade assumed center stage with the mercantilists, who placed much stress on the structure of foreign trade and the primacy of exports over imports. Recent revisionist interpretations of their belief system absolve them of the charge that they wished to accumulate a positive trade balance in the form of precious metals because they mistook money for wealth. This apparent Midas-like obsession with the balance of trade can be construed as a proxy for economically more sensible goals, such as a 'balance of labor' aimed at maximizing the level of employment, or a vehicle for a policy of import-substituting industrialization. The interest of mercantilists in a normative, as opposed to a positive, theory of comparative advantage makes them precursors of the statesmen and thinkers who, in reaction to Adam Smith's *Wealth of Nations*, established a rationale for the promotion of infant industries (Chapter 5). Whatever errors the mercantilists may have committed in their zeal to promote import substitution, this period saw the beginnings of the rationalization of a territorial division of labor between advanced and primitive economies which would be accepted for two centuries. According to Josiah Tucker, the former should specialize in manufactures and the latter in primary products, a view fervently held even by advocates of a nationalist path of development like Friedrich List. True analytical progress in formulating the gains from trade was achieved when Henry Martyn expressed with a numerical example the eighteenth-century rule that exports are an indirect means of production of importable goods.

Adam Smith deserves a place of honor for legitimizing the goal of free trade which many mercantilists had espoused, and for propounding a 'productivity' theory of trade which postulates a feedback process between trade and the enhancement of labor productivity (Chapter 3). Because of this insight, some economists now regard him as a precursor of the 'new trade theory'. Smith identified 'soil, climate, and situation' as crucial determinants of the international division of labor, and noted that the abundance of land makes agriculture 'the proper business of all new colonies'. Such hints led some observers two centuries later to see in him a precursor of the Heckscher–Ohlin theory of trade.

The discovery of comparative advantage by Robert Torrens and David Ricardo early in the nineteenth century established a separate subfield of inquiry, international economics (Chapter 4). It is somewhat paradoxical that while Ricardo's name is associated (and, for many economists, primarily associated) with comparative advantage, the concept itself played a small role in his system of thought. Trade in the *Principles of Political Economy and Taxation* takes mainly the form of trade in corn, since Ricardo wished to focus attention on its effects on the rates of profit and capital accumulation. Ricardo and other classical economists held that the pressure of population on the land in Britain would lead to an increasing comparative disadvantage in agricultural goods. His later parliamentary support of the repeal of the Corn Laws was clearly motivated by the benefits he expected to accrue from the enhancement of Britain's comparative advantage in manufactures, assisting her transformation into the Workshop of the World. His implicit trade model was a growth-and-trade model, consistent with the 'magnificent dynamics' for which Ricardian economics has also been justly celebrated. Comparative advantage is transformed as factor endowments change, the labor force acquires greater skills, or investment occurs in labor-saving machinery. Soon after setting out his comparative cost example, Ricardo even postulated a reversal of comparative advantage between England and Portugal in response to an improvement in the English wine-making technique (1951a, pp. 137–8). In his chapter 'On Machinery', he pointed out that technological change can be expected to alter comparative advantage since 'by employing improved machinery, the cost of production of commodities is reduced, and, consequently, you can afford to sell them in foreign markets at a cheaper price' (p. 397). His dynamic view of comparative advantage went hand in hand with a belief in dynamic gains from trade, which hold pride of place over the static ones associated with a reallocation of resources.

Some classical economists went beyond Ricardo in stressing the role of trade in improving an economy's technology and the quality of its resource endowments, allowing it to grow wealthier. In his essay 'Of Commerce', Hume (1955, p. 14) noted that 'commerce with strangers ... rouses men from their indolence' and that 'imitation soon diffuses all those arts; while domestic manufactures emulate the foreign in their improvements, and work up every home commodity to the utmost perfection of which it is susceptible'. In 'Of the Jealousy of Trade', he added that 'notwithstanding the advanced state of our manufactures, we daily adopt, in every art, the inventions and improvements of our neighbours' (1955, pp. 78–9), a theme also taken up by John Stuart Mill. The Hume–Mill thesis that trade stimulates the borrowing of the technology and practices of other nations has a surprisingly modern flavor. The phenomenon of technological convergence, which has been formally modeled in recent years to explain the dependence of a country's growth rate on the technological gap separating it from more advanced economies, can be regarded as a direct descendant of this thesis.

In 1835 Mountifort Longfield described the continual improvements occurring in the manufacturing sector, and spelled out their implications for the pattern of trade. He and other economists even recognized the effects of the 'Dutch disease', where an improvement in one line of economic activity leads to the decline of others. The classical economists were well aware of the international diffusion of technological discoveries, and the consequent ephemeral nature of comparative advantage in the 'high-tech' sectors of the time. An awareness of the spread of techniques to other countries and of the consequent erosion of Britain's comparative advantage in manufacturing underlay the restrictions that the British government imposed until 1844 on the export of machinery. This policy was supported even by some free-traders and well-known political economists such as Senior and Torrens, despite their recognition that such restrictions were ineffective. The opinions expressed by the classical economists about the factors motivating trade, and the mutations to which they are subject, thus went well beyond a bald statement of the theory of comparative costs. As Bloomfield ([1978] 1994, p. 23) pointed out, 'these views were seldom the subject of systematic or sustained analysis and were rarely integrated into the main body of classical trade theory'. But the leitmotiv underlying them was a belief that comparative advantage in both the agricultural and industrial sectors of the economy was subject to change, even rapid change.[1]

The infant industry argument for protection represents an exceptionally dynamic view of comparative advantage, since it can be created with the assistance of policymakers who wish to advance their country's relative economic standing (Chapter 5). Its rationale for this argument was advanced by dissenters from some of the teachings of Adam Smith, such as Alexander Hamilton and John Rae, and incorporated into political economy thanks to J. S. Mill's persuasive advocacy. This view was further developed by national economists such as Friedrich List who speculated on ways to alter their country's comparative advantage so as to allow it to catch up with Britain, the leading industrial power of that time. They blazed a trail which was followed by other advocates of protectionism, such as Henry Carey in the US, Mihail Manoilescu in Romania and Raúl Prebisch in Argentina. Their driving vision was the identification of economic development with industrialization, with notable variations not only from each other but from their predecessors.[2] The infant-industry argument was accepted by eminent neoclassical economists such as Marshall, Taussig, Haberler and (in his last work) even Pareto. The view that comparative advantage can be created has been reincarnated in the new theories of trade and growth that emerged in the past two decades.

After the discovery of comparative advantage, the classical economists illustrated it with numerical examples and examined at great length its normative implications, but did not seek to elucidate its ultimate causes. Attention shifted from arguments in favor of free trade, which after Smith and Ricardo had become part of the conventional wisdom, to the division of the gains from trade between the trading countries. Despite J. S. Mill's youthful attribution of the entire gains from trade to both countries, it soon became apparent that these gains are shared between them, and that each country's share is a function of the terms of trade. Mill's law of international values for determining the latter depends on the strength of reciprocal demand (Chapter 6). While the sources of comparative advantage remained unexplained, autarky price ratios played a modest role in setting upper and lower limits for the terms of trade, as James Penningon intimated in 1840. James Whewell's 1850 formula for the terms of trade provided a more complete description than that offered by Mill's rudimentary algebraic formula, which depended on the assumption of unitary price elasticities of demand in both countries. In addition to demand-side parameters for the 'susceptibilities' of demand in the two countries, Whewell's formula contained supply-side ones such as gap between the two countries' autarky price ratios, which measures the difference in comparative advantage between them. Whatever the extent of his indebtedness to Whewell, Mill used the law of international values imaginatively in his *Principles of Political Economy* in exploring such issues as the change in comparative advantage resulting from an 'improvement' in a country's manufacturing process, with its implications for the terms of trade and hence for the division of the gains from the improvement between the trading partners.

As the classical period was drawing to an end, increasing dissatisfaction was felt with the formulation of comparative advantage in terms of labor costs. The existence was recognized of heterogeneous types (or 'non-competing groups') of labor in the same country, whose costs were not simply proportional to hours of embodied labor, and of capital as an additional category of costs. Ricardo himself had painstakingly analyzed in the third edition of his *Principles* how the labor theory of value must be modified when capital-labor ratios differ among sectors. Labor costs were accordingly expanded into 'real costs', but no convincing expedient was advanced for aggregating costs in this manner. Alfred Marshall's deferential respect for Ricardian economics did not allow him to make the decisive break with this theory needed to implement in the area of international trade the neoclassical revolution which he epitomized in so many other areas of economics. His invention of offer curves to represent Mill's law of international values was of course a landmark discovery, though it is noteworthy that (unlike Edgeworth) Marshall never succeeded in relating their construction to supply-side determinants such as the trading countries' autarky prices and hence their comparative advantage (Chapter 7). His aggregation of export and import commodities into 'representative bales' was a well-meaning but ultimately sterile attempt to aggregate bundles of heterogeneous inputs as well as outputs. As both Haberler and Ohlin commented, it would have been better if Marshall had adhered to a labor theory of value in his formulation of trade theory.[3]

A decisive break with the classical theory of trade was effected by Vilfredo Pareto, who was the first to generalize the Walrasian general equilibrium model to two trading economies. He also generalized the concept of comparative advantage by giving an exact expression to Cairnes's cost of commodities in terms of labor and 'abstinence'. Pareto related such costs to individuals rather than to amorphous national entities, and postulated that two individuals trade until they equate the ratios of their 'ophelimity costs' of two commodities. The Ricardian model, however, held a lingering fascination for Pareto, just as it did for Marshall and Haberler, and retains for the current generation of economists. To trace how monetary flows aid an economy's adjustment to a disturbance, Pareto 'resolutely sacrifice[d] rigor for clarity' by considering labor to be the only factor of production. He also analyzed in depth Ricardo's footnote example of two individuals, one of whom holds an absolute advantage over the other in two activities and a comparative advantage in one. He thereby elucidated 'Pareto's paradox', that full specialization by these individuals may lower overall welfare compared to autarky since the total output of one of the commodities they jointly produce may decline. Pareto's friend Enrico Barone not only drew the first neoclassical diagram depicting an economy's trade equilibrium and the associated gains from trade, but speculated about the dynamic losses that arise if the terms of trade fluctuate on either side of the autarky price ratio, causing reversals of comparative advantage and the associated destruction of capital. According to Barone, dynamic factors of this type qualify the gains arising from a free trade equilibrium, so that free trade should not be erected into a dogma.

The theory of comparative costs was regarded in diametrically opposed ways by the second generation of neoclassical trade theorists. Eli Heckscher and Gottfried Haberler, like Marshall and Pareto before them, respected Ricardo's insights and wished to reconcile them with the emerging neoclassical theory of value (Chapter 8). Haberler rejected the constant-cost tradeoff between commodities of real cost theorists in favor of increasing opportunity costs. Unaware of Barone's diagram, he drew a concave transformation curve and justified its shape in terms of the stickiness of factors of production, and the time they take to move between sectors in response to price changes. While Haberler's role in formulating the specific-factors model has not been sufficiently recognized in the literature, he did not use this model to create a new theory of the sources of comparative advantage. His aim was the more modest (though still important) one to show that the concept of comparative advantage and the existence of gains from trade survive in a neoclassical economy, and to outline how the passage of time modifies these gains when there are obstacles to factor mobility. Like Haberler, Heckscher portrayed himself as a reformer and improver of the Ricardian theory. He used a model based on dissimilar factor endowments among countries and differential factor intensities in the production of commodities in order to explain the differences in comparative costs among countries and to analyze the impact of trade on income distribution.

In sharp contrast, Heckscher's student Ohlin assumed the mantle of a revolutionary bent on the annihilation of the classical model by critiquing its very foundations, to the point even of refusing to use the term 'comparative advantage' and denouncing the theory of comparative costs as a mere *deus ex machina*. It is ironic that Ohlin's book ended up being the first full-length study of the causes of comparative advantage, as Paul Samuelson (1948) was quick to recognize. Ohlin succeeded so well in advancing a paradigm alternative to the classical one that his (and Heckscher's) assumption of internationally identical techniques of production eliminated the possibility of a country having an absolute advantage in all traded goods as well as a comparative advantage in some. Therefore, the Heckscher–Ohlin theory could not produce an example similar to the wine–cloth one of Ricardo.[4] Its inability to mimic comparative advantage in the Ricardian sense is consistent with the possibility that (given incomplete specialization in both countries) factor prices become equalized by trade in absolute as well as relative terms. By contrast, in Ricardo's numerical example the country with an absolute advantage in both commodities is marked by a higher post-trade wage than its trading partner.

10.2 The Heckscher–Ohlin theory in the twilight of the twentieth century

In view of its importance as the mainstream theory of international trade, it is appropriate to devote some space to an evaluation of the current status of the Heckscher–Ohlin theory, with its H–O–S and HOV variants, in light of the empirical evidence that has accumulated to date. The widely different views on its validity held by economists depend in part (as is true of many other issues in economics) on the intellectual capital that they have spent on the elaboration of this theory or of alternative theories. In the most ambitious empirical study to date of the HOV model, Leamer (1984) championed the Heckscher–Ohlin assumption that technology is internationally identical and criticized the conventional interpretation of Ricardian comparative advantage:

> An economist ought to be uncomfortable assuming technological differences, and Ricardo is treated unfairly when his name is associated with this idea. According to the classic Ricardian example, Portugal exchanges wine for cloth from Britain because Portugal is relatively efficient in the production of wine. The source of this comparative advantage was not Ricardo's concern, but it has been interpreted by many modern writers as 'technological differences.' This very superficial account of the causes of international trade seems to suppose that there are either biological differences between the Portuguese and the British that preclude each from emulating the productive techniques of the other or rather effective counterintelligence agents.
>
> The Heckscher–Ohlin model is much more satisfying, since it accounts for comparative advantage without having to appeal to the 'demon' of technological differences. Namely, Portugal is relatively well endowed in land with a Mediterranean climate. The British indeed have the knowledge; but they lack the resources for efficient production of wine. (Leamer, 1984, pp. 36–7)

At the end of his landmark study, he concluded:

> What emerges from this data analysis is a surprisingly good explanation of the main features of the trade data in terms of a relatively brief list of resource endowments. There

are apparent problems with measuring some of the resources, and there is some evidence of nonlinearities, but overall the simple linear model does an excellent job. It explains a large amount of the variability of net exports across countries, and it also identifies sources of comparative advantage that we all 'know' are there. (Leamer, 1984, p. 187)

In a later study (Bowen et al., 1987) of the factor endowments theory with data relating to 27 countries and 12 factors of production, the authors (who included Leamer) found that for eight of these factors trade ran in the direction predicted by the HOV theory less than 70 per cent of the time. A textbook on international economics co-authored by Krugman, one of the pioneers of the new trade theory, commented on these findings that

this result confirms the Leontief paradox on a broader level: trade just does not run in the direction that the Heckscher–Ohlin theory predicts.... The best answer at this point seems to be to return to the Ricardian idea that the trade pattern is largely driven by international differences in technology rather than resources. For example, the United States exports computers and aircraft not because its resources are specially suited to these activities, but because it is simply relatively more efficient at producing these goods than it is at automobile or steel production. This still leaves the reasons for technology differences unexplained. Understanding the sources of technological differences between countries is now a key topic of research. (Krugman and Obstfeld, 1994, pp. 78–9)

Students of technical change have also been struck by the extent to which the techniques used in the world economy differ among countries and show no sign of becoming more uniform. Comparative advantage based on different technologies seems to them much more realistic than one based on different factor endowments in a world of identical techniques of production.[5]

These skeptical views were corroborated by recent empirical work on the HOV trade model, which concludes that the empirical failure shown by previous tests of that model can be traced to its assumptions of factor price equalization, identical and homothetic tastes, and internationally identical production functions. Trefler (1993), proving that the last word has not yet been said about the Leontief paradox, subtitled his paper 'Leontief Was Right!'. He thereby wished to ratify Leontief's attribution of his own paradox to American labor being more productive than foreign labor, so that the US is in fact a labor-abundant country. Given the HOV model's assumption of identical technologies, Leamer (1984) had found paradoxically that developed countries are scarce in almost all factor endowments, while developing countries are abundant in most factor endowments. Trefler (1995) named this finding 'the endowments paradox', and the fact that factor service trade is much smaller than its prediction based on factor endowments 'the case of the missing trade'. He concluded that 'empirically, the HOV theorem has been repeatedly rejected over the years and rightfully so: it performs horribly.... A goal of this paper is to demonstrate that the HOV theorem is rejected because factor service trade departs from its endowments-based prediction in *systematic* and informative ways' (1995, p. 1029). One of these ways is that developed countries' endowments are on average more productive than those of less developed countries. Departures from the HOV theorem can be satisfactorily explained by postulating international differences in technology as well as a home bias in consumption. When he modified the HOV model so as to allow for factor-augmenting international productivity differences, Trefler found that this revised model explains both the factor content of trade and the large variations in factor prices across countries.

As the twentieth century draws to a close, the accumulated empirical evidence appears to reject the conclusions of models based on the assumptions of internationally identical production functions and identical homothetic tastes, which are the building blocks of the H–O–S explanation of trade flows and comparative advantage. Ricardian technological differences between economies at different stages of economic development retain an important supplementary role. Of course, this does not imply the ultimate victory of Ricardo over the two Swedish pioneers of the factor endowments theory. Trefler's work argues in favor of a synthesis of the Ricardian and Heckscher–Ohlin models, with the offspring assuming characteristics of both parents.

10.3 The new views of comparative advantage

Even before the advent of a new generation of trade models, the Ricardian principle of comparative costs and the very notion of comparative advantage had come under attack for the reasons outlined in previous chapters and summarized in section 10.1. As argued in section 10.2, the explanation of comparative advantage offered by the Heckscher–Ohlin theory has become increasingly harder to maintain. The cloud cast over comparative advantage turned even more threatening in the past two decades with the emergence of the new trade theory examined in section 9.5. One of the remarkable features of that theory is that it could, at last, provide an intellectually satisfactory explanation for the phenomenon of intraindustry trade, which the Heckscher–Ohlin paradigm was powerless to explain. As Krugman characterized it, this was truly a 'noncomparative-advantage trade', since its volume increases with the similarity between the trading countries' factor endowments. Has the new trade theory then weakened or even abrogated the principle of comparative advantage? Some of its pioneers have claimed that its insights can be traced to Adam Smith's division of labor giving rise to dynamic economies of scale. In the introduction to *Rethinking International Trade*, a collection of his papers, Krugman (1990, p. 4) noted that 'the long dominance of Ricardo over Smith – of comparative advantage over increasing returns – was largely due to the belief that the alternative was necessarily a mess. In effect, the theory of international trade followed the perceived line of least mathematical resistance'.[6]

In Chapter 3 we noted that Smith's 'productivity theory' of trade has been hailed as a precursor of the new models based on increasing returns and dynamic comparative advantage. It implies that an industry's competitive advantage over other nations is not fixed but depends on the history of its production, which is itself affected via an evolutionary or feedback process by the amount it has exported in the past. It thereby contrasts not only with the textbook Ricardian trade theory based on a given technology, but with the Heckscher–Ohlin theory predicated upon exogenously given factor endowments and internationally identical production functions. Its form appears surprisingly in tune with recent models based on Marshallian external economies. Smith's perception that the division of labor is limited by the extent of the market, which includes the world market as well as the domestic one, has inspired the construction of models that can be viewed as lineal descendants of his productivity theory. For example, the model in Krugman (1987a) can be regarded as a prototypical Smithian model. Other models where history and initial conditions determine the pattern of an economy's evolution, such as those of Grossman and Helpman (1991), can also claim a Smithian antecedent.

Adam Smith's name was invoked in a different connection by Ethier (1979), who distinguished between two concepts of economies of scale, the 'traditional' ones which require concentration of production in one country, and 'internationally decreasing costs [which depend] on the size of the international market rather than national output'. Moreover, 'international specialization is not really central to this argument [the generation of economies of scale], if free trade in intermediate goods is possible. This view of scale economies as largely, or at least substantially, a matter of the division of labor is central to Adam Smith and subsequent extensions, such as Young (1928)' (Ethier, 1979, p. 2). Since externalities are static in scope and the role of factor endowments looms large in determining trade and specialization, this yields a very different interpretation of Smithian increasing returns, though one consistent with Smith's dictum that the division of labor depends on the extent of the market. Ethier used the term comparative advantage in an idiosyncratic sense to indicate that a larger country can produce a commodity subject to increasing returns more cheaply than a smaller one.[7]

Models based on Chamberlinian monopolistic competition have also yielded interesting insights into the nature of and gains from trade, by reconciling increasing returns with a degree of interfirm competition. But while Chamberlin's model 'corresponds much more closely to Smith's vision than does the perfectly competitive model ... it retains a static character foreign to Smith; preferences and production possibilities are given and the equilibrium appropriate to them represents a configuration of production that will remain the same so long as they do not change' (Richardson, 1975, p. 355). Richardson's conclusion (which refers to Chamberlin's original model rather than to the models of the new trade theory based on it) flows from his belief that Smith postulates 'a disequilibrium theory in the sense that he views the economy as in a state of constant and internally generated change' (1975, p. 351). This view is inconsistent with models yielding the economic analog of a mechanical state of equilibrium, whether a static or a dynamic steady-state equilibrium. Since many of the new trade models do yield such a long-run steady state, a purist cannot regard them as truly Smithian in nature.

Despite the claims of several new trade theorists to find in Smith an intellectual forefather, such claims do not imply that Ricardo should be consigned to play second fiddle in the Valhalla of international trade theorists. As pointed out in Chapters 3 and 5, in the *Wealth of Nations* Smith was unsympathetic to a policy of protection for infant industries even though, according to some of the new (and most of the old) trade theorists, it is possible to create comparative advantage where it did not exist before.[8] Smith's failure to recognize the temporary nature of 'acquired' advantages is indeed surprising in someone who advocated a productivity theory of trade based on learning by experience. An important strand of the new trade theory was indirectly inspired by Rae, Mill and List rather than by Smith.

While some models of the new trade theory dispense altogether with comparative advantage as a rationale for trade, this concept plays a vital role in a large subset of others. As pointed out in the next section, it has been used in a neo-Ricardian sense to describe the fact that differences in technology among countries are created over time, whether by the invisible hand of competition digging deeper furrows of expertise via learning-by-doing, or by public intervention in accordance with the infant-industry argument. While Krugman correctly characterized intraindustry trade as 'noncomparative-advantage trade', he himself constructed models illustrative of what he describes as dynamic Ricardian comparative advantage. His respect for models based on Ricardian differences in technology was highlighted in section 10.2. Such differences are also inherent in the family of models based on a product cycle or technological gap, where the innovating North has by default a comparative advantage in new goods which the South can produce only after a lapse of time.

Far from disqualifying comparative advantage from a key role in the determination of trade flows, the new trade theory has thus reinvigorated and given a new meaning to this concept. In some of its models comparative advantage due to dynamic economies of scale coexists with comparative advantage of the Heckscher–Ohlin type, since an economy's endowment of physical or human capital determines the sectors in which it initially specializes. Some of the models based on Marshallian external economies or Chamberlinian monopolistic competition thus successfully combine both the principal reasons for trade that Ohlin emphasized in his 1933 book. Having moved beyond the H–O–S paradigm to incorporate economies of scale, they can thus be described as Ohlinian *par excellence*. The renewed emphasis on dynamic gains from trade reveals that the 'new' trade theory is not as new as its name suggests, but a legitimate descendant of the theories of the classical economists, consigned to oblivion after the advent of neoclassical economics. In their different ways, David Hume, Adam Smith, David Ricardo, John Rae and John Stuart Mill all stressed the important dynamic gains which a country can derive from the international economy by participating in trade in goods and services, and being open to the flows of technology and of new ideas.

Historically the analysis of the gains from trade has always proceeded hand in hand with the explanation of trade itself. After investigating phenomena such as learning-by-doing and increasing returns, it is not surprising that the new trade theory should emphasize dynamic gains, which affect the rate of technical innovation in a country or in the world as a whole. Consumers' welfare is portrayed as a function not only of the volume of consumption but of the variety of manufactures available, whose number increases at different rates in open and closed economies. These models typically assume that the cost of innovation varies inversely with the number of varieties produced in a country (in the case of national spillovers) or in the world (in that of international spillovers).

The new trade theory was later joined by a new (or endogenous) growth theory which also took its cue from advances in the theory of industrial organization, modeling growth in the presence of increasing returns to scale, R & D and human capital formation (Romer, 1986, 1990; Lucas, 1988, 1993). This theory sought to endogenize technical progress, treated as an unexplained residual in the earlier generation of growth models (Solow, 1956, 1957). It was inevitable that the new growth theory should find a common meeting ground with the new trade theory since many studies have concluded that total factor productivity, and hence growth itself, is affected by an economy's degree of openness. This has been borne out empirically and attributed to the workings of dynamic comparative advantage.[9] The key to growth is seen to reside in human capital accumulation, which is fostered mainly by learning on the job. Moreover, 'for this to be done on a large scale, the economy must be a large scale exporter' (Lucas, 1993, p. 270). The new growth theory again points to a feedback process where the accumulation of knowledge and human capital interact with an economy's degree of openness, and an important function of policymakers is to encourage the creation of comparative advantage in accordance with an economy's potentialities. With its assumption of relatively effortless and endogenous technical change, the new growth theory has in a sense won too easy a victory over the old one. The attainment of a steady growth state is unencumbered by the exhaustibility of resources or other vexatious limits to growth, and marked instead by the proliferation of new varieties of manufactures and the rise of consumer welfare into the indefinite future. Despite this lack of attention to basic resource constraints, the new growth theory had the salutary effect of drawing attention to the lack of convergence between developed and developing countries, and highlighting the need to explore new ways to transform comparative advantage so that laggard countries can compete in an increasingly globalized world economy.

10.4 Varieties of neo-Ricardian trade models

David Ricardo occupies a central position in the history of economic thought in part because he was the co-discoverer of comparative advantage and the economist with whom this concept is primarily associated. His name has been invoked on many occasions and in many different contexts in the past two centuries, and there is a rich literature on 'neo-Ricardian' models. To use Rutherford's (1986) apt expression, 'Ricardo's mantle' has several claimants with regard to issues that extend well beyond the context of international trade, so that their exploration would not be appropriate here. It is useful, however, to review briefly the several trade models which claim (or whose labels suggest they may claim) a Ricardian pedigree.

There is no question that the textbook 'Ricardian' model is an excellent pedagogical device to represent the motivation and the advantages of trade. However, for the reasons outlined in Chapter 4, it is very questionable if it captures the implicit trade model underlying Ricardo's *Principles* and his other writings. This reservation applies even more strongly to the ingenious extensions of the two-commodity Ricardian model to several commodities and countries (McKenzie, 1954; Jones, 1961). For example, consider the case of three countries and three commodities. In situations of complete specialization by each country in one commodity, there are six possible assignments of commodities to countries. The most efficient of these, and the only one supported by the invisible hand of competition, is that which minimizes the product of the three labor coefficients.[10] In cases of unequal numbers of commodities and countries, linear programming techniques can be used to assign commodities to countries in the most efficient manner (Dorfman, Samuelson and Solow, 1958; Takayama, 1972). On the strength of such models, Takayama (1972, p. 113) went so far as to claim that 'the Ricardian analysis ... can be considered one of the earliest forerunners of the theory of linear programming and activity analysis'. This anachronism is reminiscent of Chipman's (1965a) earlier claim, examined in Chapter 6, that in formulating the law of international values J. S. Mill had implicitly solved a problem in nonlinear programming.

Another mathematical 'Ricardian' model that attracted the attention of the profession in recent years is that integrating the monetary and real sides of trade theory in an economy with a continuum of goods (Dornbusch, Fischer and Samuelson, 1977). While this model features only one primary factor, labor, and ignores diminishing returns in the agricultural sector, it has the virtue of allowing for an infinite number of commodities, and can be used to analyze changes in the factoral terms of trade and in the range of commodities produced by each country after a perturbation such as technical change.

As pointed out in section 10.3, several models of the new trade theory are based on endogenously determined technological differences among countries, and can therefore be said to evince Ricardian comparative advantage. Though these differences are of a short-run rather than a long-run nature, this does not detract from their Ricardian pedigree, since Ricardo himself had readily allowed for reversals of comparative advantage.

Besides the 'Ricardian' model that is usually the centerpiece of chapter 2 of international trade texts, another model that has become a favorite of such texts is sometimes referred to as the 'Ricardo–Viner' model, though (as argued in Chapter 8) it deserves to be associated with the name of Haberler rather than those of Ricardo or Viner. In the simplest version of this specific-factors model, each sector of the economy uses a factor of production specific to it as well as a 'mobile' factor common to all sectors, usually taken to be labor. In the chapter of their textbook where they discuss this model, Krugman and Obstfeld (1994) include a 'Box' entitled 'Specific Factors and the Beginnings of Trade Theory' where they comment that 'yet almost surely the British economy of 1817 was better described by a specific factors model than by the one-factor model Ricardo presented' (p. 56). Their implicit assumptions are that the agricultural (corn) sector uses land as its specific factor, 'capital' is specific to the manufacturing sector, and both sectors share the mobile factor, labor. They go on to discuss the distributional implications of the Corn Laws for landlords and capitalists, and the reasons for Ricardo's opposition to these Laws. Despite Ricardo's explicit statement (1951a, p. 5) that 'to determine the laws which regulate this distribution [between rent, profits and wages], is the principal problem in Political Economy', Krugman and Obstfeld make the surprising claim that instead of elaborating a model based on specific factors, Ricardo for political reasons 'chose to present his argument in the form of a model that assumed away issues of internal income distribution' (p. 56), namely, his wine–cloth example of comparative advantage.

A third alternative representation of an open Ricardian system is the class of open-economy 'neo-Ricardian' models developed in the 1970s. Since they were inspired by the work of Sraffa (1960), they are sometimes, perhaps more appropriately, referred to as 'Sraffian'. The list of economic inputs includes heterogeneous capital goods (produced means of production) in addition to labor (and possibly another primary input). A lag occurring between the application of these inputs and the resulting output gives rise to a profit component in total cost. One of the distributive variables, the wage or the profit rate, is assumed to be exogenously given. The advantages and limitations of neo-Ricardian models are nicely described in the introductory chapter of Steedman (1979a). The advantages claimed for them are the depiction of growing as opposed to stationary economies, and the allowance for the role of time and capital goods in the production of commodities. Their limitations are that they often focus on steady growth equilibria, usually ignore technical progress and do not allow for imperfections in competition. In order to ensure the attainment of steady growth, they omit inputs of land and other non-reproducible resources, a feature shared in common with neoclassical models whose authors also seem mainly interested in computing steady-growth equilibria. This 'internal' critique of neo-Ricardian theory is echoed by some neoclassical economists, who at the same time acknowledge its undoubted contributions.[11]

In considering the appropriateness of neo-Ricardian models as possible characterizations of Ricardo's implicit trade model, note first that the primary aim of neo-Ricardian authors was rather to challenge the dominant H–O–S trade model. One of the basic issues they examine is whether the $2 \times 2 \times 2$ Heckscher–Ohlin theorem remains applicable when the factor of production 'land' is replaced by 'capital' consisting of a heterogeneous bundle of goods. While this is not the place to review the heated controversies on the theory of capital of the 1970s (Harcourt, 1972), the inclusion of heterogeneous capital goods among a country's inputs is an important extension of the standard H–O–S theory in which capital is either ignored or assumed to be a homogeneous putty-like substance on the same footing as land or labor. Neo-Ricardian authors disavow any claim to depict Ricardo's comparative cost example in chapter 7 of the *Principles* based on the labor theory of value. In fact, they have pointed out the errors implicit in Ricardo's procedure. Since positive profits usually cause prices to diverge from labor values, Steedman and Metcalfe (1973) showed that, in contrast to Ricardo's assumption, countries may specialize in the 'wrong' commodity (that in which they have a comparative disadvantage) and experience a lower welfare than under autarky. Consistency with the conclusions about the causes and consequences of trade asserted by Ricardo in chapter 7 thus depends crucially on his assuming in chapter 1 'all the great variations which take place in the relative value of commodities to be produced by the greater or less quantity of labour which may be required ... to produce them' (1951a, pp. 36–7).

A fourth trade model with a Ricardian label is a growth-and-trade model of the type outlined in section 4.4, based on Findlay's (1974) extension to the open economy of the mathematical representations of a closed Ricardian system of Pasinetti (1960) and Samuelson (1959). The economy is divided into 'corn' and manufacturing sectors, where corn is produced by land and labor, and manufactures by labor subject to constant returns. Profits are earned on wages (circulating capital, consisting of corn) advanced at the beginning of the period of production. In a closed economy, the price of corn in terms of manufactures rises over time as labor is used more intensively, and hence with diminishing returns, on the fixed stock of land. Money wages rise, and the rates of profit and capital accumulation fall until the economy eventually reaches the stationary state. But if an open economy can import corn at a fixed price in exchange for manufactures, the stationary state can be delayed indefinitely.

Findlay aptly commented on the appropriateness of this 'Ricardian' model in the chapter on 'Growth and Development in Trade Models' in the *Handbook of International Economics*:[12]

> It is a strange irony, however, that Ricardo himself had constructed an implicit dynamic model of growth and trade, linked by the distribution of income, in [Ricardo, 1951b]. His interest in the repeal of the Corn Laws was motivated not so much by a static 'gains from trade' argument but from a 'gains from growth' consideration underlying the effect of the repeal in raising the rate of profit and reducing the rent of land, capitalists being thrifty and landlords profligate in his stylized representation. The Ricardo of pure trade theory is a pale shadow of the real one. The very neatness and elegant simplicity of the chapter 7 analysis seems to have diverted attention from the more complex, but also in my opinion very rich and deep ideas contained in the *Essay* [*on Profits*], and also, for that matter, in the rest of chapter 7. (Findlay, 1984, p. 186)

Pasinetti (1981, 1993) also took a dynamic view of the Ricardian theory when he developed a *general* as well as a *special* 'principle of comparative productivity-change advantage'. Instead of comparing Ricardo's four 'magic numbers' consisting of labor coefficients of two commodities in two countries, Pasinetti's 'special principle' compares the rates of growth of productivity of industry η in country H and in the rest of the world (W), $\rho_{\eta H}$ and $\rho_{\eta W}$, to their average rates of growth of productivity in producing all other internationally traded commodities, R_H and R_W. If, for example, $\rho_{\eta H}/R_H > \rho_{\eta W}/R_W$, industry η in country H improves its competitive position *vis-à-vis* the rest of the world. This principle has a policy implication for developing countries following in the footsteps of Japan and Europe: by imitating technical methods used abroad in a particular industry, their firms can achieve higher rates of productivity that allow them to become more competitive than the current industrial leaders, displacing their exports. Echoing David Hume and John Rae, Pasinetti (1993, p. 173) argued that 'the acquisition of technical knowledge by poor economic systems, i.e. international mobility of information and of technical knowledge, represents the fundamental factor, in truth the crucial factor, that may put the poor countries on the way first of all to set a check to the widening, and later on to actually head towards the elimination, of the huge disparities in per-capita incomes that are nowadays observed throughout the world'. Trade is needed to accomplish this goal since 'to the extent that the low-income countries succeed in finding markets abroad, they will be in a position to extend their learning (and thus their ability for production) to all that range of goods which are demanded at higher incomes – something they could not do if they were to rely exclusively on internal markets. This source of stimulus to production for export, and to learning, represents an explanation of international trade ... by far more relevant than the one (based on comparative costs) so far considered in all treatises of international trade' (1993, pp. 157–8). While this recalls the Smithian principle that the division of labor is limited by the extent of the market, Pasinetti went beyond both Smith and Rae by postulating a hierarchy between the benefits from learning and the gains from trade: 'it is only when all possible efforts to increase learning have been made ... that an underdeveloped country can hope to obtain further gains from international trade. In other words, possible benefits from international trade are subordinated to the benefits from international learning' (1993, p. 160).

   Despite the role which actual and potential comparative advantage can play in mobilizing a country's resources for economic development, some economists and policymakers in less developed countries have regarded it with suspicion as a static concept which depends on exogenous parameters such as the technology of production or a given endowment of factors of production. Some displayed an openly critical attitude towards the theory of comparative costs, viewing it as a rationalization for a frozen international division of labor in which their countries are assigned the role of 'drawers of water and hewers of wood', or providers of primary products for the developed countries which end up garnering the lion's share of the gains from trade. The classical and neo-Ricardian models discussed in this chapter, and those described in Chapters 4, 5 and 9, should go some way towards alleviating such fears by showing that most models of comparative advantage, past and present, are dynamic in nature.

Another critique levied against Ricardian models is that they do not allow for the market failures observed especially in developing countries. One such failure is the existence of non-competing groups of labor already pointed out by Cairnes (1874), which led to a modification of the law of comparative costs examined in Chapter 6. It has been increasingly realized that comparative advantage is influenced by market distortions as well as by fundamental economic circumstances such as given technologies or factor endowments. The first economist who related distortions to comparative advantage and economic development in a systematic way was Mihail Manoilescu (1931), who argued that the marginal value product of labor is higher in manufacturing than in agriculture. The fact that the wage rate in manufacturing exceeds that in agriculture, however, prevents an agricultural country from realizing a potential comparative advantage it may have in manufacturing. Unless its industrial sector is granted protection, it is condemned to remain an exporter of agricultural goods and forgo the positive externalities associated with manufacturing. Manoilescu's book was the first of many contributions to the subject of economic distortions which have enriched the literature, and led to the articulation of optimal policies which governments can use to offset them. These policies allow countries at any stage of development to neutralize the distortions affecting them, enabling them to reap the benefits of free trade in accordance with their natural comparative advantage.[13]

10.5 Comparative advantage: a many-splendored thing

What can we conclude about the validity of comparative advantage as an explanatory principle of international trade? The first conclusion that emerges is that there is no agreement in the profession about the meaning of this term, which is used in a variety of different, often incompatible, ways.[14] In the 2 × 2 × 2 case, it often simply expresses the fact that a country's autarky price is lower than its trading partner's. In the multicommodity case, one must resort to the broader Deardorff–Dixit–Norman formulation of the law of comparative advantage in terms of a positive correlation between net exports and low autarky prices. Other economists employ the term comparative advantage in the old Ricardian sense of exogenously given technological differences among countries, or in a neo-Ricardian sense that allows such differences to be created over time, whether by the invisible hand of competition or the visible hand of public intervention in favor of an industry. Others use the term in the Heckscher–Ohlin sense that countries have an edge in the production of commodities intensive in their abundant factor endowments. Comparative advantage is sometimes simply meant to indicate that, thanks to a large market, a country can produce commodities subject to increasing returns more cheaply than a smaller country.

Although David Ricardo has not been supplanted by Adam Smith as the patron saint of international trade theory, Smith's insight that the division of labor is limited by the extent of the market, which includes the export market, has added significantly to the arsenal of models used by trade theorists. A theory of trade based on increasing returns is different from, and complementary to, one based factor endowments. This was also a basic tenet of Bertil Ohlin for which he has not received sufficient credit. Ohlin emphasized the chance elements which condition the geographic location of industries subject to economies of scale, and the hysteresis effect or 'friction' that allows them to endure even after the conditions which originally gave rise to them have disappeared. The rediscovery of the importance of historical antecedents by the new trade theorists restores the theory of international trade to its Ohlinian and Smithian roots. An economist with a deep historical sense such as Adam Smith must be smiling in his grave over the fact that economists, as the twentieth century draws to a close and a new millennium approaches, have rediscovered that 'history matters' after all.

Notes

1. Among present-day historians of economic thought, one finds diametrically opposed attitudes towards this issue. On the one hand, Blaug (1985, p. 210) maintains that 'it is curious that classical theory, generally oriented as it was to problems of long-run development, should have developed an almost wholly static theory of international trade'. On the other hand, O'Brien (1975, as cited by Bloomfield, [1978] 1994, p. 22) argued that 'there are many elements in Classical trade theory, particularly in its interconnection with growth and development, which have been almost entirely neglected in the modern treatments of that theory'. In agreement with O'Brien and Bloomfield, I believe that the classical economists viewed growth, trade and comparative advantage as inextricably intertwined.

2. As Georgescu-Roegen (1987, p. 300) stated of Manoilescu, 'his argument was about the advantage not only of industrialization for an agrarian and overpopulated economy but also of industrialized nations able to purchase food for less labour than that of its exports.... By now hardly any economist would deny that industrialization was responsible for economic development from the Tennessee Valley to Korea'.

3. This was the course that Marshall took when he generalized the Ricardian model to trade in many commodities between two 'islands' in Appendix H of *Money Credit and Commerce* (1923, p. 323). By neglecting 'differences in the skill required for different occupations, and in the

amount of capital by which each man's labour needs to be assisted ... so that the real cost of production of any commodity in either island can be regarded as proportional to the amount of the standard labour of that island', Marshall derived a chain of comparative advantage similar to that which Edgeworth (following Mangoldt's lead) had obtained before him.

4. Findlay (1970a, chapter 3) constructed a hybrid model combining the H–O–S assumptions with Hicks-neutral differences in countries' technologies. Since differences in factor endowments can be offset by those in technology, it can make no clear-cut predictions about the pattern of trade.

5. In examining the relation between technical change and international trade, Dosi, Pavitt and Soete (1990, pp. 3, 10) state that their analysis '*starts* from differences of technological capabilities and innovativeness between countries and then focuses on the effects of such differences on international patterns of trade and growth.... The century of economic discussion which has focused primarily on allocative optimality *for given techniques* has obscured the importance of differences in techniques and product characteristics between countries, and has neglected the analysis of their origin'.

6. Krugman's reflection echoes an earlier comment by Richardson (1975, p. 353) on the failure of theorists to incorporate in their models dynamic economies of scale as described by Smith: 'The theorist has come to attend to the things he can most easily handle and in this way our perception of reality has adapted to the development of our mental machinery'. See also Young (1928).

7. The term was used in that sense in a model with a single productive factor, where technology is internationally identical and subject to increasing returns in the manufacturing sector. Ethier (1982b, p. 1246) argued that 'the large country has a comparative advantage in that good subject to increasing returns and the small country a comparative advantage in the other'.

8. In an article significantly entitled 'Import protection as export promotion: international competition in the presence of oligopoly and economies of scale', Krugman (1984, p. 191) argued that 'a protected domestic market gives firms a base for successful exporting'. In a later article, Krugman (1987a) used the term 'narrow moving band' to describe the policy allegedly used by the Japanese government to engineer a permanent shift of comparative advantage via temporary protection in a succession of industries.

9. See Edwards (1992) and World Bank (1993), among many such studies.

10. An analogous assignment rule applies to the case of n countries and n commodities. Jones ([1977] 1979, p. 295) showed that if the same rule is applied to the 2×2 case, the assignment of goods to countries is consistent with Ricardian comparative advantage.

11. For a sampling of neo-Ricardian trade models, see Steedman (1979a, 1979b, 1987), Mainwaring (1984) and Evans (1989). Evans (1989) provides an excellent outline of such models, and his book usefully compares them to Ricardian, neoclassical and Marxian ones. For evaluations of neo-Ricardian trade models by mainstream economists, see Dixit (1981) and Smith (1984). In his review of Steedman (1979a, 1979b), Dixit (1981) paid tribute to them for calling attention to issues related to trade, growth and capital ignored or downplayed in the mainstream literature. He believes, however, that 'models which confine themselves to steady states are ... simply inappropriate for answering real-world policy questions', and that while neo-Ricardians 'have opened up useful avenues for further research ... I do not think success lies in the neo-Ricardian direction' (1981, pp. 282, 294). In his survey of trade theory and capital theory, Smith (1984, pp. 318–20) recognized that the neo-Ricardian contribution 'is substantial and useful, and that at least some of the 'neoclassical' theoretical developments surveyed above would have been different and poorer without the stimulus provided by the neo-Ricardians. On the grand question of whether we really are given an alternative 'vision' of international trade, only a personal view can be expressed and my answer is negative'.

12. See also Findlay (1987a).

13. On Manoilescu's contributions, see Haberler (1936), Viner (1937), Georgescu-Roegen (1987) and Irwin (1996, chapter 10). Hagen (1958) converted Manoilescu's confusing numerical

examples into an elegant model illustrating the effects of intersectoral wage differentials on resource allocation and comparative advantage. Two classic articles outlining the modern theory of distortions and its implications for policy are Johnson (1965) and Bhagwati (1971).

14. MacDonald and Markusen (1985) even argued that comparative advantage can be a misleading guide to policy in the context of optimal assignment decisions, and attempted to rehabilitate the concept of absolute advantage.

References

Allen, W. R. (1968), 'The Position of Mercantilism and the Early Development of International Trade Theory', in R. V. Eagly (ed.), *Events, Ideology and Economic Theory*, Detroit: Wayne State University Press, pp. 65–106.

—— (1970), 'Modern Defenders of Mercantilist Theory', *History of Political Economy*, **2** (2), 381–97.

—— (1973), 'Rearguard Response', *History of Political Economy*, **5** (2), 496–8.

Angell, J. W. (1926), *The Theory of International Prices: History, Criticism and Restatement*, Cambridge, MA: Harvard University Press.

Anson-Meyer, M. (1982), *Un économiste du développement au XIXe siècle. Friedrich List* [*A Development Economist in the 19th Century: Friedrich List*], Grenoble.

Appleyard, D. R. and J. C. Ingram (1979), 'A Reconsideration of the Additions to Mill's "Great Chapter"', *History of Political Economy*, **11** (4), 459–76.

Arrow, K. J. (1962), 'The Economic Implications of Learning by Doing', *Review of Economic Studies*, **29** (3), 155–73.

Baldwin, R. E. (1969), 'The Case Against Infant Industry Protection', *Journal of Political Economy*, **77** (3), 295–305.

—— (1982), 'Gottfried Haberler's Contributions to International Trade Theory and Policy', *Quarterly Journal of Economics*, **97** (1), 141–8.

Barone, E. (1908), *Principi di economia politica*, Rome: G. Bertero.

Bastable, C. F. (1903), *The Theory of International Trade*, 4th ed., London: Macmillan.

Bensel, T. and B. Elmslie (1992), 'Rethinking International Trade Theory: A Methodological Appraisal', *Weltwirtschaftliches Archiv*, **128** (2), 249–65.

Bhagwati, J. (1971), 'The Generalized Theory of Distortions and Welfare', in J. N. Bhagwati et al. (eds), *Trade, Balance of Payments, and Growth: Papers in International Economics in Honor of Charles P. Kindleberger*, Amsterdam: North-Holland, pp. 69–90.

—— (1972), 'The Heckscher–Ohlin Theorem in the Multicommodity Case', *Journal of Political Economy*, **80** (5), 1052–5.

Blaug, M. (1985), *Economic Theory in Retrospect*, 4th ed., Cambridge: Cambridge University Press.

—— (1987), 'Classical Economics', in J. Eatwell, M. Milgate and P. Newman (eds), *The New Palgrave: A Dictionary of Economics*, vol. 1, London: Macmillan, pp. 434–45.

—— (1990), 'Introduction', in M. Blaug (ed.), *The History of Economic Thought*, Aldershot: Edward Elgar.

—— (1992), *The Methodology of Economics: Or How Economists Explain*, 2nd ed., Cambridge: Cambridge University Press.

Bloomfield, A. I. ([1938] 1994), 'The Foreign-Trade Doctrines of the Physiocrats', in Bloomfield (1994), pp. 205–32.

—— ([1975] 1994), 'Adam Smith and the Theory of International Trade', in Bloomfield (1994), pp. 109–44.

—— ([1978] 1994), 'The Impact of Growth and Technology on Trade in Nineteenth-Century British Thought', in Bloomfield (1994), pp. 22–6.

—— (1994), *Essays in the History of International Trade Theory*, Aldershot: Edward Elgar.

Bourne, E. G. (1894), 'Alexander Hamilton and Adam Smith', *Quarterly Journal of Economics*, **8** (April), 328–44.

Bowen, H. P., E. E. Leamer and L. Sveikauskas (1987), 'Multicountry, Multifactor Tests of the Factor Abundance Theory', *American Economic Review*, **77** (5), 791–809.

Burgstaller, A. (1986), 'Unifying Ricardo's Theories of Growth and Comparative Advantage', *Economica*, **53** (212), 467–81.

Burns, A. F. (1928), 'A Note on Comparative Costs', *Quarterly Journal of Economics*, **42** (May), 495–500.

Caffè, F. (1987), 'Barone, Enrico', in J. Eatwell, M. Milgate and P. Newman (eds), *The New Palgrave: A Dictionary of Economics*, vol. 1, London: Macmillan, pp. 195–6.

Cairnes, J. E. (1874), *Some Leading Principles of Political Economy*, London: Macmillan.

Casarosa, C. (1978), 'A New Formulation of the Ricardian System', *Oxford Economic Papers*, **30** (1), 38–63.

Caves, R. E. (1960), *Trade and Economic Structure: Models and Methods*, Cambridge, MA: Harvard University Press.

——, J. A. Frankel and R. W. Jones (1993), *World Trade and Payments: An Introduction*, 6th ed., New York: HarperCollins.

—— and H. G. Johnson (eds) (1968), *Readings in International Economics*, Homewood, IL: Irwin.

Chenery, H. B. (1961), 'Comparative Advantage and Development Policy', *American Economic Review*, **51** (1), 18–51.

Chipman, J. S. (1965a), 'A Survey of the Theory of International Trade: Part 1, The Classical Theory', *Econometrica*, **33** (3), 477–519.

—— (1965b), 'A Survey of the Theory of International Trade: Part 2, The Neo-Classical Theory', *Econometrica*, **33** (4), 685–760.

—— (1966), 'A Survey of the Theory of International Trade: Part 3, The Modern Theory', *Econometrica*, **34** (1), 18–76.

—— (1979), 'Mill's "Superstructure": How Well Does It Stand Up?', *History of Political Economy*, **11** (4), 477–500.

—— (1987), 'Haberler, Gottfried (born 1900)', in J. Eatwell, M. Milgate and P. Newman (eds), *The New Palgrave: A Dictionary of Economics*, vol. 2, London: Macmillan, pp. 581–2.

Coats, A. W. (1973), 'The Interpretation of Mercantilist Economics: Some Historiographical Problems', *History of Political Economy*, **5** (2), 485–95.

Cochrane, J. L. (1970), 'The First Mathematical Ricardian Model', *History of Political Economy*, **2** (2), 419–31.

—— (1975), 'William Whewell's Mathematical Statements', *The Manchester School*, **43** (4), 396–400.

Cooke, J. E. (1964), *The Reports of Alexander Hamilton*, New York: Harper & Row.

—— (1982), *Alexander Hamilton*, New York: Charles Scribner's Sons.

Corden, W. M. (1957), 'Tariffs, Subsidies and the Terms of Trade', *Economica*, **24** (95), 235–42.

Cornes, R. (1992), *Duality and Modern Economics*, Cambridge: Cambridge University Press.

Coustillac, M. (1996), 'Die List-Rezeption in Frankreich' [List's Reception in France], in E. Wendler (ed.), *'Die Vereinigung des europäischen Kontinents': Friedrich List: Gesamteuropäische Wirkungsgeschichte seines ökonomischen Denkens ['The Unification of the European Continent': Friedrich List: A History of the Influence of his Economic Thought throughout Europe*], Stuttgart: Schäffer-Poeschel, pp. 203–89.

Creedy, J. (1986), *Edgeworth and the Development of Neoclassical Economics*, Oxford: Blackwell.

—— (1989), 'Whewell's "Translation" of J. S. Mill', *Scottish Journal of Political Economy*, **36** (3), 266–81.

—— (1990), 'Marshall and Edgeworth', *Scottish Journal of Political Economy*, **37** (1), 18–39.

—— (1992), *Demand and Exchange in Economic Analysis: A History from Cournot to Marshall*, Aldershot: Edward Elgar.

Dalal, A. J. (1979), 'A Note on Mill's Theory of International Values', *Journal of International Economics*, **9** (4), 583–7.

Deardorff, A. V. (1979), 'Weak Links in the Chain of Comparative Advantage', *Journal of International Economics*, **9** (2), 197–209.

—— (1980), 'The General Validity of the Law of Comparative Advantage', *Journal of Political Economy*, **88** (5), 941–57.

—— (1994a), 'Exploring the Limits of Comparative Advantage', *Weltwirtschaftliches Archiv*, **130** (1), 1–19.

—— (1994b), 'Overview of the Stolper–Samuelson Theorem', in A. V. Deardorff and R. M. Stern (eds), *The Stolper–Samuelson Theorem: A Golden Jubilee*, Ann Arbor: University of Michigan Press, pp. 7–34.

De Marchi, N. (1976), 'Anomaly and the Development of Economics: The Case of the Leontief Paradox', in S. J. Latsis, *Method and Appraisal in Economics*, Cambridge: Cambridge University Press, pp. 109–27.

Dickey, L. (1993), '*Doux-Commerce* and the "Mediocrity of Money" in the Ideological Context of the Wealth and Virtue Problem', Appendix IV in A. Smith, *An Inquiry into the Nature and Causes of the Wealth of Nations*, Indianapolis: Hackett, pp. 243–59.

Dixit, A. K. (1981), 'The Export of Capital Theory', *Journal of International Economics*, **11** (2), 279–94.

—— and V. Norman (1980), *Theory of International Trade*, Digswell Place: Cambridge University Press.

Dorfman, R., P. A. Samuelson and R. M. Solow (1958), *Linear Programming and Economic Analysis*, New York: McGraw-Hill.

Dornbusch, R., S. Fischer and P. A. Samuelson (1977), 'Comparative Advantage, Trade, and Payments in a Ricardian Model with a Continuum of Goods', *American Economic Review*, **67** (5), 823–39.

Dosi, G., K. Pavitt and L. Soete (1990), *The Economics of Technical Change and International Trade*, New York: New York University Press.

Drabicki, J. Z. and A. Takayama (1979), 'An Antinomy in the Theory of Comparative Advantage', *Journal of International Economics*, **9** (2), 211–23.

Edgeworth, F. Y. (1894), 'The Pure Theory of International Values', *Economic Journal*, **4** (13, 15, 16), 35–50, 424–43, 606–38.

—— (1899), 'On a Point in the Theory of International Trade', *Economic Journal*, **9** (March), 125–8.

—— (1925), *Papers Relating to Political Economy*, vol. II, London: Macmillan.

Edwards, S. (1992), 'Trade Orientation, Distortions and Growth in Developing Countries', *Journal of Development Economics*, **39** (1), 31–57.

Einaudi, L. (1929), 'James Pennington or James Mill: An Early Correction of Ricardo', *Quarterly Journal of Economics*, **44** (1), 164–71.

Ellis, H. S. and L. A. Metzler (eds) (1949), *Readings in the Theory of International Trade*, Homewood, IL: Irwin.

Elmslie, B. T. (1994), 'Positive Feedback Mechanisms in Adam Smith's Theories of International Trade', *European Journal of the History of Economic Thought*, **1** (2), 253–71.

—— (1995), 'Retrospectives: The Convergence Debate Between David Hume and Josiah Tucker', *Journal of Economic Perspectives*, **9** (4), 207–16.

—— (1996), 'The Role of Joint Products in Adam Smith's Explanation of the "Vent-for-Surplus" Doctrine', *History of Political Economy*, **28** (3), 513–23.

—— and A. M. James (1993), 'The Renaissance of Adam Smith in Modern Theories of International Trade', in R. Hébert (ed.), *Perspectives on the History of Economic Thought*, vol. IX, Aldershot: Edward Elgar, pp. 63–76.

Ethier, W. J. (1974), 'Some of the Theorems of International Trade with Many Goods and Factors', *Journal of International Economics*, **4** (2), 199–206.

—— (1979), 'Internationally Decreasing Costs and World Trade', *Journal of International Economics*, **9** (1), 1–24.

—— (1982a), 'National and International Returns to Scale in the Modern Theory of International Trade', *American Economic Review*, **72** (3), 389–405.

—— (1982b), 'The General Role of Factor Intensity in the Theorems of International Trade', *Economics Letters*, **10** (3/4), 337–42.

—— (1982c), 'Decreasing Costs in International Trade and Frank Graham's Argument for Protection', *Econometrica*, **50** (5), 1243–68.

—— (1984), 'Higher Dimensional Issues in Trade Theory', in R. W. Jones and P. B. Kenen (eds), *Handbook of International Economics*, vol. I, Amsterdam: North-Holland, pp. 131–84.

Evans, H. D. (1989), *Comparative Advantage and Growth: Trade and Development in Theory and Practice*, New York: Harvester Wheatsheaf.

Findlay, R. (1970a), *Trade and Specialization*, Harmondsworth: Penguin Books.

—— (1970b), 'Factor Proportions and Comparative Advantage in the Long Run', *Journal of Political Economy*, **78** (1), 27–34.

—— (1974), 'Relative Prices, Growth and Trade in a Simple Ricardian System', *Economica*, **41** (161), 1–13.

—— (1984), 'Growth and Development in Trade Models', in R. W. Jones and P. B. Kenen (eds), *Handbook of International Economics*, vol. I, Amsterdam: North-Holland, pp. 185–236.

—— (1987a), 'Comparative Advantage', in J. Eatwell, M. Milgate and P. Newman (eds), *The New Palgrave: A Dictionary of Economics*, vol. 1, London: Macmillan, pp. 514–7.

—— (1987b), Review of Haberler (1985b), *Journal of Economic Literature*, **25** (3), 1346–7.

Flam, H. and M. J. Flanders (1991), 'Introduction' to Heckscher and Ohlin (1991).

Fortrey, S. (1673), *England's Interest and Improvement*, London: Nathanael Brook; reprinted in J. R. McCulloch (ed.), *Early English Tracts on Commerce*, Cambridge: Cambridge University Press, 1954, pp. 211–49.

Georgescu-Roegen , N. (1966), *Analytical Economics: Issues and Problems*, Cambridge, MA: Harvard University Press.

—— (1987), 'Manoïlescu, Mihail (1891–?1950)', in J. Eatwell, M. Milgate and P. Newman (eds), *The New Palgrave: A Dictionary of Economics*, vol. 3, London: Macmillan, pp. 299–301.

Gherity, J. A. (1988), 'Mill's "Friendly Critic" – Thornton or Whewell?', *The Manchester School*, **56** (3), 282–5.

Gomes, L. (1987), *Foreign Trade and the National Economy: Mercantilist and Classical Perspectives*, New York: St. Martin's Press.

—— (1990), *Neoclassical International Economics: An Historical Survey*, New York: St. Martin's Press.

Goodwin, C. D. W. (1961), *Canadian Economic Thought: The Political Economy of a Developing Nation 1814–1914*, Durham: Duke University Press.

Graham, F. D. (1923), 'The Theory of International Values Re-examined', *Quarterly Journal of Economics*, **38** (November), 54–86.

—— (1932), 'The Theory of International Values', *Quarterly Journal of Economics*, **46** (May), 581–616.

—— (1948), *The Theory of International Values*, Princeton: Princeton University Press.

Grampp, W .D. (1952), 'The Liberal Elements in English Mercantilism', *Quarterly Journal of Economics*, **66** (4), 465–501.

Groenewegen, P. (1983a), 'Turgot's Place in the History of Economic Thought: A Bicentenary Estimate', *History of Political Economy*, **15** (4), 585–616.

—— (1983b), 'Turgot, Beccaria and Smith', in P. Groenewegen and J. Halevi (eds), *Altro Polo: Italian Economics Past and Present*, Sydney: Frederick May Foundation for Italian Studies, pp. 31–78.

Grossman, G. M. and E. Helpman (1991), *Innovation and Growth in the Global Economy*, Cambridge, MA: MIT Press.

Haberler, G. (1929), 'The Theory of Comparative Costs Once More', *Quarterly Journal of Economics*, **43** (February), 376–81.

—— (1930), 'Die Theorie der komparativen Kosten und ihre Auswertung für die Begründung des Freihandels', *Weltwirtschaftliches Archiv*, **32** (2), 349–70.

—— (1933), *Der internationale Handel*, Berlin: Julius Springer.

—— (1936), *The Theory of International Trade*, Edinburgh: William Hodge.

—— ([1950] 1968), 'Some Problems in the Pure Theory of International Trade', reprinted in Caves and Johnson (1968), pp. 213–29.

—— (1961), *A Survey of International Trade Theory*, rev. ed., Special Papers in International Finance, No. 1, Princeton University.

—— (1985a), 'The Theory of Comparative Costs and Its Use in the Defense of Free Trade', in Haberler (1985b), pp. 3–19.

—— (1985b), *Selected Essays of Gottfried Haberler*, ed. by A. Y. C. Koo, Cambridge, MA: MIT Press.

Hacker, L. M. (1957), *Alexander Hamilton in the American Tradition*, New York: McGraw-Hill.
Hagen, E. E. (1958), 'An Economic Justification of Protectionism', *Quarterly Journal of Economics*, **72** (4), 496–514.
Hamilton, A. (1964), 'Report on Manufactures', in Cooke (1964).
—— (1966), 'Report on the Subject of Manufactures', in Syrett et al. (1966).
Harcourt, G. C. (1972), *Some Cambridge Controversies in the Theory of Capital*, Cambridge: Cambridge University Press.
Harwitz, M. (1972), 'A Note on Professor Chipman's Version of Mill's Law of International Value', *Journal of International Economics*, **2** (2), 181–8.
Hayek, F. A. (ed.) (1935), *Collectivist Economic Planning*, London: Routledge.
Heckscher, E. F. (1930), 'Mercantilism', in E.R.A. Seligman and A.E. Johnson (eds), *Encyclopaedia of the Social Sciences*, New York: Macmillan, pp. 333–9.
—— (1949), 'The Effect of Foreign Trade on the Distribution of Income', in H. S. Ellis and L. A. Metzler (eds), *Readings in the Theory of International Trade*, Homewood, IL: Irwin, pp. 272–300.
—— (1991), 'The Effect of Foreign Trade on the Distribution of Income', in Heckscher and Ohlin (1991), pp. 39–69.
—— and B. Ohlin (1991), *Heckscher–Ohlin Trade Theory*, ed. and trans. by H. Flam and M. J. Flanders, Cambridge, MA: MIT Press.
Helpman, E. (1981), 'International Trade in the Presence of Product Differentiation, Economies of Scale, and Monopolistic Competition: A Chamberlinian–Heckscher–Ohlin Approach', *Journal of International Economics*, **11** (3), 305–40.
—— and P. R. Krugman (1985), *Market Structure and Foreign Trade: Increasing Returns, Imperfect Competition, and the International Economy*, Cambridge, MA: MIT Press.
Henderson, J. P. (1985), 'The Whewell Group of Mathematical Economists', *The Manchester School*, **53** (4), 404–31.
—— (1989), 'Whewell's Solution to the Reciprocal Demand Riddle in Mill's "Great Chapter"', *History of Political Economy*, **21** (4), 661–77.
Henderson, W. O. (1983), *Friedrich List: Economist and Visionary 1789–1846*, London: Frank Cass.
Hicks, J. R. (1939), *Value and Capital*, Oxford: Clarendon Press.
—— (1946), *Value and Capital*, 2nd ed., Oxford: Clarendon Press.
—— (1983), *Classics and Moderns: Collected Essays on Economic Theory*, vol. III, Oxford: Blackwell.
Hilton, B. (1987), 'Corn laws', in J. Eatwell, M. Milgate and P. Newman (eds), *The New Palgrave: A Dictionary of Economics*, vol. 1, London: Macmillan, pp. 670–1.
Hirschman, A. O. (1977), *The Passions and the Interests*, Princeton: Princeton University Press.
Hirst, M. E. (1909), *Life of Friedrich List and Selections from his Writings*, London: Smith, Elder & Co.
Hollander, J. H. (1910), *David Ricardo: A Centenary Estimate*, Baltimore: The Johns Hopkins Press.
—— (1911), 'Ricardo and Torrens', *Economic Journal*, **21** (September), 448–68.
Hollander, S. (1973), *The Economics of Adam Smith*, Toronto and Buffalo: University of Toronto Press.
—— (1979), *The Economics of David Ricardo*, Toronto: University of Toronto Press.

—— (1985), *The Economics of John Stuart Mill*, Oxford: Blackwell.

Hoselitz, B. F. (1960), 'Theories of Stages of Economic Growth', in B.F. Hoselitz et al., *Theories of Economic Growth*, Glencoe: Free Press, pp. 193–238.

Hume, D. (1955), *Writings on Economics*, ed. by E. Rotwein, Madison: University of Wisconsin Press.

Hutchison, T. W. (1978), *On Revolutions and Progress in Economic Knowledge*, Cambridge: Cambridge University Press.

—— (1988), *Before Adam Smith: The Emergence of Political Economy 1662–1776*, Oxford: Basil Blackwell.

Irwin, D. A. (1996), *Against the Tide: An Intellectual History of Free Trade*, Princeton: Princeton University Press.

Jaffé, W. (1972), 'Pareto Translated: A Review Article', *Journal of Economic Literature*, **10** (4), 1190–1201.

James, R. W. (1965a), *John Rae, Political Economist: An Account of his Life and a Compilation of his Main Writings*, vols I and II, Aylesbury: University of Toronto Press.

—— (1965b), 'Rae on Political Economy', Chapter 11 of James (1965a), vol. I. Reprinted in *The Scottish Contribution to Modern Economic Thought*, ed. D. Mair, Aberdeen: Aberdeen University Press.

—— (1965c), 'Reactions to Rae's Book in the Nineteenth Century', Chapter 12 of James (1965a), vol. I.

Johnson, E. A. J. (1937), *Predecessors of Adam Smith: The Growth of British Economic Thought*, New York: Prentice-Hall.

Johnson, H. G. (1965), 'Optimal Trade Intervention in the Presence of Domestic Distortions', in R. E. Baldwin et al. (eds), *Trade, Growth and the Balance of Payments*, Chicago: Rand McNally, pp. 3–34.

Jones, R. W. ([1956] 1979), 'Factor Proportions and the Heckscher–Ohlin Theorem', reprinted in Jones (1979), pp. 5–19.

—— (1961), 'Comparative Advantage and the Theory of Tariffs: A Multi-country, Multi-commodity Model', *Review of Economic Studies*, **28** (3), 161–75.

—— (1965), 'The Structure of Simple General Equilibrium Models', *Journal of Political Economy*, **73** (4), 557–72.

—— (1971), 'A Three-Factor Model in Theory, Trade, and History', in J. N. Bhagwati et al. (eds), *Trade, Balance of Payments, and Growth*, Amsterdam: North-Holland, pp. 3–21.

—— (1974), 'The Small Country in a Many-Commodity World', *Australian Economic Papers*, (December), 225–36.

—— ([1977] 1979), '"Two-ness" in Trade Theory: Costs and Benefits', reprinted in Jones (1979), pp. 289–326.

—— (1979), *International Trade: Essays in Theory*, Amsterdam: North-Holland.

—— (1980), 'Comparative and Absolute Advantage', *Swiss Journal of Economics and Statistics*, **3**, 235–60.

—— (1987), 'Heckscher–Ohlin Trade Theory', in J. Eatwell, M. Milgate and P. Newman (eds), *The New Palgrave: A Dictionary of Economics*, vol. 2, London: Macmillan, pp. 620–7.

—— and J. P. Neary (1984), 'The Positive Theory of International Trade', in R. W. Jones and P. B. Kenen (eds), *Handbook of International Economics*, vol. I, Amsterdam: North-Holland, pp. 1–62.

Kemp, M. C. (1960), 'The Mill–Bastable Infant-Industry Dogma', *Journal of Political Economy*, **68** (1), 65–7.

—— (1964), *The Pure Theory of International Trade*, Englewood Cliffs: Prentice-Hall.

Kenen, P. B. (1994), *The International Economy*, 3rd ed., Cambridge: Cambridge University Press.

Keynes, J. M. (1936), *The General Theory of Employment, Interest and Money*, London: Macmillan.

Kirman, A. P. (1987), 'Pareto as an Economist', in J. Eatwell, M. Milgate and P. Newman (eds), *The New Palgrave: A Dictionary of Economics*, vol. 3, London: Macmillan, pp. 804–9.

Kravis, I. B. (1956), '"Availability" and Other Influences on the Commodity Composition of Trade', *Journal of Political Economy*, **64** (2), 143–55.

Krugman, P. R. (1979a), 'Increasing Returns, Monopolistic Competition, and International Trade', reprinted in Krugman (1990), pp. 11–21.

—— (1979b), 'A Model of Innovation, Technology Transfer, and the World Distribution of Income', reprinted in Krugman (1990), pp. 139–51.

—— (1984), 'Import Protection as Export Promotion: International Competition in the Presence of Oligopoly and Economies of Scale', reprinted in Krugman (1990), pp.185–98.

—— (1986), 'A "Technology Gap" Model of International Trade', reprinted in Krugman (1990), pp. 152–64.

—— (1987a), 'The Narrow Moving Band, the Dutch Disease, and the Competitive Consequences of Mrs. Thatcher: Notes on Trade in the Presence of Dynamic Scale Economies', reprinted in Krugman (1990), pp. 106–20.

—— (1987b), 'Increasing Returns and the Theory of International Trade', reprinted in Krugman (1990), pp. 63–89.

—— (1990), *Rethinking International Trade*, Cambridge, MA: MIT Press.

—— (1991), 'History versus Expectations', *Quarterly Journal of Economics*, **106** (2), 651–67.

—— and M. Obstfeld (1994), *International Economics: Theory and Policy*, 3rd ed., New York: HarperCollins.

Kurz, H. (1992), 'Adam Smith on Foreign Trade: A Note on the "Vent-for-surplus" Argument', *Economica*, **59** (236), 475–81.

Lancaster, K. (1980), 'Intra-Industry Trade under Perfect Monopolistic Competition', *Journal of International Economics*, **10** (2), 151–75.

Leamer, E. E. (1980), 'The Leontief Paradox, Reconsidered', *Journal of Political Economy*, **88** (3), 495–503.

—— (1984), *Sources of International Comparative Advantage: Theory and Evidence*, Cambridge, MA: MIT Press.

Leontief, W. W. (1933), 'The Use of Indifference Curves in the Analysis of Foreign Trade', *Quarterly Journal of Economics*, **47** (May), 493–503.

—— (1953), 'Domestic Production and Foreign Trade: The American Capital Position Re-examined', *Proceedings of the American Philosophical Society*, **97** (September), 331–49.

Lerner, A. P. (1932), 'The Diagrammatical Representation of Cost Conditions in International Trade', *Economica*, **12** (37), 346–56.

—— (1934), 'The Diagrammatical Representation of Demand Conditions in International Trade', *Economica*, N. S. **1** (3), 319–34.

Lindert, P. H. (1986), *International Economics*, Homewood: Irwin.

Lipsey, R. G. and K. Lancaster (1956), 'The General Theory of Second Best', *Review of Economic Studies*, **24** (63), 11–32.

List, F. (1827), *Outlines of American Political Economy*, Philadelphia: Samuel Parker.

—— (1856), *National System of Political Economy*, trans. G. A. Matile, Philadelphia: J. B. Lippincott & Co.

—— (1885), *The National System of Political Economy*, trans. S. S. Lloyd, London: Longmans, Green, and Co.

Longfield, M. (1834), *Lectures on Political Economy*, New York: A. M. Kelley, 1971.

—— (1835), *Three Lectures on Commerce, and One on Absenteeism*, New York: A. M. Kelley, 1971.

Lucas, R. E. (1988), 'On the Mechanics of Economic Development', *Journal of Monetary Economics*, **22** (1), 3–42.

—— (1993), 'Making a Miracle', *Econometrica*, **61** (2), 251–72.

MacDonald, G. M. and J. R. Markusen (1985), 'A Rehabilitation of Absolute Advantage', *Journal of Political Economy*, **93** (2), 277–97.

Macleod, C. (1983), 'Henry Martyn and the Authorship of "Considerations upon the East India Trade"', *Bulletin of the Institute of Historical Research*, **56** (November), 222–9.

Magee, S. P. (1980), 'Three Simple Tests of the Stolper–Samuelson Theorem', in P. Oppenheimer (ed.), *Issues in International Economics*, London: Oriel Press, pp. 138–53.

Magnusson, L. (ed.) (1993), *Mercantilist Economics*, Norwell, MA: Kluwer Academic Publishers.

—— (1994), *Mercantilism: The Shaping of an Economic Language*, London: Routledge.

Mainwaring, L. (1984), *Value and Distribution in Capitalist Economies: An Introduction to Sraffian Economics*, Cambridge: Cambridge University Press.

Maloney, J. (1987), 'Real Cost Doctrine', in J. Eatwell, M. Milgate and P. Newman (eds), *The New Palgrave: A Dictionary of Economics*, vol. 4, London: Macmillan, pp. 103–4.

Maneschi, A. (1983) 'Dynamic Aspects of Ricardo's International Trade Theory', *Oxford Economic Papers*, **35** (1), 67–80.

—— (1992), 'Ricardo's International Trade Theory: Beyond the Comparative Cost Example', *Cambridge Journal of Economics*, **16** (4), 421–37.

—— (1993a), 'Ricardian Comparative Advantage and the Perils of the Stationary State', in M. Baranzini and G. C. Harcourt (eds), *The Dynamics of the Wealth of Nations: Growth, Distribution and Structural Change: Essays in Honour of Luigi Pasinetti*', London: Macmillan, pp. 124–46.

—— (1993b), 'Pareto on International Trade Theory and Policy', *Journal of the History of Economic Thought*, **15** (Fall), 210–28.

—— (1998a), 'Comparative Advantage With and Without Gains from Trade', *Review of International Economics*, **6** (1), 120–28.

—— (1998b), 'John Rae on Trade, Inventions and Infant Industries: A Capital–Theoretic Perspective', *History of Political Economy*, **30** (3).

—— and W. O. Thweatt (1987), 'Barone's 1908 Representation of an Economy's Trade Equilibrium and the Gains from Trade', *Journal of International Economics*, **22** (3/4), 375–82.

Mangoldt, H. (1871), *Grundriss der Volkswirthschaftslehre*, 2nd ed., Stuttgart: Verlag von Julius Maier.

Manoilescu, M. (1931), *The Theory of Protection and International Trade*, London: P. S. King.

Marshall, A. (1879), *The Pure Theory of Foreign Trade*, Clifton: A. M. Kelley, 1974.

—— (1919), *Industry and Trade*, London: Macmillan.

—— (1920), *Principles of Economics*, 8th ed., London: Macmillan.

—— (1923), *Money Credit and Commerce*, London: Macmillan.

Martyn, H. ([1701] 1954), *Considerations on the East-India Trade*, in J. R. McCulloch (ed.), *Early English Tracts on Commerce*, Cambridge: Cambridge University Press, pp. 541–629.

Mason, E. S. (1926), 'The Doctrine of Comparative Cost', *Quarterly Journal of Economics*, **41** (November), 63–93.

Mayer, W. (1974), 'Short-run and Long-run Equilibrium for a Small Open Economy', *Journal of Political Economy*, **82** (5), 955–68.

McKenzie, L. W. (1954), 'Specialization and Efficiency in World Production', *Review of Economic Studies*, **21** (3), 165–80.

Meade, J. E. (1955), *Trade and Welfare*, London: Oxford University Press.

Melvin, J. R. (1969), 'Mill's Law of International Value', *Southern Economic Journal*, **36** (2), 107–16.

Mill, James (1818), 'Colony', in *Encyclopaedia Britannica*, Supplement to the 4th, 5th and 6th eds, 257–73.

—— (1821), *Elements of Political Economy*, London: Baldwin, Cradock, and Joy.

Mill, John Stuart (1844), *Essays on Some Unsettled Questions of Political Economy*, London: London School of Economics and Political Science reprint, 1948.

—— (1920), *Principles of Political Economy*, 7th ed., ed. by W.J. Ashley, London: Longman, Green and Co.

Mirowski, P. (1984), 'Physics and the "Marginalist Revolution"', *Cambridge Journal of Economics*, **8** (4), 361–79.

Moss, L. S. (1976), *Mountifort Longfield: Ireland's First Professor of Political Economy*, Ottawa, IL: Green Hill.

Mun, T. ([1664] 1954), *England's Treasure by Forraign Trade*, in J. R. McCulloch (ed.), *Early English Tracts on Commerce*, Cambridge: Cambridge University Press, pp. 115–209.

Mundell, R. A. (1957), 'International Trade and Factor Mobility', *American Economic Review*, **47** (3), 321–35.

Mussa, M. (1974), 'Tariffs and the Distribution of Income: The Importance of Factor Specificity, Substitutability, and Intensity in the Short and Long Run', *Journal of Political Economy*, **82** (December), 1191–1203.

Myint, H. (1958), 'The "Classical Theory" of International Trade and the Underdeveloped Countries', *Economic Journal*, **68** (270), 317–37.

—— (1977), 'Adam Smith's Theory of International Trade in the Perspective of Economic Development', *Economica*, **44** (175), 231–48.

Myrdal, G. (1957), *Economic Theory and Underdeveloped Regions*, London: Duckworth.

Neary, J. P. (1978), 'Short-Run Capital Specificity and the Pure Theory of International Trade', *Economic Journal*, **88** (351), 488–510.

O'Brien, D. P. (1970), *J. R. McCulloch: A Study in Classical Economics*, London: G. Allen.

—— (1975), *The Classical Economists*, Oxford: Oxford University Press.

244 Comparative Advantage in International Trade

Ohlin, B. (1927), 'Ist eine Modernisierung der Aussenhandelstheorie erforderlich?' ['Is a Modernization of Foreign Trade Theory Necessary?'], *Weltwirtschaftliches Archiv*, **26** (2), 97–115.

—— (1933), *Interregional and International Trade*, Cambridge, MA: Harvard University Press.

—— (1967), *Interregional and International Trade*, rev. ed., Cambridge, MA: Harvard University Press.

—— (1991), *The Theory of Trade*, in Heckscher and Ohlin (1991), pp. 71–214.

Oniki, H. and H. Uzawa (1965), 'Patterns of Trade and Investment in a Dynamic Model of International Trade', *Review of Economic Studies*, **32** (1), 15–38.

Pantaleoni, M. (1898), *Pure Economics*, trans. by T. Boston Bruce, London: Macmillan.

Pareto, V. (1894), 'Teoria matematica dei cambi forestieri', *Giornale degli Economisti*, **8** (February), 142–73.

—— (1895), 'Teoria matematica del commercio internazionale', *Giornale degli Economisti*, **10** (April), 476–98.

—— (1896, 1897), *Cours d'économie politique*, vol. I and vol. II, Lausanne: Rouge.

—— (1906), *Manuale di economia politica*, Milan: Società Editrice Libraria.

—— (1935), *The Mind and Society [Trattato di sociologia generale]*, New York: Harcourt, Brace.

—— (1971), *Manual of Political Economy*, New York: Kelley.

Pasinetti, L. L. (1960), 'A Mathematical Formulation of the Ricardian System', *Review of Economic Studies*, **27** (2), 78–98.

—— (1981), *Structural Change and Economic Growth: A Theoretical Essay on the Dynamics of the Wealth of Nations*, Cambridge: Cambridge University Press.

—— (1993), *Structural Economic Dynamics: A Theory of the Economic Consequences of Human Learning*, Cambridge: Cambridge University Press.

Peake, C. F. (1994), 'A Note on John Stuart Mill, William Thornton and William Whewell', *The Manchester School*, **62** (3), 319–23.

Pennington, J. (1840), *A Letter to Kirkman Finlay, Esq., on the Importation of Foreign Corn*, London: London School of Economics and Political Science reprint, 1963.

Pigou, A. C. (1953), *Alfred Marshall and Current Thought*, London: Macmillan.

Posner, M. V. (1961), 'Technical Change and International Trade', *Oxford Economic Papers*, **13** (3), 323–41.

Power, S. (1987), 'The Origins of the Heckscher–Ohlin Concept', *History of Political Economy*, **19** (2), 289–98.

Rabbeno, U. (1895), *The American Commercial Policy*, Cleveland: The Arthur H. Clark Co.

Rae, J. (1834), *Statement of Some New Principles on the Subject of Political Economy, Exposing the Fallacies of the System of Free Trade, and of Some Other Doctrines Maintained in the 'Wealth of Nations'*, Boston: Hilliard, Gray, and Co. Vol. II of James (1965a) is a facsimile reproduction of Rae (1834).

Rashid, S. (1977), 'William Whewell and Early Mathematical Economics', *The Manchester School*, **45** (4), 381–91.

Ricardo, D. (1951a), *On the Principles of Political Economy and Taxation*, in P. Sraffa (ed.), *The Works and Correspondence of David Ricardo*, vol. I, Cambridge: Cambridge University Press.

—— (1951b), *An Essay on the Influence of a Low Price of Corn on the Profits of Stock*, in P. Sraffa (ed.), *The Works and Correspondence of David Ricardo*, vol. IV, Cambridge: Cambridge University Press, pp. 9–41.

—— (1951c), *Letters, 1810–1815*, in P. Sraffa (ed.), *The Works and Correspondence of David Ricardo*, vol. VI, Cambridge: Cambridge University Press.

—— (1951d), *Letters, 1816–1818*, in P. Sraffa (ed.), *The Works and Correspondence of David Ricardo*, vol. VII, Cambridge: Cambridge University Press.

Richardson, G. B. (1975), 'Adam Smith on Competition and Increasing Returns', in A. S. Skinner and T. Wilson (eds), *Essays on Adam Smith*, Oxford: Clarendon Press, pp. 350–60.

Robbins, L. (1958), *Robert Torrens and the Evolution of Classical Economics*, London: Macmillan.

—— (1968), *The Theory of Economic Development in the History of Economic Thought*, London: Macmillan.

Robinson, J. (1974), *Reflections on the Theory of International Trade*, Manchester: Manchester University Press.

Romer, P. M. (1986), 'Increasing Returns and Long-Run Growth', *Journal of Political Economy*, **94** (5), 1002–1037.

—— (1990), 'Endogenous Technological Change', *Journal of Political Economy*, **98** (5), S71–102.

Rutherford, R. P. (1986), 'Ricardo's mantle', *Australian Economic Papers*, **25** (47), 206–21.

Rybczynski, T. M. (1955), 'Factor Endowment and Relative Commodity Prices', *Economica* **22** (84), 336–41.

Samuels, W. J. (1987), 'Taussig, Frank William (1859–1940)', in J. Eatwell, M. Milgate and P. Newman (eds), *The New Palgrave: A Dictionary of Economics*, vol. 4, London: Macmillan, p. 596.

Samuelson, M. C. (1939), 'The Australian Case for Protection Re-examined', *Quarterly Journal of Economics*, **54** (1), 143–49.

Samuelson, P. A. (1947), *Foundations of Economic Analysis*, Cambridge, MA: Harvard University Press.

—— (1948), 'International Trade and the Equalisation of Factor Prices', *Economic Journal*, **58** (230), 163–84.

—— (1949), 'International Factor Price Equalisation Once Again', *Economic Journal*, **59** (234), 181–97.

—— (1953), 'Prices of Factors and Goods in General Equilibrium', *Review of Economic Studies*, **21** (1), 1–20.

—— (1959), 'A Modern Treatment of the Ricardian Economy, I, II', *Quarterly Journal of Economics*, **73** (1, 2), 1–35, 217–31.

—— (1969), 'The Way of an Economist', in P.A. Samuelson (ed.), *International Economic Relations: Proceedings of the Third Congress of the International Economic Association*, London: Macmillan, pp. 1–11.

—— (1971), 'Ohlin Was Right', *Swedish Journal of Economics*, **73** (4), 365–84.

—— (1981a), 'Bertil Ohlin 1899–1979', *Journal of International Economics*, **11** (2), 147–63.

—— (1981b), 'Summing Up on the Australian Case for Protection', *Quarterly Journal of Economics*, **96** (1), 147–70.

—— (1994), 'Tribute to Wolfgang Stolper on the Fiftieth Anniversary of the Stolper–Samuelson Theorem', in A. V. Deardorff and R. M. Stern (eds), *The Stolper–Samuelson Theorem: A Golden Jubilee*, Ann Arbor: University of Michigan Press, pp. 343–9.

Schumpeter, J. A. (1951), *Ten Great Economists from Marx to Keynes*, New York: Oxford University Press.

—— (1954), *History of Economic Analysis*, New York: Oxford University Press.

Semmel, B. (1970), *The Rise of Free Trade Imperialism: Classical Political Economy, the Empire of Free Trade, and Imperialism*, Cambridge: Cambridge University Press.

Shoup, C. S. (1960), *Ricardo on Taxation*, New York: Columbia University Press.

Smith, Adam (1976), *An Inquiry into the Nature and Causes of the Wealth of Nations*, Oxford: Clarendon Press.

Smith, Alasdair (1984), 'Capital Theory and Trade Theory', in R. W. Jones and P. B. Kenen (eds), *Handbook of International Economics*, vol. I, Amsterdam: North-Holland, pp. 289–324.

Solow, R. M. (1956), 'A Contribution to the Theory of Growth', *Quarterly Journal of Economics*, **70** (1), 65–94.

—— (1957), 'Technical Change and the Aggregate Production Function', *Review of Economics and Statistics*, **39** (3), 312–20.

Spengler, J. J. (1960), 'Mercantilist and Physiocratic Growth Theory', in B. F. Hoselitz *et al.*, *Theories of Economic Growth*, Glencoe, Ill.: The Free Press, pp. 3–64.

Sraffa, P.(1930), 'An Alleged Correction of Ricardo', *Quarterly Journal of Economics*, **44** (3), 539–44.

—— (1951), 'Introduction', in Ricardo, D. (1951a), pp. xiii–lxii.

—— (1960), *Production of Commodities by Means of Commodities*, Cambridge: Cambridge University Press.

Steedman, I. (1979a) (ed.), *Fundamental Issues in Trade Theory*, London: Macmillan.

—— (1979b), *Trade Amongst Growing Economies*, Cambridge: Cambridge University Press.

—— (1987), 'Foreign Trade', in J. Eatwell, M. Milgate and P. Newman (eds), *The New Palgrave: A Dictionary of Economics*, vol. 2, New York: Stockton Press, pp. 406–11.

—— and J. S. Metcalfe (1973), 'On Foreign Trade', *Economia Internazionale*, **26** (3–4), 516–28.

Stigler, G. J. (1965), *Essays in the History of Economics*, Chicago: The University of Chicago Press.

Stolper, W. F. and P. A. Samuelson ([1941] 1949), 'Protection and Real Wages', in H. S. Ellis and L. A. Metzler (eds), *Readings in the Theory of International Trade*, Homewood, IL: Irwin, pp. 333–57.

Syrett, H. C. et al. (1966), *The Papers of Alexander Hamilton*, vol. X, New York: Columbia University Press.

Takayama, A. (1972), *International Trade*, New York: Holt, Rinehart and Winston.

Tarascio, V. J. (1968), *Pareto's Methodological Approach to Economics*, Chapel Hill, NC: University of North Carolina Press.

Taussig, F. W. (1927), *International Trade*, New York: Macmillan.

Theocharis, R. D. (1968), 'William Whewell', *International Encyclopedia of the Social Sciences*, pp. 531–2.

—— (1983), *Early Developments of Mathematical Economics*, 2nd ed., London: Macmillan.

—— (1993), *The Development of Mathematical Economics: The Years of Transition: From Cournot to Jevons*, Houndmills: Macmillan.

Thornton, W. (1869), *On Labour: Its Wrongful Claims and Rightful Dues, Its Actual Present and Possible Future*, London.

Thweatt, W. O. (1976), 'James Mill and the Early Development of Comparative Advantage', *History of Political Economy*, **8** (2), 207–34.

—— (1986), 'James and John Mill on Comparative Advantage: Sraffa's Account Corrected', in H. Visser and E. Schoorl (eds), *Trade in Transit*, Dordrecht: Martinus Nijhoff, pp. 33–43.

Tinbergen, J. (1945), *International Economic Cooperation*, Amsterdam: Elsevier.

Torrens, R. (1815), *An Essay on the External Corn Trade*, 1st ed., London: Hatchard

—— (1827), *An Essay on the External Corn Trade*, 4th ed., London: Longman, Rees, Orme, Brown and Green.

Trefler, D. (1993), 'International Factor Price Differences: Leontief Was Right!', *Journal of Political Economy*, **101** (6), 961–87.

—— (1995), 'The Case of the Missing Trade and Other Mysteries', *American Economic Review*, **85** (5), 1029–46.

Tucker, J. ([1774] 1973), *Four Tracts, on Political and Commercial Subjects*, Tract I, in R.L. Meek (ed.), *Precursors of Adam Smith*, Totowa, N.J.: Rowman and Littlefield, pp. 173–96.

Vaggi, G. (1987a), 'Physiocrats', in J. Eatwell, M. Milgate and P. Newman (eds), *The New Palgrave: A Dictionary of Economics*, vol. 4, New York: Stockton Press, pp. 869–76.

—— (1987b), *The Economics of François Quesnay*, Durham: Duke University Press.

Vanek, J. (1968), 'The Factor Proportions Theory: The N-Factor Case', *Kyklos*, **21** (October), 749–54.

Varian, H. R. (1992), *Microeconomic Analysis*, 3rd edition, New York: Norton.

Vernon, R. (1966), 'International Investment and International Trade in the Product Cycle', *Quarterly Journal of Economics*, **80** (2), 190–207.

Viner, J. (1926), 'Angell's Theory of International Prices', *Journal of Political Economy*, **34** (5), 597–623.

—— (1931), 'Cost Curves and Supply Curves', *Zeitschrift für Nationalökonomie*, **3** (1), 23–46.

—— (1937), *Studies in the Theory of International Trade*, New York: Harper.

—— (1958), Review of E. Salin and A. Sommer, *Friedrich List, Schriften, Reden, Briefe*, vol. IV, in J. Viner, *The Long View and the Short*, Glencoe: Free Press, pp. 389–91.

—— (1968), 'Mercantilist Thought', in *International Encyclopedia of the Social Sciences*, New York: Macmillan and Free Press.

—— (1972), *The Role of Providence in the Social Order*, Princeton: Princeton University Press.

—— (1991), *Essays on the Intellectual History of Economics*, ed. by D. A. Irwin, Princeton: Princeton University Press.

Virgil [Publius Vergilius Maro] (1990), *The Georgics*, trans. C. Day Lewis, Chicago: Encyclopaedia Britannica.

Walsh, V. C. (1979), 'Ricardian Foreign Trade Theory in the Light of the Classical Revival', *Eastern Economic Journal*, **5** (3), 421–27.

Whewell, W. (1850), 'Mathematical Exposition of Some Doctrines of Political Economy – Second Memoir', New York: A. M. Kelley, 1971.

Whitaker, J. K. (1975), *The Early Economic Writings of Alfred Marshall, 1867–1890*, vol. 1, New York: The Free Press.

—— (1987), 'Marshall, Alfred (1842–1924)', in J. Eatwell, M. Milgate and P. Newman (eds), *The New Palgrave: A Dictionary of Economics*, vol. 3, New York: Stockton Press, pp. 350–63.

Williams, J. H. ([1929] 1949), 'The Theory of International Trade Reconsidered', in American Economic Association *Readings in the Theory of International Trade*, Homewood, IL: Irwin, pp. 253–71.

Woodland, A. D. (1982), *International Trade and Resource Allocation*, Amsterdam: North-Holland.

World Bank (1993), *The East Asian Miracle: Economic Growth and Public Policy*, New York: Oxford University Press.

Wu, C.-Y. (1939), *An Outline of International Price Theories*, London: Routledge.

Young, A. A. (1928), 'Increasing Returns and Economic Progress', *Economic Journal*, **38** (152), 527–42.

Index

258   *Comparative Advantage in International Trade*

Printed and bound by CPI Group (UK) Ltd, Croydon, CR0 4YY

23/04/2025

14660982-0005